Routledge Revivals

State Apparatus

Originally published in 1984, *State Apparatus* contributes to the debate on the theory of the state through posing questions regarding the state's form, function, and apparatus.

The book begins by setting out the theoretical and methodological problems and reviewing the various Conservative, Liberal and Marxist theories in light of these. It discusses state activity, using specific case studies to clearly illustrate key points, such as the development of welfare systems in North America and Western Europe. It also explores the use of language under the state, the role of the legal apparatus within a capitalist system, and the "local state". The book concludes with a discussion of democracy and the crisis of legitimacy, and the issue of justice and the state.

State Apparatus is a detailed and comprehensive text, ideal for those with an interest in the history, theory, form, and function of the state.

State Apparatus

Structures and Language of Legitimacy

By Gordon L. Clark and Michael Dear

First published in 1984
by George Allen & Unwin Ltd

This edition first published in 2020 by Routledge
2 Park Square, Milton Park, Abingdon, Oxon, OX14 4RN
and by Routledge
605 Third Avenue, New York, NY 10017

Routledge is an imprint of the Taylor & Francis Group, an informa business

© G. L. Clark and M. J. Dear 1984

All rights reserved. No part of this book may be reprinted or reproduced or utilised in any form or by any electronic, mechanical, or other means, now known or hereafter invented, including photocopying and recording, or in any information storage or retrieval system, without permission in writing from the publishers.

Publisher's Note
The publisher has gone to great lengths to ensure the quality of this reprint but points out that some imperfections in the original copies may be apparent.

Disclaimer
The publisher has made every effort to trace copyright holders and welcomes correspondence from those they have been unable to contact.

A Library of Congress record exists under LCCN: 83022357

ISBN 13: 978-0-367-63439-1 (hbk)
ISBN 13: 978-1-003-11919-7 (ebk)

State Apparatus

Titles of related interest

The British system of government
A. H. Birch

Town and country planning in Britain
J. B. Cullingworth

Water planning in Britain
D. J. Parker & E. C. Penning-Rowsell

The countryside: planning and change
M. Blacksell & A. Gilg

Coal in Britain: an uncertain future
G. Manners

National parks: conservation or cosmetics
A. & M. MacEwen

Perspectives on drought and famine in Nigeria
G. J. van Apeldoorn

British dogmatism and French pragmatism
D. E. Ashford

Inspectorates in British government
G. Rhodes

The political economy of the welfare state
T. & D. J. Wilson

Planning the urban region
P. Self

The local government system
P. G. Richards

Approaches to public policy
S. Leach & J. Stewart (eds)

Policy styles in western Europe
J. Richardson (ed.)

The community of states
J. Mayall (ed.)

Disaster and reconstruction
R. Gelpel

Outcast Cape Town
J Western

Living under apartheid
D. M. Smith (ed.)

London's Green Belt: containment in practice
R. J. C. Munton

Manipulating the machine: changing patterns of ministerial departments, 1960–83
C. Pollitt

Planning in Europe
R. H. Williams

The state in capitalist Europe
S. Bornstein, D. Held & J. Krieger (eds)

The city in cultural context
J. Agnew, J. Mercer & D. Sopher (eds)

State Apparatus

Structures and Language of Legitimacy

Gordon L. Clark

University of Chicago

Michael Dear

McMaster University

Boston

ALLEN & UNWIN, INC.

London   Sydney

© G. L. Clark and M. J. Dear, 1984
This book is copyright under the Berne Convention. No reproduction without permission. All rights reserved.

Allen & Unwin Inc.,
9 Winchester Terrace, Winchester, Mass. 01890, USA

George Allen & Unwin (Publishers) Ltd,
40 Museum Street, London WC1A 1LU, UK

George Allen & Unwin (Publishers) Ltd,
Park Lane, Hemel Hempstead, Herts HP2 4TE, UK

George Allen & Unwin Australia Pty Ltd,
8 Napier Street, North Sydney, NSW 2060, Australia

First published in 1984

Library of Congress Cataloging in Publication Data

Clark, Gordon L.
    State apparatus.
Bibliography: p.
Includes index.
1. Legitimacy of governments.   2. Capitalism.
3. Social justice.   I. Dear, M. J. (Michael J.)
II. Title.
JC328.2.C57   1984   320.2   83–22357

British Library Cataloguing in Publication Data

Clark, Gordon L.
    State apparatus.
1. Capitalism
I. Title   II. Dear, Michael
330.12′2   HB501
ISBN 0–04–320159–8
ISBN 0–04–320160–1 Pbk

Set in 10 on 12 point Bembo by
Phoenix Photosetting, Chatham

For Shirley and Heather

Preface and acknowledgments

This book examines the apparatus of the capitalist state. It is concerned to develop a theory of the state, to explain the character and evolution of the capitalist state apparatus, and to show how that apparatus determines the sociospatial structure of contemporary society. Ultimately, the book shows how the state apparatus operates as a complex system to ensure the political legitimacy of capitalist society.

Beginning with our earliest work on the theory of the state, we have been fascinated with the state as an institution and with its relationship to wider capitalist society. As teachers and researchers of urban phenomena, we have often needed to rationalize what the state ought to do to solve a particular planning problem and what the state actually does. Understanding this dissonance has led us from the simple answers (for example, "the state comprehends neither the problems nor the solution") to more subtle and enveloping answers, as when the state is implicated in the creation of the supposed "problem" and is incapable of superseding the set of wider social processes. Simultaneously, therefore, we have sought concrete explanations of state actions grounded in the logic of institutional behavior, as well as abstract theoretical explanations of the state grounded in social and philosophical theory. These twin concerns have been preserved in the writing of this book.

The result is a book which attempts to integrate the sociospatial consequences of state activity with the wider theoretical framework of capitalist society. It would be overly simple to assert that state activity is merely the result of social forces mediated through specific institutional forms. On the other hand, the view of the state as an autonomous entity, capable of setting its own goals, must clearly be tempered by the particular political and economic context within which the state is embedded. The tension between state and society, and how this is manifest in a specific sociospatial form, are the subjects of this book.

The specific goals of this book are threefold: to outline a theory of the form and function of the capitalist state; to explain the concrete structure of the contemporary state apparatus; and to examine the impact of the apparatus on the spatial organization of society. The book proceeds thematically in its treatment of these issues. We have preferred to avoid any artificial division between state theory and sociospatial outcomes;

viii PREFACE AND ACKNOWLEDGMENTS

instead, these two themes intersect frequently throughout the book in order to explain the organization of society as a *composite* outcome of state and sociospatial process. Since the argument that follows is necessarily long and complex, it is important at this point to rehearse briefly the main dimensions of this argument.

In Chapter 1, the major theoretical and methodological tenets of our approach are laid down in a very general manner.

Chapter 2, entitled "The problematic of the capitalist state," introduces the key concepts and definitions required for developing a theory of the state. A critical review of the various existing theories is offered, emphasizing the variety of ideological visions implied in these analyses. Typical liberal and conservative viewpoints are set alongside the different marxist theories. For instance, notions of the "minimalist" state are considered, as is the "rule enforcer" state typical of liberal and conservative philosophy. From that point, we deal with other liberal theories, and in particular, their functional characteristics, for example, the "arbiter" mode of state intervention in social conflict. This discussion and critical appraisal then enables us to deal with the alternative marxist tradition, concentrating in particular upon the state derivation and capital-logic schools. The shortcomings of liberal theories are in their "ideal-typical" assumptions; that is, they fail principally because they rarely address the concrete relations of power and domination characteristic of capitalism. Their functional inadequacy is in sharp contrast to the marxist theories which relate a particular mode of social production to the institutional fabric of society. As will become apparent, however, we do not embrace the marxist model in total; in our approach the political and economic spheres of society remain separate. Consequently, we argue for a theory of the capitalist state premised upon notions of relative state autonomy and power.

In Chapter 3, "The capitalist state apparatus," our view of the contemporary capitalist state is considered in more depth. First, we set out the dimensions of the form and function of the state. Next, form and function are expressed in terms of concrete state apparatus. This linking of form, function and apparatus is fraught with conceptual and methodological difficulties. However, it is the keystone of the logic by which we establish a more specific correspondence between matters of abstract theory and material outcomes. By "form" we refer to the structural links between the capitalist social formation and the state. As we show in Chapter 2, it is the social and historical context that makes the state a specifically capitalist state. "Function" then refers to what the state does; here, we establish a hierarchy of necessary functions which are vital for the reproduction of the capitalist system and its attendant social relations. "Apparatus" is the term used to describe the mechanisms or instruments through which state functions are executed. Our argument is that all previous theories of the state have neglected to trace through the form–func-

PREFACE AND ACKNOWLEDGMENTS

tion–apparatus structure and as a result, have missed vital clues as to the state's agenda, power and bureaucratic design. Through this state-centered analysis we hope to link the state with other aspects of capitalist society, thereby generating a more complete picture of the rôle and behavior of the state at different social and spatial scales.

Chapter 4, "State apparatus and everyday life," marks an important point of departure. In it, we trace the impact of the state apparatus structure on people's everyday lives. Through the welfare apparatus of the state we directly trace the effect of state intervention in the everyday lives of families and individuals. Thus this chapter represents an important extension of our study into the realm of the empirical, as well as a new consideration of the rôle of the state in the reproduction of social relations. The concepts of social and spatial reproduction are central in this analysis, and are used to indicate the rôle of the various institutions of the welfare apparatus. These ideas are illustrated by reference to the growth of mental health care in North America and Western Europe, the examples of which highlight the political dimensions of the welfare problem. By this example, it becomes apparent that the state is deeply implicated in people's personal lives. While the welfare apparatus is used to illustrate the instrumental nature of the state apparatus, it should be considered as being representative of the penetration of many state apparatus into everyday life.

From a grounding in theory (Ch. 2), a definition of the form, functions and apparatus of the contemporary state (Ch. 3), and how it affects the everyday lives of individuals (Ch. 4), we then turn to examining how the state "works." Our primary point of departure is that the set of institutions and classes which compose capitalist society, including the state, invoke a special language in the conduct of their affairs. Chapter 5, "The language of the state," examines first the nature of their "political language," beginning with theoretical statements on the social context of language, the grammar of political language, and the political impacts of such language. Thereafter, the chapter examines how "community" and "space" become part of the language of the state. Essentially this chapter examines how a system of structured political discourse, bound by rules of inclusion and exclusion, facilitates capitalist accumulation and social control. This theme is expanded through an analysis of the language used to legitimize the actions of the state at various levels of community. The language of politics can be thought of as the *lingua franca* of the state apparatus. For example, the formalization of political discourse embodies a language of "proper" or acceptable political behavior, and "delegitimizes" other competing or unacceptable modes of political activity. This has far reaching consequences for the organization of political dissent as, for example, via elected political parties and for the structuration of social discourse itself.

PREFACE AND ACKNOWLEDGMENTS

Attention then turns in Chapter 6, "Law and the state," and in the following chapters, to a more detailed consideration of the rôle of specific state apparatus in the legitimacy and spatial organization of capitalism. The legal apparatus is examined, and the nature and character of law are explored, together with the central notion of individual rights and their relation to political power. Then, using this foundation, the rôle of the legal apparatus in sustaining the spatial integration of the United States of America is considered. In this chapter, we turn our attention to a theory of law and society that takes as its foundation the structure of capitalist social relations. Consequently, law is given an instrumental rôle, as a determining factor in the reproduction of the capitalist system as a whole. But it would be a mistake to assume that law is simply, or even solely, the domain of the élites. Our theory emphasizes the consensual nature of the universal rules of right and wrong. For American society in particular, these rules give precedence to individual consent; thus, as an *ideal* vision of society, law embodies Revolutionary conceptions of a "good" society. To integrate law with the systematic character of capitalist social relations, we also consider law in terms of its idealization of reality. Here, we seek an understanding of law that goes beyond a crude instrumentality; there are fundamental substantive moral values to be recognized and integrated in our analysis.

"The local state" (Ch. 7) is another element of the state apparatus which has a direct rôle in managing a spatially extensive and socially heterogeneous society. In this chapter, the theoretical foundations of the local state are first examined, and then the dimensions of local state autonomy in one particular jurisdiction (Massachusetts) is analysed in detail, emphasizing the structural and legal links between various state tiers. Finally, the political significance of the local state is assessed with respect to recent debates over the importance of local control and autonomy. Two aspects of local state autonomy are emphasized. The first is the legal framework of responsibilities and the spatial division of powers that characterizes much of American local government. Secondly, the question of autonomy is considered in the light of fiscal relationships between state tiers. Our argument is that the local state is an apparatus of national and state governments. Whatever the ideal image of local government as the crucible of democracy, its reality is one of limited autonomy and instrumental purpose designed in accordance with the objectives of higher tiers of the state. To illustrate this argument, we not only consider budgetary and legal aspects of the local state, but also a specific example, the recent case in Michigan of *Poletown v. City of Detroit*. Here, the schism between the ideal and the instrumental dependence of the local state is plainly illustrated.

The issue of the legitimacy of state actions acquires a new significance in Chapter 8, "Democracy and the crisis of legitimacy," where the relationship between democracy and capitalism is explored in detail. We emphasize the increasing rôle of consumption-based politics for the national and local states, while noting at the same time their increasingly antagonistic relations. Not only does the question of the relative autonomy of the state loom large but, more fundamentally American liberal political philosophy, which provides ideological legitimacy for the state, is argued to be bankrupt. Recurrent political crises of democracy increasingly pressurize the state and its apparatus, as the system of consumption politics is forced again and again to confront its inability to deliver the ideologically conceived "goods." In this chapter, we consider the state not only in terms of its ideal image, but also in terms of its relationships with capitalist society. It is the structure of inequality, and the complicity of the state in the reproduction of this economic and political system, that highlights the issue of legitimacy. The liberal democratic ideal of the state is reviewed, and the current problems of maintaining consent are examined. In the absence of a strong moral claim of legitimacy at both the local and national levels, the state's only recourse, apart from outright violence, is to a consumption-based politics. Here, however, there are problems of delivery, bias, cost, and garnering political support – a question of which state apparatus is to gain legitimacy from providing public goods and services. One result is internal state conflict, wherein there is a continual fight to shift, horizontally and vertically, the costs of maintaining consent while at the same time isolating electoral support.

In the concluding chapter, "Justice and the state" (Ch. 9), we begin by summarizing the major themes of the preceding chapters. The complex scenario thus constructed is then used as a basis for speculating about the rôle of the state with regard to social justice and political change. In doing so, we consider the future of the capitalist state and, in particular, the sources of its ultimate mandate. The chapter begins with two arguments: the "smash the state" notion so prevalent among radical groups, and the "state as instrument of social change" notion, which also enjoys some support among social activists. We have some sympathy with both arguments, depending on the nature of social change envisaged. It cannot be assumed that the state will be resistant to social justice in every instance. There are many examples of the state leading social change, particularly in Western Europe. The issue can only be determined by empirical reference to the state autonomy. Ultimately, we argue the case for state legitimacy which eschews notions of public goods and market failures in favor of the state as an instrument of justice. Here we are explicitly idealistic, arguing the case for a society that uses the state apparatus in purposeful and specific ways. Yet, our return here to society-centered visions of state behavior should not be mistaken as a return to liberal society-centered theory. As we hope to make clear, any theory of capital-

xii PREFACE AND ACKNOWLEDGMENTS

ist society, and consequently any theory of a just society, must confront the capitalist state as a whole.

One final point of general information is worth re-emphasizing. Any empirical analysis of the state and state apparatus is, by definition, society or culture specific. In this book, most of our real-world examples relate to experiences of the USA: consequently, our theoretical conceptualizations will be premised by the American context. On the one hand, this is obviously a virtue, in that it takes seriously the historical materialistic method. However it may, on the other hand, make our analysis quite culturally specific. Hence we introduce evidence also from Australia, Canada, and the United Kingdom and other parts of Western Europe. We believe that the gains from a culturally and historically specific analysis far outweigh any loss of generality due to our methodology.

Many people have helped us with this book. In particular, Nigel Thrift, Chris Paris, Dean Forbes and Peter Williams of the Australian National University offered constructive comments on the first drafts of Chapter 3. Barbara Horvath of Sydney University and S. Martin Taylor of McMaster University commented upon Chapter 4, while David Kennedy of Harvard University's Law School and Sue Tongue of Tufts University's Fletcher School offered comments on Chapters 6 and 7. Shirley Clark, then of the Kennedy School at Harvard, provided great assistance with Chapter 9. Thanks also to Richard Higgott of Murdoch University, Robert Sack of the University of Wisconsin, and Allen Scott of UCLA, who all read and commented on the whole manuscript. More generally, we would like to thank our colleagues in geography and planning for their support of our research.

Finally, we wish to acknowledge the permission of the Editor, *Economic Geography*, to reproduce excerpts from a paper, entitled "Rights, property and community," and Pion Ltd (publishers of *Environment and Planning A*) for allowing us to reproduce portions of two papers, "Law, the state, and the spatial integration of the United States" and "Dimensions of local state autonomy" in Chapters 6 and 7. Glenda Laws, of McMaster University, compiled the index.

GORDON L. CLARK
MICHAEL DEAR

Chicago, Ill. & Hamilton, Ont.; August 1983.

Contents

Preface and acknowledgments	*page* vii
List of tables	xv
1	**Introduction**	**1**
	The question of the state	1
	Capital, the state and space	2
	A note on methodology	6
	Requirements for a theory of the state	8
2	**The problematic of the capitalist state**	**14**
	Analytical alternatives	15
	Theories of the state in capitalism	18
	Theories of the capitalist state	23
	Synthesis and evaluation	33
3	**The capitalist state apparatus**	**36**
	Form and function of the capitalist state	37
	The capitalist state apparatus	45
	A taxonomy of the state apparatus	48
	The evolution of the state apparatus	55
4	**State apparatus and everyday life**	**60**
	Statization of everyday life	60
	Reproduction in the social formation	61
	The social structuration of class relations	65
	The spatial structuration of social relations	67
	The statization of the psychiatric profession	70
	Everyday life and psychiatric services	75
	Synthesis	81

xiv CONTENTS

5 *The language of the state* — 83

The nature of political language — 83
Concepts in linguistic theory — 84
The structure of political language — 87
The language of the state — 97
Conclusions — 102

6 *Law and the state* — 104

Interpreting law and society — 106
Law and the state — 110
Rights as contextual obligations — 113
Judicial apparatus and spatial integration — 118
Conclusions — 128

7 *The local state* — 131

The local state and capitalism — 132
Legal autonomy of the local state — 138
Fiscal dependence and control — 144
Local self-determination — 149
Conclusions — 152

8 *Democracy and the crisis of legitimacy* — 153

Democracy and capitalism — 153
Legitimacy in a decentralized democracy — 157
Taking American values seriously — 160
Spatial organization of the state — 164
Crisis of liberalism — 168

9 *Justice and the state* — 175

Two arguments about radical transformation — 176
State autonomy reconsidered — 178
Normal and crisis politics — 183
State and society — 188
Conclusions — 193

Bibliography — 195

Author index — 210

Subject index — 213

List of tables

2.1	Ideological classification of theories of the state	15
2.2	Historical forms of the capitalist state in America	32
3.1	The state apparatus	50
5.1	The structure of political language	89
5.2	The social context of political language	94
7.1	Intergovernmental transfers: national government to city of Cambridge (1978/9)	146
7.2	Intergovernmental transfers: State of Massachusetts to the city of Cambridge and vice-versa (1978/9)	147

1 Introduction

The question of the state

The purpose of this book is to examine how the state and the state apparatus structure the sociospatial organization of capitalist society. At the most general level, it is apparent that the state intervenes in virtually all aspects of everyday life. It provides the hospitals in which we are born; schools in which we are educated; jobs at which many of us labor; and social security which supports us until we are buried in a public cemetery. However, at a deeper level, there lies an uneasy suspicion held by many, radicals *and* conservatives, that the state does more than simply supply a range of public goods and services. There is an increasingly popular sentiment that it purposely controls, and even forms the fundamental processes and structures of society, such as patterns of social welfare, income distribution, and power.

For many people, the state appears as an all-embracing monolith, and they cannot be blamed for holding this perception. Consider for a moment a list of state activities, as reported in a typical daily news bulletin: several nation states have joined with the Commission of the European Economic Community to set new guidelines for the control of multinational enterprises operating within and beyond their territorial boundaries; at the same time, a new conservatism has led to sweeping electoral victories for parties committed to "less government;" but as public expenditure cuts begin to bite, many public services are threatened, leading to central state attempts to decentralize politically contentious responsibilities to lower tiers of government; the growing fiscal crisis of central cities is increasingly recognized as a geographical manifestation of the wider problems of capitalist economies, yet central governments portray themselves as reluctant saviors stepping in to "bail out" the cities; this leads to crises of federalism and arguments over the proper allocation of government duties and functions; and people secure in jobs and homes fight to preserve their status, especially resenting local government proposals to change local zoning laws, which threaten their property values and the possible future wellbeing of their children. This list could be extended but, as it stands, it gives a fairly accurate overall representation of the contemporary reality. State activities range over a

2   INTRODUCTION

multitude of functions, incorporating many different spatial scales: local, regional, national and supranational governments; diverse spheres of social life; economic, political, social and legal systems; and many levels ranging from individual through to aggregate processes. How, therefore, are we to comprehend and analyze the complex phenomenon called "the state"?

This book seeks to provide a systematic understanding of the capitalist state and its apparatus. What is the state? What does it do? How does it operate? What structures does it use to organize itself and society? And whence does it draw its legitimacy? It is obviously unreasonable to expect complete answers to all these questions in a single volume. Our particular interest here lies with understanding the spatial organization of the social system and the dominant characteristics of "western" capitalist societies and, in particular, North America. In what follows, we emphasize two themes which are at the core of our inquiry. The first concerns the theory of the capitalist state: how the forms of the state derive from the capitalist formation; what functions are performed by the capitalist state; and which apparatus are used in the execution of these functions. The second theme concerns the territorial manifestations of state involvement in national, regional and urban processes. In this instance, we focus on the spatial structure of capitalist society which occurs as a consequence of state actions. These two themes intersect throughout the book and, as a result, a concept emerges of geographical structure as a composite product of state action and sociospatial processes under capitalism.

The remainder of this chapter is devoted to outlining the problematic of the capitalist state. This preliminary statement takes the form of a simplified theoretical overview of the capitalist state; an account of our epistemological and methodological assumptions; and a statement on the requirements of a theory of the state.

Capital, the state and space

The theoretical viewpoint adopted in this book has its origins in historical materialism. One of the main precepts of this approach is that sociospatial processes are comprehensible only within the context of an historical analysis of the social relations of production and reproduction. It is also assumed that capitalism is as much a political system as it is economic, although the exact definition of the relative importance of these factors is open to debate. Finally it is also contended that state intervention in sociospatial processes is a social event, embedded within society and deriving its logic from society as a whole. These three precepts assume that human agency is contextual, that is, bound within the fabric of society and itself structured by social relations, both material and cultural. As such, human agency is socially conceived and has a past, a place, and an institutional image. In our terms, the theory of the state and sociospatial processes cannot be divorced from some wider concept of society itself.

The organizing principle of capitalism is the relationship of wage labor to capital within a system of specialized commodity production and exchange. This is a general social process whereby materials and equipment are combined with labor power to produce outputs which are then sold by their owners for profit. Capitalism is also a political system of power and domination, in which the surplus generated by labor is the source of profit, and more generally wealth. The exploitation of labor, defined as the ratio of unpaid to paid labor (see Roemer 1981, Ch. 2), is a key characteristic of capitalist production systems which depend on the fact that the value of surplus labor is withheld from labor itself. We assume a labor theory of value, although more as a basis for understanding the nature of exploitation than as a means of determining commodity prices (Harvey 1982). Here, the labor theory of value is a metric, or a criterion, for evaluating the substantive justice of exchange transactions and agreements between labor and capital (Dworkin 1981). In bilateral negotiation over the material conditions of work, employers may be willing to forgo some of their unilateral power of ownership and control. For example, a firm's dependence upon a group of uniquely skilled workers may force it to provide special working conditions and rights of job tenure. Alternatively, a firm may have so many people applying for jobs that it can dictate wages and conditions without reference to the wishes of its employees.

Capitalist society thus has a specific economic and political structure of production relations. These production relations are embodied in the basic structure of state authority and power, since the state itself is both situated in capitalism and sustains its logic through a specific pattern of private ownership. Through property ownership, capitalists are able to use, dispose of, and hold as wealth the goods created in production. Through these rights and entitlements, defined by Calabresi and Melamed (1972) as "first-order" legal structures, capitalists are able to maintain their exploitative hold over wealth and their control over the means of generating wealth. Although there is extensive competition among capitalists over ownership, these rights give capitalists a great deal of unilateral power which does not require the consent of labor for its exercise. For example, ownership rights enable capitalists to relocate production facilities against the wishes of their workers and the citizens of communities in which they are located.

Two conditions are necessary for the continued viability or reproduction of capitalism. First, the accumulation and circulation problems endemic in decentralized processes of production, market exchange and

4 INTRODUCTION

distribution must be controlled or eliminated. Secondly, there must be a constantly renewed labor force which is socialized according to the existing structure of power and domination as well as the political nature of production and exchange relations. Neither of these conditions is automatically guaranteed. On the one hand, commodity production is frequently characterized by disruptive crises of overproduction, underconsumption, restrictive trade practices, and so on. Not only do firms seek to avoid the market by constructing elaborate oligopolistic devices, but these devices often tend to restrict consumption, impoverish the working class, and threaten the economic viability of the capitalist system as a whole. On the other hand, reproduction of the labor force is subject to unpredictable social and individual political vagaries which threaten to undermine the reproduction of a disciplined workforce. In sum, the smooth operation of commodity exchange is perpetually threatened by the anarchy of production and political conflict between workers and owners over the nature and allocation of entitlements.

The inability of capitalism to guarantee its economic self-regeneration and the continuing threat of class-related political disorder imply the need for some systematic mediating agency. This agency must maintain the vital production and reproduction institutions of capitalist society, and possess the necessary political authority to protect these institutions when they are threatened. Out of this imperative, the "state" appears as the guarantor of social relations in capitalist society. For example, the state sustains the processes of accumulation by ensuring, where possible, a rational system-wide allocation of resources and by direct investment in economic infrastructure, such as the transportation network. At the same time, the state intervenes to ensure social reproduction through housing, welfare, and similar programs. In doing so, the state is also promoting its own interests. It is an institution with its own objectives, as well as an instrument for sustaining the social relations of capitalism. Thus, it seeks to legitimize its own actions and the relationships between owners and workers.

We conceive of the state as deriving equally from the economic and political imperatives of capitalist commodity production. The state is ultimately implicated in the generation and distribution of surplus value as it seeks to sustain its own power and wealth. Thus the capitalist state cannot be neutral or unbiased. However, we should not necessarily conclude that the state is the exclusive domain of privileged élites. The state interacts with society in a continuous spiral of response and counterresponse. As capitalist society encounters some new predicament, the state responds, and so society moves toward some further state of development, which in itself generates new difficulties, leading to yet a further round of state intervention.

A key aspect of the market organization of capitalist commodity production has been its particular spatial configuration. An initial trend towards the spatial concentration of industrial activity had its obverse in the spatial expansion of a decentralized commodity market. While firms clustered at the site of cheap power or resources, or took advantage of transportation nodes, commodity exchange was extended through the political integration of world and national markets. Inter-firm agglomeration economies often enhanced surplus-accumulation potentials. As workers were assembled in dense residential areas around the industrial cores, further consumption markets were created, and yet more firms gathered at the core. Through these economic and political mechanisms, a market-oriented spatial system was conceived with its own momentum for growth.

The most significant consequence of this growth dynamic was the creation of two complementary dimensions of spatial organization: first, a "core" area, a complex, integrated hierarchy of predominantly urban centers which formed the major locations of commodity production; and secondly, a "periphery," a variety of hinterlands subordinate or incidental to the demands of the core area for resources and consumption of commodities. In this way, a spatial system was created which was at once uneven but integrated in terms of growth and exchange. Because this spatial system was founded on a process of social organization for private profit, the pattern of uneven development created its own tensions and dilemmas. These "problems" have included political movements of devolution and questions of the core's legitimacy, as well as economic impoverishment and marked spatial inequality. Such predicaments have often demanded specialized state intervention, as, for example, in urban and regional planning. Regional development plans have been initiated in the United Kingdom and the US to arrest the decline of obsolescent industrial areas, to bolster flagging consumption and to coordinate the spatial map of resources and economic activity.

In recent years, a new spatial map of capitalism has emerged in North America and, to a lesser extent, in Western Europe. Spatial decentralization of production has occurred, reversing some of the earlier trends of agglomeration and concentration. As a result older industrial centers have declined, and growth in smaller centers has increased costs of providing public infrastructure and brought new problems of economic coordination. The penetration of the capitalist system into less developed countries has also created tensions in regard to external political control and economic exploitation. Not only is the state the facilitator of economic and spatial transformation, but it is also a necessary actor in ameliorating and legitimating the shifting fortunes of areas and their residents. It is not simply the planned actions of the state that are at issue; more significant, but less understood, is the state's rôle in structuring the general economic and political environment within which capitalist production relations are set.

6 INTRODUCTION

In summary, the problematic of the state, as conceived in this book, consists of two major dimensions: an economic imperative derived from the nature of decentralized commodity production, market exchange and the necessities of sustaining accumulation; and a political imperative derived from the need to legitimate class-based divisions of surplus value and the state's own rôle in protecting an inherently exploitative set of production relations. The historical and spatial specificity of these issues, coupled with a need to develop an understanding of the state itself, implies significant methodological problems.

A note on methodology

We have made a deliberate choice to utilize a historical materialist mode of analysis because this approach accords with our epistemological objectives. These objectives are that any analysis of the state (a) should be embedded within a wider theory of society, viewed as an evolving historical entity; (b) should elucidate the mechanisms whereby society, state and space are connected and evolve; (c) should demonstrate how individual human actors and state agencies impinge upon and determine specific spatial outcomes in the real world; and (d) should be capable of illuminating and thereby guiding social action. Our objectives indicate a concern with the state as an institution, an organization with its own ambitions, but at the same time embedded in a capitalist society. They also indicate a concern with the development of a theoretical perspective guided by historical specificity, but nevertheless focused upon the principles of capitalist organization.

By adopting a theoretical and historical materialist approach, we do not intend to convey acquiescence in a simple marxism or a crude economic determinism. As will become apparent, this inquiry is aligned with recent theoretical advances which are causing a resurgence of interest in historical materialism in the social sciences. Although we are not always in agreement with the neo-marxists and critical theorists, we seek a more developed debate over social science theory and method, including a reassessment of the Weberian contribution and the emerging school of structuralism. As we conceive it, a major thrust in current social theory is the search for what may be called a "middle-level" theory. This aims to link the level of appearances of society, often ideologically perceived, with the underlying social reality which produces those appearances. This gap is rarely bridged, since conventional empirical analysis usually remains at the level of appearances and takes as given the categories of social life, while theoretical analysis is often abstract to the point of analytical intractability and only tenuously related to the real-world context. The issue is then to find a method that allows

A NOTE ON METHODOLOGY

us to move between levels, from the abstract to the concrete and back again. In this book, we aim to develop a set of theoretical categories in order to understand contemporary political outcomes and debates.

We recognize that our methodological tools may be anathema to some research traditions, conservative and radical alike. Furthermore, they risk producing a confusion of different interpretations of real-world events. However, we remain convinced of the need for, and rich potential of, this broadly based attack on the problems of analyzing the state. This is especially important at a time when research in many social science disciplines is converging, and when issues relating to society, state and space are yielding to the penetrating insights of the interdisciplinary assault of new methodologies.

It has been suggested that many social sciences, including geography and urban studies, have been committed to a positivist epistemology which has profoundly isolated them from capitalist society and its culture. This isolation is cause for concern, since it makes ". . . social science an activity performed *on* rather than *in* society" (Gregory 1978, p. 51). Progress toward a critical social science, and away from the empirical–analytic traditions of positivism, depend upon the application of what Habermas has called the historical–hermeneutic approach in social science. This approach is premised upon a rejection of the possibility of an autonomous nonsocietal social science, insisting instead that concepts of science depend upon determinate social context and practice. Progress in understanding the principles of social organization thus depends upon an emancipatory dialogue between the analyst's internal and external theoretical frameworks. These two domains of reality are defined respectively by Habermas (1979, pp. 66–7) as those ". . . feelings, intentions, etc., to which an 'I' has privileged access and can express as its own subjective experiences before a public . . .," and ". . . the objectivated segment of reality that the adult subject is able (even if only mediately) to perceive and manipulate. . . ." Clearly, both domains are social, in the sense of their contextual specificity, and both presuppose a higher order of social organization beyond the individual.

In proposing a specific mode of inquiry into the theory of the state, the choice between the empirical–analytic and historical–hermeneutic approaches is a crucial point of departure. On the one hand, the former mode of inquiry offers a well defined analytical methodology which, however, succeeds only in describing the functions of the state. On the other hand, the latter offers a powerful heuristic method for integrating the relationship between the state apparatus and the underlying social formation. However, the historical–hermeneutic approach proceeds in essence by contradiction, and the interpretive mode of debate is not conducive to the establishment of scientific "findings" or "results" (on this point see Fiss 1982; and the rejoinder by Brest 1982). The methodological

8 INTRODUCTION

distinction between these two approaches is best understood by recognizing that the criteria of validity in empirical–analytical knowledge is successful prediction; in historical–hermeneutic knowledge, the criteria is successful interpretation (Gregory 1978, Table 1).

In spite of the difficulties presented by the historical–hermeneutic methodology, we are persuaded that it is the only option for developing a viable theory of the capitalist state. This is because it is a methodology that requires the analysis of state functions and form in terms of the wider social formation. In addition, there is a fundamental historical element to this inquiry. Furthermore, because spatial structure is to be interpreted in conjunction with social process, analysis of the spatial aspects of the state and its apparatus requires a theory of society as well as a theory of space as opposed to a partial analysis of human agency on the "stage" of space.

Thus, significant methodological difficulties remain. To get below the level of appearances requires much more than developing a series of propositions with respect to state structure. Obviously, such a methodology is anathema to the type of analysis envisaged by Habermas, since such a move would be grounded in positivist epistemology and its constituent ideology. Inevitably, positivist analysis takes as given the very social categories that are the subjects of domination and control. Moreover, those analysts who have attempted to generate empirical studies using marxist categories appear to have lost much of the character of marxist theory in the process. As Wright (1978) suggested, however, there is another choice which requires the development of an empirical marxism, a theory and mode of inquiry explicitly grounded in marxist theory but able nevertheless to generate propositions about the real world. We do not have to accept the "world view" of positivism to be conscious of the need for an informed, reality-based theoretical discourse. Our assumption is that building such a discourse is in itself a social act, which is inherently normative, not positive.

This sentiment has been expressed by Hirsch (1978) among others, in his study of the capitalist state. He argued for a theory of the state that could come to grips with the concrete expression of state power and activity. Simply put, we cannot be satisfied with a theory of the state in its abstract form. If specific apparatus and outcomes cannot be integrated with the theoretical argument we will have only succeeded in substituting one partial and formalistic theory for another. Given these methodological suppositions, we can now restate and clarify the desirable qualities of a theory of the capitalist state.

Requirements for a theory of the state

We wish to provide an account of the links between the capitalist state apparatus and sociospatial processes. This necessitates a clear exposition of the theory of the state and society, and also of how this theory relates to specific aspects of sociospatial structuration. In addition, the theory must be able to distinguish between the political and economic imperatives that provide the basis of state action. This necessitates an explicit recognition of the political autonomy of the state and the inevitably political nature of capitalist social relations. The difficulties of linking such abstract theory with particular facets of social existence are addressed by developing categories of state form, state functions and state apparatus. In this way, the actions of an individual state apparatus or institution may be traced back to particular theoretical categories and explanations, and vice versa.

This objective requires an *integrated* account of the state. As we define it, an integrated theory of the state should (a) provide a clear theoretical account of the state; (b) allow for concrete historical analyses and empirical evaluations of propositions regarding the state; (c) account for the operations of the state at a variety of geographical scales at both national and local levels; and (d) permit analysis of state intervention at various social scales, from individual through to aggregate or group processes. Our integrated analysis of the state aims systematically to expose the multidimensional economic and political character of the contemporary capitalist state. This will include consideration of the structure and institutions of the state (that is, its apparatus, language, ideology and culture) and how the everyday lives of groups and individuals are affected by the state and its apparatus.

Two specific emphases are important in our account of state form, function and apparatus. The first is that our theoretical stance is *state-centered*, in that we begin analysis from the viewpoint of the state as it is embedded within the structural relations of capitalism. This mode of analysis stands in sharp contrast to the more traditional theories of the state, be they marxist or liberal, which are *society-centered*. In these theories, society is the initial and principal object of inquiry, and the state's rôle is derived from the ensemble of class or individual relations. Related to this approach is a second emphasis in our research: our inquiry is essentially descriptive rather than prescriptive. Instead of pursuing the traditional goal in philosophy of defining the state's proper rôle in society, we focus on its actual performance in capitalism. In short, we are not concerned to invent a new theory of what the state should be or how it should act; rather our interest lies in understanding the origins and consequences of state actions.

It is worth pausing to consider explicitly what is implied by a state-centered mode of inquiry as against society-centered theories of the state. To be brief, the former mode of inquiry focuses upon the actual behavior of the state as an institution. Questions of bureaucratic organi-

10   INTRODUCTION

zation, relationships between contending centers of power, and the maintenance of the state's legitimacy through its own actions indicate the scope and definition of this type of analysis. For example, Wilson's (1980) work on the politics of regulation is a state-centered approach in that the objectives of state apparatus are considered in terms of the institution itself, and not some idealized vision of what the state ought to be. State-centered theories often deal with the logic of implementation, and the requirements for building constituencies in terms of public goods (see Bardach 1977).

The principal alternative to the state-centered mode of inquiry is society-centered (Nordlinger 1981). Here the analytical method focuses upon the social obligations between society's members, and hence derives the necessity of the state, and its apparatus, from social relationships. Typically, this mode of inquiry begins with individuals, sets the condition for social intercourse, then introduces the state as a social function (see Rawls 1971, Olson 1965). An example of society-centered analysis is the utilitarian notion that the state is a representative of social procedures, rules and obligations. Defined thus, the state need not even have a specific institutional form except in the particular functions that it performs. According to utilitarian theory, the state's rôle is to guarantee the potential of individual choice and utility maximization. Thus it may simply provide an arena for individual action by maintaining the neutrality of social procedures. For Nozick (1974) the state so defined is an image of social rules, and not an institution.

A more concrete example of state analysis using this mode of inquiry is to be found in the work of political scientists (for example, Verba & Nie 1972) and political geographers (for example, Johnston 1979) who have been concerned with the adjudication of competing social claims upon resources. Here, the state is derived from the existence of nonoverlapping preferences and competition among contending social groups for relative advantage. In these instances, the rôle of the state is to adjudicate competing claims, which may involve sustaining the procedures of conflict resolution as well as determining the justice of substantive outcomes. In the literature on public goods, for example, there is a great deal of debate over the "procedures v substantive outcomes" issue. Even so, whatever the merits of each position, it is assumed that agency ultimately resides with society, and the state is its collective agent. Consequently, action by the state outside these parameters is often thought to be akin to the actions of a rogue elephant, acting beyond its legitimate boundaries and smashing the delicate fabric of society itself.

Marxist theories of the state often parallel the society-centered mode of inquiry. However, they are different from liberal conceptions in that they depend upon a different conception of society, involving classes, not individuals or groups with like preferences, and irreconcilable antagonisms in place of consensual association. Poulantzas' (1973) theory of the state was essentially society-centered. His logic began with the capitalist mode of production, the dynamics of capital accumulation and class exploitation, and the imperatives of reproduction, and then developed the form of the state as being inherently capitalist out of these initial assumptions. For us this conception has a number of virtues. Obviously it is specific to a particular structure of social organization, and has the potential for historical and place specificity. Also, the mode of social organization provides a means of understanding why the state cannot be neutral or unbiased, thus directly questioning idealist conceptions of the state.

Miliband's (1973) theory of the state also shares the virtue of being derived from the logic of capitalism itself. The similarity is shared, despite their differences, by those liberal and marxist society-centered theorists who view the state as being derivative from the social formation. More specifically, both sets of theories begin with social units, individuals or classes, then build society around either shared or antagonistic preferences, and finally derive the necessary collective functions for social continuity. The state is a product of these logical derivations. Yet by itself this mode of inquiry is rarely satisfactory, and is certainly not adequate for our purposes.

The problem for liberals and marxists in following this rubric is to account for the existence of so-called "nonnecessary" functions, those economic and political functions and activities of the state that flourish beyond the necessary requirements for social harmony, as in the liberal model, or social domination, as in the marxist model. In addition, the society-centered mode runs the risk of being utopian and neither historical nor realist. Because the state is derived from a set of initial assumptions regarding the relationships between individuals and classes, causality "flows" from these initial assumptions to the existence of the state. The implied causality is logically, not historically constructed, and has little direct relevance to specific instances. After all, the legitimacy crisis of the capitalist state is as much a result of the fact that the state acts independently of society, whatever the supposed line of causality, as much as, for example, problems of fiscal instability. This is a danger shared by all society-centered theories of the state.

The issue is then to consider the capitalist state in its entirety, not only its logical derivation from class relationships, and to consider also its particular institutional form, functions, and apparatus, and not to regard it merely as a hegemonic integrated institution. Thus, in what follows, we do not deny the utility of society-centered theory, but rather seek to understand the actions of the capitalist state in specific contexts, a goal which also requires a state-centered methodology. In doing so, we are intimately concerned with the state's power and relative autonomy. As will become clear however, liberal theories are relatively weak in terms

12   INTRODUCTION

of this mode of inquiry. By their very nature liberal theories are typically concerned with abstract and ahistorical problems of individual free- dom, consent, and association. A state that acts beyond these theoreti- cally derived limits is inevitably compromised, at least according to liberal theory. The crisis of the state, in these terms (for example, Ely 1980) is due to the state's vulnerability to élites. According to con- servatives, however, the state's incapacity to govern is due to the excess demands of the masses (Huntington 1981). Otherwise, it is often thought that the state is "selfishly" concerned with its own reproduction. What- ever the descriptive power of the explanations, they are hardly adequate for explaining the relative autonomy of the state and its systematic or structural bias towards specific classes.

Too few analysts are aware of these distinctions despite their importance. Many writers, including Huntington (1981), mix their modes of inquiry indiscriminately, using society-centered notions to explain how the state should act and state-centered notions to explain discrepancies. On the one hand, theoretical elegance engenders a specific set of hypotheses, and on the other hand pragmatic empiricism explains away empirical reality. Our dichotomy is useful for analysing the various theories of the state in an uncluttered and systematic manner. But it is also evident that for our purposes, the state-centered approach must be given societal roots; this will help in explaining why the state is systematically capitalist, operating in a biased, nonneutral manner. These links are developed in Chapters 2 and 3 where we strive to develop our own theory of the state. However, when we come to explaining and understanding specific instances and state apparatus we utilize a state- centered mode of inquiry. In this manner, our theory of the state is integrated with society but at the same time its actions are considered in terms of its institutional structures.

In summary, a state-centered approach focuses upon the capitalist state as an institution within a specific historical and geographical context. Our objective is to understand how the state and the state apparatus structure capitalist society, especially the sociospatial processes which, in a recursive manner, envelop everyday life. It is obvious that such a task must necessarily concentrate on concrete historical situations. Hence, in what follows, much of our analysis is based upon contemporary North America, with more limited attention paid to Western Europe. Although this specific focus is a constraint, it also strengthens our analysis of the state and allows a deeper understanding of the wider social and political fabric of capitalism itself.

This research framework imposes major demands upon our analysis. In particular, six major requirements for a viable theory of the capitalist state can be identified. (a) The form of the capitalist state must be analysed in terms of its relationships with the economic and political structure of the wider capitalist social formation. (b) Any theory should fully account for the appearance of, and necessity for, a distinct political sphere in society, separate from the economic, social, and cultural spheres. (c) The necessity of state intervention should be examined, particularly to identify the range of state production and reproduction functions needed for the maintenance of capitalist social relations, as well as the origin and purposes of supposedly "nonnecessary" functions. (d) Any theory should be able to describe and explain the diverse functional arrangements of the state apparatus, in terms of both its sectoral and spatial organization. (e) It should be possible to anticipate and analyze the historical evolution of concrete historical forms, functions and apparatus of the state. (f) Finally, our theory should permit the generation of tractable analytical propositions about the state in the real world.

2 The problematic of the capitalist state

The literature on the state is highly diverse and often confusing. It seems that almost every discipline and every ideological persuasion has attempted to develop its own theory of the state. Moreover, very little effort has been made to synthesize and to examine the respective merits of these diverse approaches. For our part, we are surprised by the degree of commonality and overlap among the various theories; we suspect that they are not all as distinct as their protagonists would sometimes like to believe.

In this chapter, an attempt is made to classify the array of "theories of the state." This is an essential first step if we are to clear the ground for presenting our own theory in Chapter 3. We shall attempt to examine the merits and disadvantages of the various theories in the light of the methodological principles which were developed at the end of Chapter 1. It should be noted that we do not intend to construct a single general theory, although we shall require that any set of concepts be internally consistent. The attempt at a general theory would seem doomed to reductionism at either end of the theoretical-empirical continuum: on one hand, a theoretical reductionism would relieve us of the burden of proof and the necessity for historical specificity; and on the other hand, an empirical reductionism would promote a confused meandering at the level of appearances.

As a general guide to what follows in this chapter, we first intend to establish some basic definitions and clarify the available analytical alternatives for analyzing the theory of the state (Table 2.1). Secondly, we examine theories of the "state in capitalism," i.e., those theories which focus solely on the functions of the state. Thirdly, theories of the "capitalist state" are explored which focus on the form of the state, i.e., its relationship with the wider social formation. Finally, some evaluation of our synthesis is made in the light of the requirements for a theory of the capitalist state. On the basis of this "catalog," we are able to look ahead to the specific reconstitution of the theory of the state which we propose in Chapter 3.

Table 2.1 Ideological classification of theories of the state.

conservative/liberal

    supplier of public goods
    regulator and facilitator
    social engineer
    arbiter
    minimalist

classical marxist

    parasite
    epiphenomena
    cohesive force
    instrument
    institutions
    political domination

neo-marxist

    instrumentalist
    structuralist
    ideological
    input–output

state derivation debate

    capital logic
    materialist

other viewpoints

    corporatist/managerialist

Analytical alternatives

Let us begin by examining some definitions of the "state." We shall find that even the apparently simple task of identification is far from straightforward. For example, on the one hand, Miliband (1973) suggested that the term "state" actually stands for a number of institutions, including government, administration, judiciary and police which together form the state apparatus. Althusser (1971, p. 136) has similarly suggested that the state is not a unitary body and has provided taxonomy to distinguish between its repressive apparatus (the police) and its ideological apparatus (political parties, unions) – thereby implicitly using functional criteria to define the state as an agent of the ruling class. On the other hand, Harvey (1976, p. 87), following Poulantzas, placed more emphasis on the state as a relation, or process, for the exercise of power through certain institutional arrangements. According to Poulantzas, the state is defined as a condensate of class-based social relations. Social power, formed according to the capitalist mode of production, is exercised through a number of institutions including government, judiciary, and police. Again, the state is defined in relation to specific functions, albeit a socially based

16   THE PROBLEMATIC OF THE CAPITALIST STATE

definition. What is of interest in definitional terms is exactly how the power relations in society are constituted, and how they are translated through various state apparatus. At present, there seems to be a proliferation of possible answers.

In the absence of any consensus on the appropriate point of departure for analyzing the theory, let us begin with Mandel's (1975) contention that the state acts to protect and reproduce the social structure, and more particularly, the social relations of production. These functions are necessary, argues Mandel, to the extent that the capitalist system is unable to accomplish the tasks of protection and reproduction itself. In summary terms, Mandel's definition implies that the state acts on behalf of society, ensuring its aggregate reproduction. It is assumed to be a collective embodiment of general welfare, and is made necessary because of the inability of society to sustain itself through the separate, decentralized actions of its members. Mandel argued that the anarchy of capitalist competition makes cooperation impossible; each enterprise is required to attack other firms and exploit its labor if it is to survive. Mandel would also argue that the imperatives of survival threaten the whole of society, especially if labor is so impoverished that its reproduction is seriously compromised and aggregate consumption is curtailed.

Utilitarians make a parallel argument, in that individual utility maximization may not encourage individuals to maintain collective welfare but only their own. In the long run, this may lead to a collapse of the social infrastructure necessary to support and enable individual actions. More pragmatic arguments along these lines often invoke the failure of market mechanisms (the result of nonpricing, poor coordination, and faulty information, for example) to sustain optimal and equitable outcomes (see Bennett 1980). Thus Mandel's definition is shared by many theoretical perspectives, and is obviously a society-centered approach. However, even if most viewpoints could ultimately be reduced to Mandel's simple assertion, it leaves unresolved the questions of the state's motives, methods and degree of intervention necessary to maintain the social formation.

These questions can only be addressed if an analytical distinction is made between state *power* and state *apparatus* (Althusser 1971, p. 140). According to Althusser (1971), state power is the authority relation mediating between the state itself and other social class forces. It is a force which is expressed in the context of state policy or action. This translation of power into policy requires a state apparatus, which is the institutional organization or bureaucracy for the exercise of state authority. Therborn (1978, Ch. 1) recognized four types of apparatus, which reflect various state functions: the governmental apparatus (that is, the rule-making legislative and executive bodies, both central and local); the administration; the judiciary; and the repressive apparatus (police and

ANALYTICAL ALTERNATIVES

military). Note again that these types of apparatus are central to both marxist and liberal conceptions of state bureaucracy. The multi-dimensional character of the state apparatus is thus widely conceded, although many marxist scholars have preferred to focus less on apparatus and more on state power (for example, Poulantzas 1969).

The recent resurgence of interest in the state in the marxist literature has extended our appreciation of (and sometimes, our confusion over) the nature of the state. For example, the powerful *ideological* purposes of the state were given strong emphasis by Althusser (1971, pp. 143 ff.) among others. He included the institutional apparatus of religion, education and political organization as elements of the state's ideological agenda. In addition the evolution of the capitalist state and its functions has been recognized, including the tendency for growth in elements of the state apparatus. As Gramsci (1971) has noted, the democratic system has created a bureaucracy that functions far beyond the immediate requirements of capitalist reproduction. This observation concerning the bureaucratic nature of contemporary democracy has been also made by Yates (1982) from a more liberal perspective. Both writers noted the failure of their respective theoretical perspectives to deal with this phenomenon.

Research concerning the power, apparatus, growth, and functions of the capitalist state has engendered a widening debate, particularly in the marxist literature. At one level the debate has been over the validity of this agenda in its entirety. Some conventional marxist theorists have argued that because the state is part of the political superstructure, the emphasis upon the state as a separate institution is misplaced; instead, they argue, its logic is simply derived from the economic base. This argument has lost its force for two reasons. First, the contemporary crisis of capitalism has taken on an institutional image in the fiscal crisis of the state (O'Connor 1973). It has become apparent that this crisis is more than simply that of the economic base; its origins are as much to be found in the political arena, and in particular the imperatives of sustaining the political dimension of capitalist social relations. Secondly, the evolution of the state and its functions has, as indicated by Gramsci (1971), taken many dimensions which require different modes of analysis from those traditionally used in the marxist literature. The notion that state functions are determined by the economic base is too simplistic and misrepresents capitalism as a purely economic system. As we argued in Chapter 1, there exist rights and entitlements, defined and protected by state apparatus, which are political tools designed to sustain the social relations of power.

At another level, marxist debate over the state has focused upon the appropriateness of competing modes of analysis. Thus the debate has required a reconsideration of marxist theory in general, and this has created both greater appreciation of the state as well as confusion over the appropriateness of different modes of inquiry.

18 THE PROBLEMATIC OF THE CAPITALIST STATE

Previous studies of the state or, more accurately, of political power, have tended to adopt one of three approaches, according to Therborn (1978, pp. 130–1). First, there is what he termed the "subjectivist" approach, which seeks to identify those who have power in society, and is best thought of as a society-centered model. Studies of the power élite and pluralism fall under this rubric. Secondly, the "economic" approach (also society-centered) has attempted a representative theory of democracy based primarily upon exchange relationships in society (see also Downs 1957). Again, the state is derived from these relationships and the requirements for accumulation and economic coordination. Thirdly, a somewhat related, but fundamentally different approach, is the historical materialist approach, which views the state as a component of a continuing social process of production and reproduction.

Both the so-called subjectivist and economic approaches are modes of analysis which address the functional aspects of the state. That is, both describe it in a functional sense, relating activities to demands, apparatus to specific requirements, and power to function. These two approaches, as developed in liberal and conservative theory, are essentially unrelated to the form of capitalist society. These seek to derive theoretical concepts and categories which concern the optimal strategies and activities of the state. The underlying logic of capitalist social relations is left out of the analysis. We propose to categorize these modes of analysis as being concerned with the *state in capitalism*. Conversely, those modes which focus on form rather than function will be designated theories of the *capitalist state*. Our distinction is partly derived from the important epistemological distinction in marxist theory – that between the "level of appearances" and the "social reality" underlying and causing those appearances.

Theories of the state in capitalism

The state as a supplier of public goods. Perhaps the simplest theory of the state suggests that it is a supplier of public goods and services. Three particular reasons for the provision of public goods are normally noted (Bennett 1980): the existence of unwanted external pricing or distributional effects associated with market transactions leading to goods being either unpriced or inefficiently allocated; other kinds of market failure unrelated to commodity characteristics (for example monopolistic tendencies); and a preference for certain standards of community welfare. Public goods provision is often regarded as an allocative function of government. It usually has little to do with the other two functions of public finance – distribution and stabilization (Musgrave & Musgrave 1980). Typically, analysis of the allocation problem focuses upon the proper criteria for government intervention, and the optimal allocation rules for public goods provision. However, although it may be analytically convenient to isolate the allocative function, the distributive consequences of allocative decisions cannot be ignored. The separation of the two issues implicitly favors the existing distribution within society, and can only be accepted if one assumes that distributive questions are outside the legitimate rôle of the state. Ultimately, the goal of the state, according to this theory, is to increase aggregate economic welfare by correcting sub-optimal and inefficient market mechanisms (Baumol 1965).

By considering only the allocative dimension of public goods, most analysts in this tradition (and here we are talking about liberal and conservative economists and geographers) think of the supply of public goods to be a purely technical problem. Positive economics reigns supreme. Given *a priori* defined rules of efficiency, the state functions within a tightly prescribed domain. This is not to suggest that these rules are necessarily complete or inclusive of all possible circumstances. For instance, Bennett (1980) has argued that the Musgrave model is vulnerable to the geography of society. That is, the benefits of public goods are often distributed according to distance from the point of supply – a problem termed *tapering*. Also, the heterogeneity of space, politically, economically, and jurisdictionally, often creates an uneven surface of public goods provision, causing problems of distribution and biased (nonneutral) outcomes. This effect is termed jurisdictional *partitioning* by Bennett. Finally, the costs and benefits of public goods may *spill over* jurisdictions. Yet again, the solution to these problems with the provision of public goods is conceived in technical terms. The state functions within a set of boundaries defined by the society itself with regard to goods that cannot be individually supplied. The state is simply and solely a collective instrumental agent.

The state as a regulator and facilitator.   Consistent with this logic, the state may also be viewed as an instrument through which the operation of the private market is regulated and facilitated. State intervention to sustain the efficient operation of the market is based on two assumptions. First, that a well regulated and efficient market will create the best possible allocation of resources (that is a Pareto optimum; see Posner 1981); and secondly, that the market will not inevitably achieve an optimal allocation or a consistently full employment equilibrium. The Keynesian revolution in macroeconomics provided the theoretical rationale for state intervention in the economy. Stabilization policies and the maintenance of market efficiency through the use of fiscal, budgetary and monetary policies are then elements of a wider political conception of the state.

Macroeconomic policies are not the only instruments for regulating the economy and market place. The state has enforced market competition in many countries as evidenced in anti-monopoly and anti-trust legislation. However, this rôle is ultimately limited to maintaining the "rules" of the market system, which are themselves often derived from the neoclassical competitive model of the economy. Functionally, the rôle of the state then derives from more abstract requirements such as improving information flows in both time and space as well as economic growth and competitive development. These notions of state instrumentality dominate contemporary policy. For example, in the USA, Harvey and Chatterjee (1974, p. 22) have noted three typical concerns of housing policy at the national level. These are: (a) the relationship which links construction, economic growth, and new household formation (population growth); (b) the behavior of the construction industry and the housing sector as a policy instrument through which cyclical swings in the economy at large are ironed out; and (c) the relationship between housing provision and the distribution of income (welfare) in society.

The state as social engineer. A significant aspect of state action in advanced capitalist economies is the adjustment of market outcomes so as to fit its own normative goals. Such intervention involves a judgment about what society ought to be rather than what it is. This is an important concept, since according to this logic distribution becomes an element of legitimate concern for the state. Thus the state may operate to ensure distributive justice, although this is often qualified by the acceptance of the market as a means of distribution. The state as social engineer seeks to redress socioeconomic imbalances and maintain fairness for disadvantaged groups in a decentralized market society. On the basis of fairness, many diverse criteria have been developed in policies of social engineering. For example, in their analysis of school, street and library provision in Oakland, California, Levy and others (1974) noted three increasingly redistributive variations on the equity theme: market equity (expenditures in neighborhoods vary according to their tax contributions); equal results (expenditures equal irrespective of tax contributions); and equal outcomes (quality of service equal in all neighborhoods irrespective of tax contributions).

This concept of the function of the state differs from the previous two rôles in that rather than being preoccupied by questions of rules (as in the efficient operation of the market or the provision of public goods), standards of welfare are the focus of state activity. This focus implies a concern with outcomes as opposed to procedures of market behavior. Standards inevitably require definition, and as Rae and others (1982) have shown, there is an incredible variety of (for example) equality definitions. And yet it would be misleading to suppose that this function is qualitatively different from the preceding functions. All three see the state as a collective agent pursuing socially derived goals made necessary by the breakdown of the market or by an inability to derive social good out of individual actions. Moreover, the state remains outside society, although it may be situated in capitalism. Stated simply, the state has a set of rôles that define it as an entity, but which make it merely a collective actor unencumbered by a particular mode of production. There is no reason to suppose that the state in socialist countries acts any differently in terms of these functions. It remains a quintessentially socially non-specific instrument.

The state as arbiter.   The notion that the state holds a mandate to adjust outcomes in favor of particular social groups introduces a broader, more political function. This is the concept of the state as the arbiter of inter-group conflicts in a society where conflict may exist between elements of the state "system" as well as between social groups. The view of the state as arbiter consistently forces attention on three major questions: Who has the power to influence market outcomes?; Who benefits from state policy?; and How does the state reconcile conflicting interests?

Considerable ambiguity surrounds the possible approaches the state may adopt in its mediation efforts. Dye (1972) has summarized five simple models of public decision making, each of which has significant implications for the nature of state mediation. State arbitration can be viewed as rational, that is, based on some logical criterion of choice (perhaps not unlike the Musgrave approach of optimality rules); incrementalist, being founded mainly in slight shifts in position from existing practices; élitist, reflecting the interests of the ruling power groups; group-biased, implying some genuine efforts at compensation among all interested parties; or institution-based, suggesting that the state may act in its own interests, and may possess hidden objectives in entering group conflict. Whichever view (or combination of views) is eventually accepted as descriptive of the state's arbiter role, the change of emphasis from decisions in the market place to decisions in the political forum is an important distinguishing characteristic of this functional concept of the state. It reflects, more than any other choice so far considered, the reality of democratic conflict and the involvement of the state in determining outcomes.

How this notion works in practice is the subject of extensive debate. A number of authors (including Buchanan & Tullock 1962, and Downs 1957) have attempted to construct representative theories of democracy using public choice theory (often termed interest group theory). In these types of model, the voter is assumed to voice his or her preference for a group of social goods on the basis of democratic voting. Such voting is assumed to be rational in that outcomes are not arbitrary but represent "true" preference rankings in society. Thus in much the same way as traditional economics analyzes relationships between producers and con-

22 THE PROBLEMATIC OF THE CAPITALIST STATE

sumers, the economic theory of democracy attempts to define the relationship between the state (the producer of goods) and the voter (the consumer). Both groups of actors have known objective functions, although in the case of the state, attempts at maximizing the probability of re-election may be undertaken without the knowledge of consumer supporters. Votes then become voter signals, and much emphasis is placed on the ability of the state to recognize and react to changes in consumer preferences; the state derives its rôle from a consumer mandate, and limits to collective action reside in the discretionary voting of consumers.

A secondary issue that has been raised in this context concerns the cost of effective political action. It has been observed that this cost increases as group membership becomes larger and groups less cohesive. The size of the group also relates to the benefits of state activity. As the group becomes larger, the benefits to each member are likely to become smaller, and hence the individual's incentive to contribute to the group will be lessened. A group may attempt to overcome this problem by a redistribution in which all members would benefit substantially; but such redistribution will be much more costly to those outside the group who will be taxed to defray its cost, and this will increase resistance to the group's objective. From an analysis of such factors, the public choice literature has concluded that effective interest groups are usually small and directed toward a single issue. The benefits of a redistribution in their favor are concentrated, the costs of organizing the group are small, and the costs of the redistribution are so widely diffused that few will oppose it.

In describing an alternative, conflict-oriented view of society, Dahrendorf (1959) has argued that the distribution of political authority in society defines a clearly visible authority structure. At the bottom rung are the mere citizenry who occupy no political position other than that common to all members of the polity. In contrast, the three branches of authority in society (the legislature, judiciary and executive branches of government) represent the peak of the authority structure. The responsibility of the state as arbiter involves the resolution of many kinds of social conflicts which may involve all branches of authority. Hence, this view of the state is clearly related to a pluralist theory of society, associated with Dahl and others.

These functionalist definitions of the state are essentially liberal and/or conservative (see Table 2.1), and tightly define the legitimate arena of state action. For instance, those who view the state as a supplier of public goods and services tend to emphasize the importance of market failures of the economic system. Relevant theoretical questions include the proper criteria for state intervention and for allocative efficiency. The research problem in this category is concerned with issues of allocation. In contrast, the view of the state as regulator and facilitator emphasizes the stabilization function of government. It is a view which allows for rather greater, but still highly selective, intervention in the market. Those who view the state as a social engineer recognize that the state can intervene to create specific distributional outcomes. Policy questions here are predominantly of an equity or justice nature. The state as arbiter allows that the state is in a powerful position to arbitrate among conflicting group interests in society. More importantly, the approach changes the focus from decision making in the market system to decision making in the political arena although in some instances similar logic may be used to describe state action.

The minimalist state. The most significant alternative to these traditions, within the conventional literature, is Nozick's (1974) theory that the state should be interpreted as an umbrella organization and sanctuary for widely different and antagonist individual visions of the future. In his model, individuals (and their derivative collective communities of like individuals) could only coexist if the state served to enforce those minimum rights that would guarantee the maximum freedom of individuals to pursue their separate and irreconcilable utopian visions. This is a political solution (rather than an economic one to problems of market failure, and the like) which does not depend upon the failure of the aggregate system; it is the state that makes Nozick's world possible. The state would be supported, according to Nozick (1974), to the extent that it enforces this collective but minimal altruistic vision of "society."

Again we have a functionalist definition, but one that is more abstract than before. Society does not exist except in the sense of its altruistic dimension reflected in the state. In Nozick's model, the state is seen as the location of the enforcement of law; is presumed to be independent of the interests of any one set of individuals; and is dependent upon the support of all individuals for its material existence. Although the definition of law and the rights of individuals are political issues perhaps decided by argument and conflict, the solution is consensual in the sense that the state will only be supported by all individuals if it allows for the maximum freedom of individuals to pursue their separate and diverse interests. No mention is made of the economic system; the state is placed by Nozick in a mode of production that is undetermined.

Theories of the capitalist state

The only theories which self-consciously address the issue of the form of the capitalist state are to be found in marxist literature. Despite the emphasis of neoclassical economic theorists upon the market system, they do not recognize the systematic arrangement of power through un-

24 THE PROBLEMATIC OF THE CAPITALIST STATE

equal property ownership. Their models are largely idealist, and do not directly confront the organization of capitalist society. Marx himself did not develop any consistent theory of the capitalist state, but significant progress in developing a marxist theory of the state has been made during the past two decades. During this period, there have been also a number of studies which, using an historical materialist approach, have gone beyond traditional marxist categories. The resurgence of these theories of the state has resulted in a literature which is at once both stimulating and confusing. This section attempts to systematize the contemporary debate on the capitalist state by pursuing three themes: the classical marxist theory of the state; the resurgence of contemporary marxist debate; and the recent development of a derivative state theory.

The classical marxist theory of the state. The point of departure for all studies of the form of the capitalist state is to analyze the genesis and development of the state with respect to the wider set of social relations from which it derives. The historical materialist methodology proceeds by developing the structural relationships between the capitalist state and the form of social relations in capitalist society. Even so, in his review of marxist theories of the state, Jessop concluded that nowhere in the marxist classics do we find a well formulated, coherent and sustained theoretical analysis of the state (Jessop 1977, p. 357). This conclusion should not be surprising, given the famous dictum of the *Communist Manifesto* that

> the executive of the modern state is but a committee for managing the common affairs of the whole bourgeoisie (Marx & Engels 1967 edn, p. 44).

Subsequently, the conventional marxist view has been that the capitalist state is simply the coercive instrument of the ruling classes, and is a product of irreconcilable class antagonisms (Lenin 1949 edn, p. 9). Whatever their theoretical drawbacks, Jessop (1982) pointed out that these early texts contain much historical insight and were the basis for later, more rigorous analysis.

Specifically, Jessop (1977, pp. 354–7) recognised six different approaches to the theory of the state in the classical marxist literature (Table 2.1). These were:

(1) the state as a *parasitic institution,* with no essential role in economic production;
(2) the state and state power as *epiphenomena,* that is, superficial reflections of an independent economic base;
(3) the state as a *factor of cohesion* in society, regulating class conflict predominantly in the interests of the dominant class;

(4) the state as an *instrument of class rule,* a consequence of its "capture" by a dominant class;

(5) the state as a *set of institutions,* this view tends to avoid assumptions about the class character of the state, focusing more on the empirical manifestations of the state apparatus; and

(6) the state as a *system of political domination,* with special attention to the characteristics of political representation and state intervention (for example, democracy as the best political setting for capitalism).

These six approaches have some similarities and broader associations despite the distinctions utilized by many of the classical marxist writers. For example, the state as a parasitic institution, epiphenomenon, and an instrument of class rule all treat the state as very much the arena of ruling-class hegemony. In these approaches, there is often an implicit argument that the state expropriates power and resources from society, particularly the working classes, and transfers this wealth to favored classes. Hence the notion common in radical organizations that the state is a parasite, removed from the immediate tensions of class conflict. Similarly, based on the view of the state as an instrument of class exploitation, many radicals have been prone to dismiss its potential as a liberating force. The slogan "smash the state" arises out of a particular set of interpretations of the state's rôle in the past. In the other cases, the state as a factor of social cohesion, a set of institutions, and a system of political domination, it could be argued that the power of the state as an independent entity is taken more seriously. Not only is the state seen to be involved at the interstices of class conflict, but also it may structure the arena of conflict (implying some potential for radical transformation if the state can be captured or controlled). Many writers have attempted to clarify these potentials with reference to particular historical episodes (see Skocpol 1978, Wolfe 1977).

Contemporary marxist theories. Recent marxist research (Table 2.1) has attempted to extend our theoretical understanding of the functions of the capitalist state through a set of distinctions that relate to process and form more than to history. The first has been the "instrumentalist" model in which the links between the ruling classes and the state élites are systematically described and analyzed. The second model has been termed "structuralist" because it examines how and why the state functions with respect to class conflict and contradictions inherent in the social system. The third model is more explicitly "ideological" wherein emphasis is placed upon the nature of the language and ideology through which the state pursues class exploitation and control. This last approach necessarily involves the state in propagandizing the dominant ideology, and relates to attempts at mystifying reality. These three models are not

26   THE PROBLEMATIC OF THE CAPITALIST STATE

mutually exclusive, although their distinctions have been much debated in the literature (Laclau 1975, Miliband 1973, Poulantzas 1969, 1978). As Gold, Lo and Wright (1975) argued, these models tend to highlight different aspects of the state's rôle within the capitalist economy, as well as different modes of understanding the causal links between capitalist society and the state.

Miliband's (1973) work is probably the best example of the instrumentalist model. He explores the record of conspiracy between the British ruling class and the central state's bureaucratic élite (civil service). According to Miliband this conspiracy has had as its objectives the maintenance of the class system and the development of social institutions to serve capitalist interests. The focus of research in this model in many countries has been to document the extent of such links, and to recognize the individuals, corporations and families involved. Little attempt has been made in these studies to clarify whether the direct participation of the ruling class in the state is a cause or effect; it has been argued that the state acts as agent because it is enveloped in the tentacles of the ruling class.

In contrast, the structuralist view is that the functions of the state are broadly determined by the structure of society itself, rather than the people who occupy positions of power (Gold, Lo & Wright 1975, p. 36). The "state as agent" attempts to alleviate persistent class contradictions, generate accumulation and accommodate contradictions within society as the balance of power between classes shifts and changes. Poulantzas (1969, p. 73) has commented that the state is not an autonomous entity, but reflects the balance of power among classes at any given time. In more detail he argued that the direct participation of members of the capitalist ruling class in the state apparatus is not the crucial determinant of state actions. For Poulantzas, the relationship between the ruling class and the state is an objective relation which means that the functions of the state are determined in the overarching social formation. Of course, the interests of the dominant classes and the state may coincide, but this is more a product of the system itself than the direct participation of members of the ruling class. According to Poulantzas (1973a) élite associations within and without the capitalist state are "not the cause but effect."

The structuralist model is obviously a society-centered mode of analysis. Class relationships create the state and its apparatus, as well as its objectives. Just as class relationships define capitalism (owners and workers, exploiters and the exploited), so these relationships also structure the capitalist state. Within this conception of structural determination it makes no difference, in the long run, who occupies the positions of state authority. Even before individuals are appointed to the state, its rôle is necessarily capitalist. However, more detailed research

THEORIES OF THE CAPITALIST STATE

of specific instances would probably indicate that control of the state apparatus can make a difference in terms of the specific distribution of wealth within classes. Poulantzas would surely not have denied this possibility. However, he would have also argued that there are structural limits to the state's activities; it is so implicated in the relations of capitalism that it is unable to deny the basic structure of the relations themselves. As the balance of class power shifts, so does the state's behavior and membership. The state in this model is part of society – a socially determined (that is, structural) formation.

The third marxist approach reflects a wider concern with the ideology and mystification of capitalist reality. Researchers in this tradition ask the question "what is the state?" The conclusion, derived from a Hegelian–marxist perspective, is that

> the state is a mystification, a concrete institution which serves the interests of the dominant class, but which seeks to portray itself as serving the nation as a whole, by obscuring the basic lines of class antagonism (Gold, Lo & Wright 1975, p. 40).

Thus the state, as an agent of the ruling class within society, seeks to misrepresent itself in order to maintain class divisions and inequality, thereby defusing different class aspirations by delegitimizing class interests in terms of a utopian conception of society as a broad homogeneous and inclusive community.

Serious criticisms have been offered of both the instrumentalist and structuralist viewpoints. It has been argued that Miliband's instrumentalism has done little more than take account of changes in the nature of the ruling class. An empiricist focus on how the state acts, and the absence of a theoretical framework for the empirical investigation of state organization ". . . limits his (Miliband's) work to a redirection of the 'plurality of élites' into a theory of the *influence* of the ruling class" (Offe & Ronge 1975, p. 137). Moreover, while power élites undoubtedly exist, the instrumentalist approach fails to identify the logic whereby the élites themselves are constituent elements of a wider social order which is independent of specific institutions and personalities. This wider logic is the specific concern of the structuralists, who see the state as a necessary constituent part of class-based society (Poulantzas 1969, 1978). However, this model also has its failings, as for example its inability to take into consideration the historical evidence of changes in the state apparatus both in terms of its empirical reality and its functions within society (Offe & Ronge 1975). Moreover, the structuralist model abstracts from reality to the extent that it fails to relate the historical evolution of the capitalist state to contemporary social conditions. As such it is unable to distinguish between the logical necessity of certain state functions and the state's actual behavior.

28   THE PROBLEMATIC OF THE CAPITALIST STATE

More problematic, however, is the structuralists' insistence that the state has no separate existence from the economic relations between labor and capital. Too often it is assumed that the economic relations exist logically prior to the state so that, in effect, the state is dependent upon the play of class antagonisms. As we argued in Chapter 1, capitalism is equally a political system; legal entitlements and liabilities do as much to define the social relations of capitalism as the market system of commodity exchange. Without entitlement to the surplus products of labor, there could be no continuity in capitalist accumulation: and without protection of ownership of working capital, labor could simply take over production itself. There is, consequently, a two-tiered political structure to capitalism; first, the determination of entitlements, wherein the state must decide who benefits and who loses, and who is entitled to certain rôles or outcomes; and secondly, the enforcement of entitlements, wherein the state protects those who were initially given entitlement advantages.

Entitlements need not be class- or even individual-specific for the state to sustain the social relations of ownership and wage labor. For example, a universal entitlement rule of property ownership if one can afford it reinforces the existing structure of wealth without explicit coercion. The value of such a rule for the state is its ideological strength, its universality, as well as the implied separation of the state from substantive market outcomes which reinforce concentrated ownership of property (see Samuels 1971). But just because the "free" market is the tool for allocating ownership does not spare the state ultimate responsibility in the political definition of entitlement. Liability rules are more specific, and in consequence more politically vulnerable. To the extent that the state decides upon compensation (the value of rights in a normative sense) the state also is involved in setting standards of fairness and justice. Of course, prior to such liability assessments, the state must define entitlements. Nevertheless, questions of liability bring into the open the underlying distribution and the behavior of the state in sustaining a particular relationship between owners and workers. The crucial issue at this point is not the detail of legitimizing tools (this is left to subsequent chapters), rather the political imperatives faced by the state in any choice of entitlement rules. In the last instance, the state can transform entitlements through its unilateral power; whether or not the state could sustain its own legitimacy in this condition is an open question (see Ch. 9). Moreover, this potential is derived from its particular political power and autonomy.

Apart from the limitations inherent in the instrumentalist and structuralist models, we could argue that the apparent dichotomy presented by the two models may be false and misleading. That is, Miliband's analysis might easily be integrated with Poulantzas if we first accept that the structuralist model sets the arena for specific élites. In this manner, Miliband's analysis may then be thought of as a concrete example of the utilization of state power derived from the balance of class forces. In these terms, the political dimensions of the state assume a greater importance as a theoretical as well as an empirical point of departure. The work of Offe (1976) in this context provides an important example of how this concept may work in practice.

Offe's work is based in large part upon critical theorists such as Habermas (1976). The capitalist state is regarded as an input–output mechanism. Its output consists of "autocratically executed administrative decisions," for which it requires an input of "mass loyalty, as little attached to specific objects as possible." This approach has the important consequence of removing the necessity for the subject–object distinction. The state may be regarded as a "thing" and an "invisible hand" simultaneously. Consequently the state exists as an independent, identifiable entity, with its own functions and objectives; and, at the same time, it is clearly situated as a constituent element of a wider set of power relations within society. According to this reasoning, the state can act in the interests of all members of a capitalist class society, and some policies may not directly serve the interest of the capitalist class (Offe & Ronge 1975, p. 144).

From this perspective, state intervention can be viewed as a strategy of crisis avoidance, as well as a more fundamental definer of the social relations of production themselves. The political input–output system, here defined in terms of the language and structure of democracy (see Ch. 4), is a vital mechanism, structurally administered by the state, which can deal with such antagonisms – usually characterized as crises of output or of input. Output crises, relating to the state's administrative decisions, take the form of crises in rationality. Input crises take the form of crises in legitimation where the system simply does not succeed in maintaining the necessary level of mass loyalty (Habermas 1976).

The current fiscal crisis of the state is intimately linked to crises in rationality and legitimation. As O'Connor (1973, p. 6) has argued, much state effort is devoted toward maintaining societal conditions under which profitable capital accumulation is made possible. At the same time, exploitation and domination must be maintained. As a consequence, when the capitalist state uses its coercive power to enable one class to profit at the expense of another, it risks losing its own legitimacy and that of the whole capitalist system. This structural, but political, contradiction is compounded during inflationary periods when rising costs and public expenditure cutbacks cause state output to fall below expectations. A further crisis of legitimacy is thus initiated which imposes pressure upon the rationality crisis, and so on. As the legitimation, rationality and fiscal crises compound one another, crucial

30   THE PROBLEMATIC OF THE CAPITALIST STATE

variations are evidenced in the relative autonomy of the state, that is, the degree of separability and interaction between the economic and political spheres. For instance, in times of fiscal crisis, the state may impose a policy of controlling prices and incomes, thus strengthening the political dimension.

The state derivation debate.   Perhaps the most important new development in marxist theories during the past few years has been the emergence of the "state derivation" model and the subsequent debate in the German-language literature. The major essays of this debate were collected and edited by Holloway and Picciotto (1978), who noted that instead of reiterating the limits between the state and capital, the contributors to the debate have assumed the separation between the economic and political spheres as a fact of contemporary capitalism. Their goal has been to establish the reasons for this separation, theoretically and empirically, while at the same time relating it to the imperatives of capitalist social relations. Without doubt, this research is a bold departure from conventional marxist theory which takes as an article of faith the nexus between the economic base and the political/ideological superstructure (compare Urry 1981).

This need to situate the separation of the political from the economic in an analysis of the logic of capitalist social relations produced two major schools in the state derivation debate: (a) a "capital logic" school, and (b) a "materialist" school of thought. Theorists of both schools proceeded from a critique of those, such as Habermas and Offe, who have totally divorced politics from capital accumulation. Their principal research question has been: why do social relations in capitalist societies take separable forms of political and economic relations? Holloway and Picciotto (1978, pp. 18–19) quoted Pashukanis in questioning the arrangement of a state power formally separate from the domination of the ruling class. More specifically ". . . why is not the mechanism of state constraint created as the private mechanism of the dominant class? Why is it dissociated from the dominant class – taking the form of an impersonal mechanism of private authority isolated from society? . . ."

In order to answer these questions of the form of the capitalist state, the capital logic school of thought insisted upon the separation of the state and civil society. This separation is thought to be vital in the provision of the general conditions of capital accumulation and reproduction, because no individual or competing capitalist is able to ensure the reproduction of the whole. An autonomous state separate from the interests of specific capitalists is thus necessary for the reproduction of the capitalist social formation. Accordingly, the form of the capitalist state and its concomitant functions are concerned with correcting the deficiencies of private capital, and with organizing individual capitalists into viable aggregate units. These concerns translate into four specific functions: the provision of general material conditions of production; establishing general legal relations; regulation and suppression of conflict between capital and wage-labor; and safeguarding total national capital in the world market (Altvater 1978, p. 42).

The capital logic approach does not conceive of the state merely as an instrument established and controlled by capital. The state will intervene against wage-labor and/or against individual capitalists when they threaten the interests of capital as a whole (Jessop 1977, p. 363). However, in spite of the utility of this answer in explaining autonomy, the school has been subject to intense criticism. For example, it has been noted that the capital logic approach again tends to reduce the political to an epiphenomenon of the economic base, without clarifying the conditions for reciprocal influence. Equally importantly the capital logic approach is fundamentally nonhistorical. It is able only to indicate probable forms of the state, and to specify broad limits of variation within which the process of capital accumulation will not be threatened (Holloway & Picciotto 1978, pp. 21–2; Jessop 1977, p. 364).

In response to these difficulties with the capital logic approach, several writers have attempted to introduce a greater historical specificity, and an analytical focus on class struggle, in the study of the capitalist state. An emphasis upon the logical implications of competing capitals is replaced, in the materialist theory of the state, by a focus on the antagonistic relation between capital and labor in the process of accumulation (Holloway & Picciotto 1978, p. 26). As formulated by Hirsch (1978), the specific form of the state derives from the social relations of domination in capitalist society. The coercive, exploitative nature of capitalist social relations is obfuscated by the constitution of discrete "political" and "economic" spheres. Hence, official state domination universalizes capitalist social relations away from the immediate point of production (Hirsch 1978, pp. 61–4). State activity is then structurally implicated in the political relations of production but is also conditioned by more aggregate discontinuities in accumulation and market coordination.

In summary, Holloway and Picciotto (1978, p. 26) observed that the materialist approach, which begins with the relationship between capital and wage labor, provides a means for understanding not only the political autonomy of the state but also its intimate connections with the underlying mode of production. We have thus returned essentially to our point of departure, noted in Chapter 1. For our purposes, state intervention can be regarded as a response to the political repercussions of accumulation. Again, there is no necessity for such intervention always to be in the interests of capital. Instead, the structure of state intervention could be more consistently interpreted as crisis management and political

32   THE PROBLEMATIC OF THE CAPITALIST STATE

reproduction, determined by changes in the balance of class forces (see Habermas 1976, Jessop 1977, p. 306).

Corporatism. Before concluding this review, we should mention one other recent development: the "corporatist" or "managerial" view of the state. This regards the state as harbinger of a new economic system in which the state acquires and controls business, utilizing powers far in excess of those needed for support and guidance of capitalism and imposes principles of unity, order, nationalism, and success, that is, a commitment to results with scant concern for means (Westergaard 1977). These (and other) descriptions of a supposed new order provide only partial insight into the evolution of the interrelationships between the state and capitalist society. A specifically historical viewpoint is necessary if the dynamics of state and social formation are to be fully understood. This point is demonstrated by Wolfe (1977), who concluded that the political tensions of evolving US capitalism have resulted, historically, in six forms of the state (Table 2.2). According to Wolfe (1977, p. 10), all six solutions have currently exhausted themselves, but they continue to exist as legacies although no single one dominates. Late capitalism has ushered in a period of political stagnation, in which the hybrid or outmoded state forms cannot adequately satisfy the political needs they create.

Table 2.2 Historical forms of the capitalist state in America (based upon Wolfe 1977).

(1) *Accumulative state* designed to ensure active governmental intervention in early capitalist accumulation
(2) *Harmonious state,* the first "legitimation" view of the state, suggesting that all classes could benefit from activities of the dominant class
(3) *Expansionist state* which alleviated conflict through extension of political activities
(4) *Franchise state* which attempted to solve conflict by granting public power to private agencies
(5) *Dual state* which created two faces of the same state, one responsible for accumulation, the other for legitimation
(6) *Transnational state* which extended previous solutions beyond the nation–state
(7) *Corporatist state* which attempted to solve accumulation crises through direct ownership and management

Wolfe's categories represent transformations of the capitalist state at various times of crisis. In his case, the historical viewpoint is more descriptive than theoretical. For instance, the expansionist state could be thought of as a response to the great depression. For our purposes, however, these categories are not immediately relevant in resolving methodological issues around the theory of the state. And we place the notions of corporatism in the same category, as descriptive of the most recent phase of the evolution of the interrelationships between state and capitalist society (Table 2.2). We do not view corporatism as a separate theory of the state, but regard it as having the same functionalist characteristics as other theories of the state in capitalism. This issue is taken up again in Chapter 3.

Synthesis and evaluation

As a first step in synthesis, it will be useful to compare the various items in the "catalog" of state theories (Table 2.1) with the list of desirable criteria for a theory of the state developed in Chapter 1. These criteria, in abbreviated form, require that any theory should (a) link the state with the social formation; (b) account for a distinctly political sphere; (c) identify the functions of the state; (d) account for the structure of the state apparatus; (e) permit an account of the historical evolution of the state; and (f) be analytically tractable.

In assessing the various theories, it must be evident that the conservative and liberal theories of the state in capitalism focus primarily on the functions of the state, and are certainly tractable in terms of generating testable hypotheses. However, they lack insight in relating the state to the wider social formation. The classical marxist and neo-marxist theories tend to do the opposite. These theories generally provide a highly abstract account of the state and the capitalist social formation, but tend to be analytically intractable. The exceptions are the instrumentalist and input–output approaches, which have been criticized for their lack of a theoretical basis. The state derivation debate provides such a basis, while providing a foundation for a tractable analysis of concrete state formations.

From the discussion of the materialist and capital logic theories it is apparent that the state may be viewed as both capitalist and autonomous, that is, simultaneously embedded in the social relations of capitalism and as an institution of power and authority in its own right. The distinction between the political and economic spheres posed by the derivationist school is a crucial insight which immediately separates it from other theories. For example, Poulantzas's model is conceived in terms of class relations and the organization of the mode of production. At base, this structuralist model of the state is society-centered, even though it allows for the instrumental use of state power. The virtue of the derivationist conception, and in particular the materialist model, is that the state can be analysed as a separate institution and given an agenda conceived in the social relations of production; however, once it is formed as an historical entity, the state also has qualities of an autonomous actor. Here,

34   THE PROBLEMATIC OF THE CAPITALIST STATE

then, is the basis of our analysis of the capitalist state. We assume a separation between the political and economic spheres that in practice sustains the capitalist state as a distinct institution. We have little sympathy with the notion that the mode of production is the ultimate constraint on state actions. The state is a political object and actor in its own right.

The significant emphases and directions proposed by the materialist theory of the state are as follows. In spite of protestations to the contrary (for example, Holloway & Picciotto 1978, Introduction; Therborn 1978, p. 30), the materialist approach does provide for a specific theory of the political, which focuses on the derivation of the form and functions of the state from the capitalist social formation. The relationship between the economic and political spheres is properly regarded as one of mutual interaction. In addition, emphasis is placed upon an historical interpretation of the state's development. Thus in the longer term, the form of the state can be expected to alter as political conditions and modes of capital accumulation call forth new responses. Hence, state functions and apparatus, including appropriate arrangements of political representation and legislation, will also change. This notion that the state's institutional structure and its mode of action is transformed by, and transforms, the social formation is of course the basis of recent characterizations of the historical evolution of the form of the American state apparatus (proposed by Wolfe 1977). His work has implied that the precise form of the capitalist state can be based, in theory, upon the stage of development of the relevant mode of production, and the internal political and economic relationships of capitalism itself.

While the materialist theory isolates crises in capital accumulation as a primary catalyst for state intervention, it is also intended to cope with the equally important political repercussions of social relations and the fundamental problem of sustaining legitimacy (Habermas 1976, Offe & Ronge 1975). Such emphasis lays stress on the rôle of the state in a system of political domination, although the separation of the economic and the political may at first sight obscure the form and purpose of state domination.

The materialist theory also places renewed importance upon ideological and repressive functions of the state. As Therborn (1978, p. 173) has suggested, the process of social reproduction is a synthesis of "economic, political and ideological processes." Ideology tells individuals what exists, what is possible, and what is right and wrong. The state plays a vital rôle in designing and implementing ideology, convincing the ruled of the legitimacy of the rulers. The aspirations and interests of the mass of people must therefore be incorporated into the dominant ideology if the social order is to be maintained in a noncoercive manner (see Jessop 1977, pp. 367–8).

Finally the materialist theory of the state allows for a clear focus on the functions of the state. Following Offe, emphasis is placed on the processes of transformation whereby demands upon the state apparatus (inputs) are translated into administrative decisions (outputs), and on how crises of legitimacy and rationality are managed in these processes. Henceforth, observed problems in specific categories of state intervention, such as urban and regional planning, should no longer be regarded as failures of particular mechanisms. Instead they should be traced to the systematic, structural contradictions in the form and function of the state, and their relationship to the capitalist mode of production (see Dear and Scott 1981, Scott 1980).

3   The capitalist state apparatus

Our objective in this chapter is to derive a systematic framework which will account for the origins and functions of the state apparatus. Is the system a monolithic object with a consistent purpose? Or is it a disparate collection of loosely related institutions with conflicting objectives? How are its organizational limits structured by state power, and how does the individual apparatus react upon the agents which established it? To begin to answer these questions, it may be useful to reconsider the problematic of the state apparatus within the framework developed in Chapter 2. A proper analysis of *state apparatus* requires an understanding of *state functions* which in turn must be derived from analysis of *state form*. Recall that the question of "form" examines how a specific state structure is constituted by, and evolves within, a given social formation; state "function" refers to those activities undertaken in the name of the state, that is, what the state actually does in capitalist society; and state "apparatus" refers to the mechanisms through which these functions are executed. Therefore, the proper analytical logic would begin with issues of form, proceed to derive notions of function, and end by reading off the set of apparatus.

In the existing literature, the first two steps in this logic are well defined; the latter step is virtually ignored. In fact, it is only very recently that research attention has been directed toward the state apparatus as such. In one early study, Therborn (1976) argued strongly for a typology of state interventions and a typology of state structures in order to guide analysis of what the state does, and the methods it uses. This plea was echoed by Wright (1978) who stressed the need for a theory which will relate social structure to the internal organization of the state. One particularly noteworthy absence in analyses of the state apparatus is a systematic description of the apparatus itself. From the evidence of the accumulation of lists of institutions and organizations, it appears that most analysts regard the apparatus as a monolithic ensemble of diverse organizations representative of state power. A notable exception is Therborn (1978), who attempted to outline a set of "characteristic organizational forms" associated with the input, transformation, and output operations of the capitalist state. However, a clear taxonomy of the mechanisms of the state apparatus did not result from his analysis.

FORM AND FUNCTION OF THE CAPITALIST STATE

Our form–function–apparatus logic imposes a fairly rigid framework on the analysis which follows in this chapter. Any model which addresses the origin and structure of the state apparatus must:

(a) be clearly embedded in the theoretical hierarchy implied by the sequence of state form, state function and state apparatus;
(b) provide a comprehensive taxonomy of the internal organizations of the state; and
(c) permit historical analysis of the evolution of the state apparatus as it intersects with a changing social reality.

The remainder of this chapter is organized around each of these three precepts.

Form and function of the capitalist state

Form of the contemporary state. The question of form is directed toward understanding how and why a particular state structure derives from a given social formation. In theory, a capitalist social formation should give rise to a distinctively capitalist state form, and an evolving social formation should realize concomitant change in the state structure. Thus, the state is a specifically capitalist state to the extent that the character of the society in which it is embedded is a capitalist society. However, this generalized, essentially functionalist, interpretation of the capitalist state needs a fuller elaboration if it is to explain any specific state formation. What we require is an explanation of exactly how the power relations of capitalism are constituted, and translated into institutions of the state apparatus.

Let us take as a point of departure the now familiar notion that the state is a relation, or process, for the exercise of power through certain institutional arrangements. The state may thus be viewed as a condensate of class-based social relations (Poulantzas 1969), acting for ". . . the protection and reproduction of the social structure . . . insofar as this is not achieved by the automatic processes of the economy" (Mandel 1975, p. 474). The state is not neutral in the exercise of power, but is bound by its structural connections with the capitalist economy to secure the conditions for capital accumulation and the reproduction of the social formation. The force of these structural imperatives is buttressed by the common class allegiances between the state and business élites, and by the latter's control over economic resources (Miliband 1973). Although capital has a "structurally privileged" position in the social formation, it would be misleading to deduce from this that the state is subordinate to capital (Crouch 1979, p. 38). The state is depen-

38   THE CAPITALIST STATE APPARATUS

dent upon accumulation, and has to maintain the conditions which permit it. However, capital also needs the state in order to secure the conditions for accumulation (Offe 1975). Capital's need for an agency to ensure the conditions for accumulation is the primary reason why social relations in capitalism take the form of separable political and economic spheres.

Hirsch (1978) argued that the separation of the economic and political spheres is vital because no individual capitalist is able to ensure the reproduction of the social formation. Reflecting the dominant pattern of social relations, discrete spheres are established, thereby abstracting the coercive relations of force from the regular processes of production. The ultimate motivation in state intervention is the need to respond to the political repercussions of the crises of capitalism in what Crouch (1979, p. 40) terms as "the pursuit of stability." In this particular period of "late capitalism," the pursuit of stability has led to a growing hypertrophy and an increased relative autonomy of the state. According to Mandel (1975, Ch. 15), these were the consequences of the increasing concentration and centralization of capital under monopoly capitalism, and the subsequent domination of international capital flows by multinationals. Such economic arrangements have had two consequences. First, the state has increasingly incorporated various productive and reproductive sectors into its general sphere of operations, under growing pressure to socialize the costs of production. Habermas (1970, 1975) refers to this as the "repoliticization" of social relations, as the state extends its market-constituting, market-complementing and market-replacing activities. The first activity establishes the basic rules of capitalist exchange; the second extends the limits of exchange; and the third involves the state in directly steering market operations. Secondly, the late capitalist state has become more involved in "crisis management," as the contradictions of the capitalist economy cause escalating political crises. Offe (1975) interpreted the reorganization of the internal structure of the state, the state apparatus, as part of a crisis-management strategy. These changes have taken the form of increased bureaucratization, increased state planning, and an increased democratization. Mandel (1975, pp. 484–6) also highlighted the importance of the machinery of ideological hegemony in integrating the dominated classes into society.

A key element of contemporary capitalism was, therefore, the extension of relative autonomy and an expansion of the functions of the state (Frankel 1978). As a consequence, all social factions are obliged to become politically active in order to defend their particular interests and to voice their opinions on collective decisions (Mandel 1975, p. 480). Under conditions of heightening economic and political crises, the state has responded by attempting to reduce the intensity of conflict through institutionalizing their aspirations into the political process (Scase 1980, pp. 16–20). This is a trend which has been termed *corporatism*. Corporatism is a term which has been much abused and confused (Martin 1983). The clearest and most useful synthesis appears to have been achieved by Panitch, who defines corporatism as

> a political structure within advanced capitalism which integrates organized socioeconomic producer groups through a system of representation and cooperative mutual interaction at the leadership level and mobilization and social control at the mass level (Panitch 1980, p. 173).

A corporatist political structure is partial, existing alongside parliament, bureaucracy and interest groups. Panitch argues that the appearance of corporatism is associated with an attempt to control the political and economic strength of the working class, and follows Offe in concluding that ". . . corporatism is primarily about state-induced class collaboration" (Panitch 1980, pp. 174–5, 1981, pp. 30–40). Although corporatist structures have proven to be quite resilient (Crouch 1979, Ch. 1, Panitch 1981), it would be misleading to apply the label "corporatist" to all social relations or to total societies. Corporatism is non-homogeneous in its causes and its effects, and is only one dimension of the complex social relations of contemporary capitalism (Panitch 1980, pp. 178–81). However, there is certainly a growing evidence of the strength and importance of corporatist structures in many countries, especially in Western Europe (Scase 1980).

What has been the impact of these corporatist trends? The empirical evidence from Britain (CSE State Group 1979, Jessop 1980, Saunders 1980) and the rest of Western Europe (Panitch 1980, 1981, Scase 1980) suggests that there have demonstrably been:

(a)   an increased intervention in the restructuring and maintenance of production relations;
(b)   an increased centralization of state functions;
(c)   a widening of the representation of labor and capital in institutionalized conflict; and
(d)   a corresponding expansion of the state apparatus.

The systematic impact of these trends has been widely interpreted as an increase in the relative autonomy of the state. This has taken the form of a decline in the power and legitimacy of parliamentary representation, and a corresponding consolidation of both cabinet dominance and of the administrative state apparatus (CSE State Group 1979, Jessop 1980, Poggi 1978).

The swing in the pendulum of power away from the economic and

40 THE CAPITALIST STATE APPARATUS

toward the political sphere has had the effect of blurring the distinction between state and civil society. In Britain, at least, this has led to the appearance of the "strong state" which relies on a complex administrative and repressive machinery to manage its programs and policies. Its appearance in Britain may be explained

> because parliamentarism has already lost, and corporatism has not yet acquired, the faculty of securing bourgeois rule (Jessop 1980, p. 82; see also, CSE State Group 1979, p. 39).

Elements of the strong state appear to be present in other countries of Western Europe, Australia and Canada. However, this manifestation should not be taken to imply that corporatism has within itself the ability to displace liberal democracy as the appropriate "shell" for capitalism. In some countries, corporatist arrangements are currently suitable for capital and labor, and facilitate the activities of the state in its crisis-management rôle.

American corporatism has both similarities and dissimilarities with European trends. Until very recently the federal government held a great deal of power with respect to its level of intervention and its responsibilities towards other tiers of government (see Table 2.2). Ever since the New Deal era that followed the Great Depression of the 1930s, the state has rapidly expanded its apparatus and increasingly centralized its organization and control of the economic system (Horowitz 1983). However, labor's representation in this process has always been problematic. Although the New Deal made some concessions to labor, it has increasingly lost ground when compared with the centralist tendencies of both the state and US corporate capitalism. The balance of power implied in European corporatism among labor, capital, and the state has not been replicated in the United States. In spite of this, in all countries these trends were widely interpreted as an increase in the relative autonomy of the state. Indeed, it is quite apparent that as capital has become increasingly concentrated, the power of the state has been centralized, and, to a lesser extent in the United States, labor more highly organized, so the state itself has come to play a key rôle in establishing the context and procedures of class collaboration.

As a result, the relative power and legitimacy of the various parliamentary systems has to some extent been circumvented. The consolidation of cabinet and executive domination and of the power of the state apparatus have removed from the democratic political arena some of the more problematic questions of negotiation and distribution. Corporatism has provided a convenient mechanism for consolidating and rationalizing competing claims upon the state from both capital and labor. Moreover, through the cooperation of élites from all these institutions, an internal ordering of the priorities of each contending group is accomplished without necessarily directly invoking state power. In this manner, legitimation crises may be controlled and circumvented, although at the cost of the veracity of democratic politics. At the same time it should be recognized that corporatism is not inherent in capitalism, since the necessary degree of cooperation is not automatically achieved. For example, Prime Minister Thatcher (United Kingdom) and President Reagan (United States) have used their power and autonomy to attempt a reordering of state apparatus and their priorities, often against the interests of many of the élites. In these instances, corporatism hardly describes the massive rearrangement of power and state functions. It is in the light of these volatile fluctuations in the structure of state relations that the question of state functions must be reconsidered.

Functions of the contemporary state. The question of function addresses those activities which are undertaken in the name of the state. The term commonly refers to what the state actually does. However, we wish to adopt a rather more specific definition of "function" as a *statement concerning the operational objective(s) of the state*. If the term "goal" is understood to mean a general purpose, then "operational objectives" refer to the means by which this purpose is attained. Thus, the goal of the capitalist state is the protection, maintenance and reproduction of the capitalist social formation, a construct which is derived from the question of form. Then, by extension, the question of function addresses the means, or operational objectives, by which this goal is achieved. When we speak of objectives or means, we do not intend to refer to the specific mechanisms by which these objectives are attained; this is a question of the state apparatus, which will be deferred until the next section.

The logic of form–function–apparatus implies that it ought to be possible to read off the set of state functions from an analysis of state form. However, this is possible only in the most general terms because historical forms of the state may continue to exist in a rudimentary condition and may hinder the growth of new institutions (Wolfe 1977). For instance, the state is older than capital and the functions of the capitalist commodity production (Mandel 1975, p. 477). Hence, a simple correspondence between form and function is not to be expected, and we do not intend to search for it in this chapter. Instead, we seek to establish some basic propositions that summarize the major functions of the contemporary capitalist state.

The literature on state functions is extensive and complex. However, the criterion that a function should represent an operational objective of the state eases the search for consensus. As we noted in Chapter 2, one of the simplest classifications of state functions has been provided by

42 THE CAPITALIST STATE APPARATUS

Musgrave and the public finance literature. Three classes of public expenditure were identified: the allocation function, which essentially refers to decisions regarding the particular mix of public goods chosen by government; the distribution function, referring to the redistributive efforts undertaken by government to compensate for the inequities in capitalist economies; and the stabilization function, which refers largely to fiscal measures designed to regulate economic growth. Although this "trinity" of state functions is enormously popular, we prefer a functional taxonomy which is more clearly derived from a structured view of capitalist social relations. A simple but powerful taxonomy of state expenditure, and hence state function, is provided by O'Connor (1973) who isolated the following: social investment to increase the productivity of labor; social consumption to lower the reproduction costs of labor power; and social expenses to maintain social cohesion.

Even greater explanatory power, in keeping with the purpose of this chapter, is offered by Mandel (1975, pp. 457–8) who describes the main functions of the late capitalist state as: provision of the general conditions of production which cannot be guaranteed by individual capitalists; repression of threats to the prevailing social order by means of the army, police, judiciary and prison system; and integration of the subordinate classes to ensure that the ruling class's ideology continues to dominate so that the exploited classes accept their subordination. Mandel understands the first category to include ensuring the technical preconditions of production, such as transport, the social preconditions, such as law and currency, and the continuous reproduction of intellectual labor necessary for economic production.

A similar approach is adopted by Saunders (1980, p. 147) in his study of the local state in urban politics. He combines the syntheses of O'Connor (1973) and Cockburn (1977) to provide the following taxonomy of key local state functions:

(a) sustenance of private production and accumulation through provision of infrastructure; reorganization and restructuring of production in space; investment in human capital; and demand orchestration;
(b) reproduction of labor power through collective consumption by means of the material and cultural conditions of existence, for example, low-cost housing and parks respectively; and
(c) maintenance of order and social cohesion through coercion; support of the "surplus" population; and support of the agencies of legitimation, such as schools.

Although Mandel and Saunders capture the essence of the state's functions, there is a significant variation in emphasis between their taxonomies. Rather than attempt to reconcile this, we prefer to establish a priority in the classification of functions of the contemporary capitalist state. The operational objectives of the state, in order of importance, may be characterized as follows:

(1) *to secure social consensus* by guaranteeing acceptance of the prevailing contract by all groups in society (Type I);
(2) *to secure the conditions of production* by regulating (a) social investment to increase production in the public and private sectors, and (b) social consumption to ensure the reproduction of the labor force (Type II); and
(3) *to secure social integration* by ensuring the welfare of all groups, but especially the subordinate classes (Type III).

This ordering of functional objectives implies a set of priorities and contingencies in state actions. Social consensus is the primary condition for two reasons. First, consensus provides order, stability and security. State–defined rules of ownership, relations between classes, and definitions of legitimate and illegitimate activities are just a few examples of vital conditions for the stability of any society. Secondly, only when these relations are established can production and exchange take place with any degree of continuity. Thus social consensus is the key constituent of any society as a collective entity. At one level, the priority we have assigned to the consensus function has a philosophical basis, and our view is in basic agreement with others as diverse as Locke, Burke and Marx. However, at another level, the issue is also contextual, in that the particular form of capitalist commodity production requires an especially high degree of coordination in exchange and a stability in class and social relations that enables highly interdependent and organized production systems to operate. Without this essential social consensus, the fabric of social relations and capitalist exchange would collapse. We shall refer to this consensus objective as the Type I function.

Securing the conditions of production and reproduction (a Type II function) is contingent upon the efficiency of Type I functions. By securing the conditions of production, the state guarantees the material survival of all classes as well as the continuity of its own power. For capital, Type II functions essentially provide the infrastructure for economic growth and coordinated market exchange. In doing so, the state provides the conditions for creating profit, and hence ensures the allegiance of the capitalist élites. By securing the conditions of production, the state also reinforces its own power and legitimacy. Since workers, the mass of people, do not directly control or own the processes of production, the state is also involved in securing their reproduction (in the interests of both capital and labor). Consequently, the state is intimately involved in the structure and nature of production and reproduction, for its own interests and those of élites and workers. Inevitably, the state is then also implicated in maintaining a systematic régime of exploitation and domination. Type II functions provide a means of legitimating its own behavior. By securing the conditions of production and reproduction, the state is also able to stimulate the creation of social wealth that can then be redistributed through its social integration apparatus.

The significance of, and rationale for, the state's integration (Type III) function can be interpreted in many different ways. For instance, Posner (1981) argued that, in order to generate maximum social welfare, some degree of inequality may be needed as an inducement for investment and economic activity. From this perspective, it is the social surplus which enables the state to compensate those harmed or exploited as the state acts to secure the conditions of production. Posner's argument implied that the state voluntarily chooses social welfare on behalf of all members of society. However, we wish to argue that, given the initial conditions of ownership, the unequal distribution of economic power, and control over the production process, maximizing social wealth is a necessary state objective because such wealth provides the means for "buying" social integration. Type III integration can be accomplished through taxation, redistribution, welfare programs or other means. However, none of these programs would in themselves sustain social integration in a class-based society in the absence of Types I and II functions.

The exact mechanisms by which these functions are executed are the focus of the next section. For the moment, it is important to reemphasize that this construct of state functions places the major emphasis on the need for consensus among social groups. Consensus is regarded here as the single most important objective of the contemporary capitalist state. To be sure, the production and integration functions may facilitate the search for consensus, but they are qualitatively distinct objectives. They aim specifically at the structure of the economy and the welfare of its citizens. All three functions are necessary for the state to be able to sustain itself and the ensemble of social and economic relations that constitute capitalist society. By ordering these functions, we have suggested the priorities of the state. For instance, without social consensus the processes of production and exchange would be, at best, highly problematic. In reality, of course, the state undertakes all three functions simultaneously, a situation which is fraught with the potential for crisis. This is because, in response to specific demands, the state may face a confusion of priorities and functional responses. For instance in response to an unemployment problem, the state may increase welfare (Type III) expenditures in preference to its Type I and II functions. The priorities represented by these latter functions are thereby compromised, and the state is faced with rationalizing the competing claims of its diverse functions.

The capitalist state apparatus

Generally speaking, the term "state apparatus" refers to the set of institutions and organizations through which state power is exercised. Despite the recent resurgence of interest in the capitalist state, little attention has been devoted to the question of the state apparatus. For instance, in his important study, Miliband (1973) was content simply to list a set of constitutive apparatus, such as the police, army, and judiciary. There may be at least two reasons for the general neglect of this issue. First, the revitalized interest in the state sprang largely from marxist sources which hitherto had rarely focused on the complex relationship between state power and state apparatus (Jessop 1977). Secondly, it is likely that a focus on a separable category of "state apparatus" was perceived as a fetishistic abstraction, diverting attention away from more fundamental analytical categories, "state power," for example. Whatever the precise causes, the net effect was to relegate the study of the state apparatus to the realm of the empirical. This had led to a number of useful studies of isolated apparatus in specific social instances. However, the synthesis of this empirical reality with the underlying social structure has been slow to develop. It was left to the recent work of Hirsch, Offe, Therborn and Wright among others to overcome this misleading legacy.

There are, of course, important exceptions to the preceding observations. The work of Poulantzas (1978) on the state apparatus represents an attempt to provide a framework for an internal analysis of the state structure. His analysis, as well as that of other more orthodox theorists such as Wilson (1975), owes a great deal to Weber. The concept of simultaneous state instrumentality and exercise of power is a crucial Weberian insight that has influenced many political theorists of bureaucracy. Wilson (1975) begins in much the same manner as Weber, concentrating on the institution of the state, its power with regard to civil society, and its internal structure. Bureaucracy in the Weberian model is a set of concrete institutions, apparatus in our terms, which by their very nature both represent and exercise power. However, the Weberian model falls short of being an integrated theory of the state, despite the explicit object-oriented or nonnormative mode of analysis (see Portis 1983). The form of the capitalist state is only loosely related to its functions and apparatus. As will become apparent, attempts at linking form and apparatus tend to be highly ideological, and rarely substantive in terms of theoretical precision.

A most important impetus for the explicit analysis of the state apparatus was provided by Althusser (1971), who distinguished between the repressive state apparatus (RSA) and the ideological state apparatus (ISA). The former is a unitary public body, incorporating government, administration, army, police, courts and prisons, and functioning

46   THE CAPITALIST STATE APPARATUS

primarily through "violence." The latter is a plurality of essentially private agencies, religion, education, family, law, politics, trade unions, communications and culture, which function by "ideology." According to Althusser, the family and education have currently replaced the family and church as the dominant ISA. He also recognizes that the RSA has an ideological component, and that the ISA functions secondarily by repression. The distinction between the ISA and the RSA appears to be one of emphasis, and Althusser has acknowledged the overlap between these categories. Other analysts have recognized the universal ideological component of most state functions, and tend to ignore the ISA as a distinct analytical concept. However, the term persists in usage, probably because of the undoubted significance of ideology as such (Frankel 1978, Therborn 1980).

The structure of the current debate around the state apparatus has been profoundly influenced by the work of Claus Offe. He observed that every state intervention implies a dual process; the state

> organizes certain activities and measures directed toward the *environmental* and it adopts for *itself* a certain organizational procedure from which the production and implementation of policies emerge. Every time a state deals with a problem in its environment, it deals with a problem of itself, that is, its internal mode of operation (Offe 1975, p. 135).

The significance of isolating this internal mode of operation as a separable analytical category was recognized by Wright and his associates who argued that the structural and organizational limits of the state had already far exceeded that which was necessary for the reproduction of capitalist society (Wright 1978, Ch. 4). The "hypertrophy" of the contemporary capitalist state had been recognized decades earlier by Gramsci. In order to explain the relationship between social structure and the internal organization of the state,

> First, it is necessary to elaborate the nature of the internal structure of the state. . . . Second, it is necessary to understand the ways in which class struggle shapes, and is shaped by, those very structures (Esping-Anderson *et al.* 1976, p. 190).

The major thrust in these new writings was to focus attention on the state apparatus and its relationship with the class structure of capitalist society. In the first major monograph devoted solely to the question of the state apparatus, Therborn (1978) acknowledged the contribution of Anderson, who argued that the passage from feudalism to capitalism was accompanied by the establishment of a distinctly capitalist state apparatus. This included the introduction of

THE CAPITALIST STATE APPARATUS

standing armies, a permanent bureaucracy, national taxation, a codified law, and the beginnings of a unified market (Anderson 1974, p. 17).

Therborn himself related the development of the contemporary apparatus to the specific functions undertaken by the state in "late capitalism." The functions of coercive defense, political governance, administrative management, and judicial regulation translate into a governmental apparatus, administration, judiciary, and repressive apparatus (Therborn 1978, pp. 22–42). In his analysis, Therborn not only isolated the need to derive the structure of the state apparatus from the wider context of state functions under capitalism, but he also emphasized the revolutionary dynamics of the apparatus as it confronts a changing social reality:

> . . . although the variance between state power and the state apparatus is limited by the fact that they express the class relations of the same society, at any given moment significant disjunctures appear between the two. The possibilities of variances are substantially increased by the coexistence within a particular state system of several apparatuses, in which different sets of class relations may have crystallized (Therborn 1980, p. 35).

This vital insight emphasizes that contradictions between state power and state apparatus are potentially a powerful force in the social formation (compare the potential for conflict among the various state functions noted in the previous section). Offe (1974) recognized that this issue may assist in reconceptualizing the base/superstructure relationship. It was left to Hirsch (1978) to articulate most forcefully the need for study of the state apparatus. He wrote (p. 107):

> If one starts from the fact that the bourgeois state apparatus appears as a relatively homogeneous conglomerate of governing cliques, party apparatuses and bureaucratic mass organizations and that it is fundamentally necessary to recognize the complex functional cohesion in which these state apparatuses relate to one another and to the classes, the present deficits in theory become fairly clear. . . . it will be vital for any theory of the state not to derive the state apparatus always only on a general level as an abstract form, but to come to grips with it as the concrete social organizational nexus which it represents in practice.

It is to this task that we now turn our attention.

A taxonomy of the state apparatus

There are three main reasons for isolating the state apparatus as a distinct category. First, the set of apparatus cannot simply be read off from the list of state functions; this is because, over time,

> the state apparatuses come to crystallize determinate social relations and thus assume a material existence, efficacy and inertia which are to a certain extent independent of current state policies and class relations (Therborn 1978, p. 35).

Such inertia in the apparatus may encourage the perpetuation of obsolescent structures and hinder the introduction of the new. It may also encourage innovation in the apparatus, as new structures are invented to bypass the old, which may nevertheless continue to operate often with a revised mandate. Secondly, state power takes on a tangible, concrete form as an apparatus which mediates the exercise of power:

> the state exists, it is a definite apparatus to be confronted. . . . Outside specific institutional forms state power does not exist: institutions represent the means of its existence and exercise (Saunders 1980, pp. 187–8, quoting P. Hirst).

In short, the apparatus acts as a medium through which the exercise of state power is "filtered" and inevitably transformed. Thirdly, because of its material existence, the state apparatus can be influenced by those with privileged positions in both the economic and political spheres. At any time, the relative autonomy of the state will depend upon the degree of control exercised by each sphere over the state apparatus. In summary, therefore, specific analysis of the state apparatus is justified because the apparatus is an imperfect, and at times obsolescent, manifestation of changing social relations; as a medium, it possesses the power to transform the exercise of state power; and, as a set of institutions, it offers the potential for strategic intervention by powerful social groups.

Analysis of the state apparatus is plagued by the lack of precision in the definition of terms. Such confusion is easy to understand since it is often difficult to decide exactly what characteristics, in what quantity, constitute a state apparatus. For example, some agencies are run by privately employed, but state-funded employees (for example, some medical clinics); others have varying degrees of public accountability in their operating procedures (for example, public broadcasting authorities); and other bodies are merely regulated by public laws (for example, the professions). It is often a matter of some fine judgment to determine whether or not any agency is appropriately regarded as a state apparatus.

In order to avoid confusion, we begin by conceding that it is likely to be impossible to provide a clear definition of the limits of the state apparatus. Instead, we prefer to establish that there is a spectrum of state intervention, along which there exists a set of apparatus which, to a greater or lesser extent, are state-controlled. At one end of this spectrum, representing total state control of an apparatus, we observe such institutions as the armed forces and the professional civil service. At the other end of the spectrum, we have the private organization of civil society such as service clubs. Between these two extremes lies an ill defined public/private interface. Hence, most quangos are still clearly dominated by a state-centered function, but trade unions are not. But how do we classify a trade union which has opted into some well defined corporatist structure of wage- and price-fixing? And how do we regard private lawyers whose profession is nevertheless regulated by state rules?

We hope to avoid confusion by adopting the following schema: *state apparatus* is a collective noun generally referring to the set of mechanisms through which state power is exercised and state functions realized; *sub-apparatus* is the more specific term for the collection of agencies, organizations and institutions which together constitute the means by which state functions are attained; and *para-apparatus* refers to the set of auxiliary agencies constituted separately from the state and other state apparatus, and possessing some degree of operational autonomy, for example, in hiring, reporting, general accountability, but retaining those functions characteristic of state sub-apparatus. While these categories are still imperfect, they will allow us to speak with greater clarity about the state apparatus, especially with respect to the manifest attenuation of the degree of state intervention in institutions as the civil society end of the spectrum is approached. The terms "part-apparatus," "sub-apparatus," and "para-apparatus" have already been used in the literature without precise definition (see, respectively, Hirsch 1978, Frankel 1978, Jessop 1980).

In this section, we wish to outline a comprehensive taxonomy of the apparatus of the contemporary capitalist state. The taxonomy has two ultimate purposes: first, to describe comprehensively the system of sub-apparatus; and secondly, to provide a heuristic tool whereby historical development of the state apparatus may be interrogated and analysed. Any taxonomy of the capitalist state should be derived from the hierarchy of state functions outlined in the previous sections; that is, specific sub-apparatus should be identifiable as the mechanisms through which those consensus, production and integration functions of the state are achieved. However, the taxonomy outlined here describes an apparatus which is more extensive and complex than at first may be anticipated. This is in keeping with the logic which suggests that links between state form, function and apparatus are more than a simple conflation or cor-

50 THE CAPITALIST STATE APPARATUS

respondence. In order to facilitate discussion, the taxonomy is initially presented in tabular form (Table 3.1), although its full rationale will not become evident until later. It should also be noted that, in what follows, we shall not devote equal attention to all aspects of the apparatus. The purpose and operation of certain sub-apparatus are already extensively documented, while others will require a fuller explanation.

Table 3.1 The state apparatus.

	Functions			
	Type I *Consensus*	*Type II* *Production*	*Type III* *Integration*	*Type IV* *Executive*
sub-apparatus	political	public production	health, education and welfare	administration
	legal	public provision	information	regulatory agencies
	repressive	treasury	communications and media	

Table 3.1 identifies the 13 sub-apparatus which we consider to form the core of the state apparatus. In order to facilitate discussion, these 13 sub-apparatus are grouped according to four functional categories. These are the three categories which we have already identified as consensus, production and integration, together with a new category, executive function. This addition will be explained below.

Each of the 13 sub-apparatus was allocated to the functional category which seems to reflect its dominant mode of operation. Hence, the politics sub-apparatus is conceived as mainly functioning to ensure the social consensus. However, it is clear that each sub-apparatus also has multiple functions; thus, politics also serves to integrate groups into society. The allocation of each sub-apparatus to any one functional division is a matter of analytical convenience only. In general terms, each apparatus may, at different times and to differing degrees, serve all four functions. With this warning in mind, we can now begin a systematic description of the taxonomy of the state apparatus.

Consensus sub-apparatus. The purpose of the consensus-seeking mechanism is to ensure that all social groups have access to the processes of the social contract as well as simultaneously defining the conduct of proceedings. This functional level includes the following sub-apparatus: politics, law and repression. The *political sub-apparatus* incorporates the whole panoply of parties, elections, government, and constitutions. It is responsible for both internal and external relations, the latter referred to as the foreign office. Parliamentary democracy has long been regarded as one of the best possible "shells" for capitalism, providing a powerful ideological buttress to the structure of capitalist social relations (Jessop 1978). One increasingly important element of the political sub-apparatus is the local state. This is usually interpreted simply as a "creature" of the central state, but it is a vital cog in the maintenance of social control (Corrigan 1979, Cockburn 1977). It represents an attenuation of the political apparatus in order to permit the exercise of state power at the local level. In this way, state control over a spatially extensive and socially nonhomogeneous jurisdiction is facilitated (see Ch. 7). External affairs are also a responsibility of the political sub-apparatus. They are qualitatively different from regulation of internal affairs because they are explicitly based upon nationalistic principles. The mechanisms of the foreign office, and its range of executive agencies such as consulates, are increasingly important in managing the complex fiscal, industrial and political arrangements of a multinational-dominated world economy.

The *legal sub-apparatus* is the mechanism which mediates between various social groups, providing them with the means to settle conflicts peaceably. The sub-apparatus consists of the statutes of law, and the court system including the whole corpus of community law structures outside the courts. The law may be used by all groups, including subordinate classes, to secure their rights (Therborn 1978, pp. 234–6). However, the legal sub-apparatus, like all others, is unable to transcend the social structure in which it is embedded, and therefore reflects the class biases inherent in that structure (Gabel 1977, Ch. 6).

The more general category of *repressive sub-apparatus* refers to the mechanisms of the internal (intranational) and external (international) enforcement of stat power. They include the civilian police and military armed forces, backed by such institutions as prisons. In general terms, repression function; in four modes: prohibition of opposition, restriction of opposition, harassment and terror, and surveillance (Therborn 1978, p. 222). Although the repressive sub-apparatus is usually regarded as the "ultimate" source of state authority, in contemporary capitalism it is firmly viewed as part of the consensus-seeking mechanism, taking its place alongside the equally important political and legal machinery.

Production sub-apparatus. The production functions of the capitalist state require a set of sub-apparatus devoted to securing the conditions of capitalist accumulation by regulating social investment and social consumption. Part of this task is achieved by other sub-apparatus such as welfare, insofar as they contribute toward the reproduction of the labor force. However, the production sub-apparatus concentrate specifically on the "welfare" of the economic system, as distinct from the welfare of the labor force. The economy is maintained by three relatively well documented means: *public production,* referring to the range of state-manufactured and state-distributed "public goods;" *public provision,* whereby the state contracts with other agencies for the production and distribution of particular goods or services; and *treasury* controls which refer to the range of state fiscal and monetary policies designed to regulate internal and external economic relations (see Bennett 1980). These three production sub-apparatus are vital because no individual capitalist is able to maintain the aggregate conditions for capital accumulation or the reproduction of the social formation. In short, the production sub-apparatus ensure the continued profitability of capitalism through infrastructure investment.

Integration sub-apparatus. The integrative mechanisms of the state are intended to promote the physical and social wellbeing of all groups in society, as well as their ability and willingness to participate in the social contract. This objective is achieved through five sub-apparatus: health, education, welfare, information, and communications and media.

The operations of the *health, education and welfare sub-apparatus* require little elaboration here. They include the hospital system, all levels of education, and a full range of social welfare programs, for instance, unemployment benefits. These welfare-oriented activities have two functions: the reproduction of labor power and the maintenance of the non-working population. The former includes not only providing the appropriate number and type of workers, but also the rearing and socialization of children, and the inculcation of suitable work and behavior patterns. The latter involves the transfer of a portion of the social wealth in support of nonproductive groups. The health, education and welfare sub-apparatus emphasize that material support offered by the state to most social groups. While providing support, however, these apparatus also involve some degree of regulation or control over the serviced population. This not only promotes the social integration of the serviced group, but it also has a profound ideological effect. It situates social pathology at the level of the individual, group or community, and has resulted in the penetration of state regulation deep into the fabric of social relations, even to the level of the family and individual (see for example Donzelot 1979, Lasch 1979, Gaylin *et al.* 1978, and Ch. 4 below).

This is a convenient point to clarify some confusion that has arisen about the concept of an "ideological state apparatus" (ISA). It now seems that there is little to be gained by isolating the ISA as a distinct analytical category (Frankel 1978, p. 26, Therborn 1980, p. 85). The nature of ideology has been shown to consist of three dimensions:

(a) a system of beliefs characteristic of a particular class or group;
(b) a system of illusory benefits, false ideas or false consciousness, which can be contrasted with true or scientific knowledge;
(c) the general process of the production of the meaning and ideas (Williams 1977, p. 55).

Ideologies tell people what exists, what is possible, and what is right or wrong. They structure the limits of discourse in society, and are present in all aspects of everyday life, including family, school, neighborhood and workplace (Therborn 1980, pp. 83–9). In some sense, therefore, every object, every act carries some ideological sign, in that it contributes toward the formation of social attitudes. Despite the existence of "counter-apparatus" which express resistance to the discourse of the ruling class, the dominant ideology in society is that of the ruling classes. In order to achieve the ideological hegemony of the ruling class, the interests and aspirations of the subordinate classes must be incorporated into the dominant ideology (Jessop 1977, pp. 367–8, Mandel 1975, Chs 15–16). The integrative purpose of ideology is therefore to promulgate the belief that the "system" is capable of overcoming the contradictions of capitalist social relations.

Although there may be no separable ISA, there are two specific integration sub-apparatus which contribute directly toward the manufacture of ideology: these are the *information sub-apparatus* and the *communications and media sub-apparatus*. The former consists of the state-sponsored and state-controlled mechanisms for information dissemination. These apparatus may be conspicuous for what they try to achieve as well as what they try to avoid. Hence, at one extreme, the information sub-apparatus may encourage the release of data or may peddle a particular ideological viewpoint. At the other extreme, active state censorship may strangle the sources of information.

The communications and media sub-apparatus includes the newspaper, television and radio, and telecommunications industries. In capitalist countries, they are normally constituted with some degree of autonomy in decision making, that is, they may be termed para-apparatus. However, in practice, they are universally subject to a varying degree of state regulation. This regulation may be achieved through law or direct political "guidance," as exemplified respectively by the libel laws and by notorious "D notice" procedures both constraining the content of British news, or through careful manipulation as in political campaigns. In contemporary capitalism, both the medium and the message become part of the state apparatus (Williams 1976). This

54 THE CAPITALIST STATE APPARATUS

orchestration of the individual's ideological integration into society extends into the field of *culture*, as the state penetrates further into other fields of individual endeavor, such as the arts (Williams 1981).

Executive sub-apparatus. So far, the system of sub-apparatus was derived from the established structure of state functions, consensus, production and integration. Now we wish to introduce a new category, the executive "function." This is not a state function in the strict sense of an operational objective; it is more an "enabling" activity. The executive sub-apparatus ensures the operation and overall compatibility of the various state sub-apparatus, and monitors the reproduction of the state apparatus itself. Neither of these objectives can be achieved by the administrative coteries which are attached to each individual sub-apparatus. Hence, a distinctive administrative sub-apparatus has evolved, and has experienced a large scale hypertrophy in the conditions of contemporary capitalism (Mandel 1975, Ch. 15). This growth has long been anticipated. For instance, Marx and Engels acknowledged the tendency toward the "parasitic autonomy" of the bureaucratic apparatus (quoted in Stepan 1978, p. 24), and Lenin predicted that the bureaucracy would become the "real center" of power and that we would be unable to survive without the associated apparatus (quoted in Wright 1978, pp. 206–20). Among contemporary analysts, Poulantzas (1973b) refers to the possibility of the state bureaucracy becoming a distinct political force. Whatever the precise causes of its development, the modern administrative bureaucracy is a potent force in the social order. Based on managerial and technical expertise, the administrative sub-apparatus is now so large and complex that it is relatively insulated from political control (Poggi 1978, Ch. VI).

One very significant development in the recent expansion of the state's executive activities was the growth of a *regulatory agencies sub-apparatus*. These are agencies which were created to organize and extend state intervention into nonstate activities, especially industrial relations. They are typically para-apparatus, in the sense that they are ancillary agencies constituted separately from government and other state apparatus, and with a certain degree of autonomy. The legitimacy of these agencies, which include quangos, product marketing boards and similar boards and commissions, resides in their perceived insulation from political pressure and in their technical expertise. Regulatory agencies simultaneously represent and regulate their constituent groups; they are potentially an important element in the current thrust toward corporatism. They tend to be created to neutralize or control a threat which cannot be contained within the normal process of the state apparatus, thus allowing a compromise to be negotiated in an isolated, insulated environment (Mahon 1980).

The evolution of the state apparatus

The preceding remarks regarding the growth of the executive apparatus emphasize the need for a dynamic analysis of the state apparatus within the evolving social formation. The nature of this evolution depends upon many factors including the developmental stage in the relevant mode of production and its relationship with the international social order. As the historical process unfolds, conflict and contradiction within the state apparatus is inevitable. Some of the reasons for this have already been outlined: the inertia of existing but increasingly obsolescent sub-apparatus; the creation of new, innovative apparatus to overcome this inertia; the reciprocal impact of the state apparatus on the structure of capitalist relations; and the extent to which certain sub-apparatus are implicated by the class interests of the groups they represent. In this final section of the chapter, we would like to consider briefly what is happening to the contemporary state apparatus as the state's crisis-management rôle becomes increasingly infused by corporatist structures.

Currently, the capitalist state appears to be "enjoying" a relatively high degree of autonomy. Recent reference has been made to the state as "supercapitalist," and to the "statization of social life" (see respectively, Therborn 1978, p. 167, Poulantzas 1978, p. 238). Many studies have confirmed the tightening hierarchical control of the state apparatus, as well as its overall expansion. In Britain, for example, these trends have altered the pattern of institutional representation leading to

> . . . first, the official sponsorship of carefully structured "participation" in government . . . ; second, the proliferation of para-state bodies not formally accountable to Parliament . . . ; third, the strengthening of the military and police repressive powers; and lastly the development of transnational administrative . . . institutions through the EEC (CSE State Group, 1979, p. 37).

Such developments have significantly blurred the distinction between the state and groups outside the state. The various branches of the state apparatus have penetrated increasingly deeply into the social fabric, requiring a sensitive attenuation, or "fine-tuning," of the apparatus in order to ensure specific exercise of state power over a spatially extensive and heterogeneous jurisdiction. This has largely been achieved through expansion of the para-apparatus, which has itself encouraged the growth of corporatist structures (see Gough 1979, pp. 149–50). As a corollary, there has been a decline in the importance of parliament and a corresponding increase in the rôle of cabinet and the executive apparatus (Poggi 1978, p. 143).

The trends toward hypertrophy and autonomy in the capitalist state,

56 THE CAPITALIST STATE APPARATUS

and the proliferation of corporatist arrangements have many important consequences. The most significant of these, for present purposes, is that the state apparatus becomes the major arena for group conflict in capitalist social relations. Class or group interests have increasingly become constituted within specific sub-apparatus, which thus reflect the relations of power between these groups. *Intra-apparatus conflict* thus becomes the primary manifestation of the way in which class or group interests are constituted, represented and mediated. The outcome of such conflicts depends upon the balance of power between the class forces represented by diverse sub-apparatus (Hirsch 1978, pp. 104–6, Mahon 1980). Offe has outlined a model for analysing the strategies adopted by state apparatus in dealing with intra-apparatus conflict. It focuses on the structure of the conflict: its process; its interaction with prevailing ideology; and the repression encountered by the protagonist (see Offe 1974, pp. 39–40).

During the present crisis, the volume of intra-apparatus conflict is likely to escalate. The apparatus itself is under increasing scrutiny as political priorities shift and sub-apparatus are forced to adjust accordingly. It has been suggested that the state can no longer enforce and guarantee the "rules of the game" (Ferraresi 1981), and that increasingly intractable political and economic problems threaten the viability of the apparatus (Poggi 1978, Ch. VI). Associated discontent in the community-at-large is likely to be part of the reason for the almost universally acknowledged expansion of the repressive apparatus of the state (Hirsch 1978, Jessop 1980, Littlejohn *et al.* 1978 among others). Other responses by the "strong state" to current crises include unprecedented cuts in personal taxation and public expenditure, as well as increasing government intervention in industrial relations. The relative autonomy of the beleaguered state is mirrored in the mutual mistrust between business and government which has led to the increasing use by business of consultants who are able to advise on the likely course of future political developments. Such mistrust is not unreasonable. In one recent dispute in Australia, the Prime Minister and the national leader of the trade union organization negotiated an end to the dispute in the absence of business representatives. Business, as a consequence, seems to have adopted an increasingly belligerent attitude toward government (see the Australian *National Times* 12–18 July 1980, p. 55).

Finally, within the state apparatus itself, both changing priorities and the attempted closure of obsolete institutions and agencies result in conflict, and increase the potential for unintended consequences and contradictory outcomes from actions of the sub-apparatus. The state faces severe problems of rationalizing the priorities of its apparatus but, at the same time, has a wide set of options in carrying out its functional objectives. For example, the state can reorder the priorities of an existing and adaptive apparatus, thereby changing its functional intent from, for example, Type I to Type III. Alternatively, the state can create new apparatus, thereby bypassing old apparatus which may be so institutionalized and bureaucratic that priority shifts are impossible. Another option is to capture an existing apparatus, and by taking advantage of its personnel, power and position, force changes in its functions and its operation.

Reordering the priorities of an existing and adaptive apparatus was, of course, a favored option in many historical instances. For example, during the depression era of the 1930s, President Roosevelt's radical restructuring of government intervention (the New Deal) took place within a broader institutional framework that was hostile to the objectives of the Executive. The Supreme Court in particular sought to show that many new Acts were unconstitutional. One strategy of Roosevelt's was to reorder the priorities of the Interstate Commerce Commission (ICC), away from essentially Type I objectives (maintenance of the procedures and rules of interstate commerce), to a mix of Type II and Type III functions. Through the ICC's constitutional mandate, Roosevelt was able to intervene directly in the economy, going far beyond its original and essentially nonactivist rôle. Production and economic development programs were initiated, as were job creation programs oriented towards social integration. Roosevelt's control and reordering of the state apparatus was highly controversial among conservatives on the Supreme Court. But, for the state apparatus as a whole, restructuring could be seen as a way of ensuring the state's survival through the rejuvenation of the American economy.

Bypassing existing state apparatus through the creation of new institutions and arrangements also has quite a long history. One of the best examples is illustrated in the work by Piven and Cloward (1971) on the decentralization of Federal welfare apparatus during the 1960s. Instead of going through existing State level apparatus, the Federal government went directly to local governments as the conduit and administrative body for dispersing Federal welfare grants. This involved a shift in the priorities of existing local agencies away from primarily Type II functions (basic infrastructure) to Type III functions, but it was also a highly innovative policy that circumvented the established and resistant State-level apparatus. By virtue of the power and influence inherent in the control of resources, this institutional arrangement was able to supplant the existing apparatus. And, because the Federal government retained a high degree of control over its decentralized network of local state apparatus, through regulation of standards of implementation, accounting and eligibility, it was able to sustain its own power. Clearly, the effectiveness of this strategy was dependent upon the resilience of the local state apparatus in taking on and administering its new functions.

58 THE CAPITALIST STATE APPARATUS

So far our discussion has centered upon two strategies where changing priorities were either accomplished by reordering the applicable apparatus or by circumventing an essentially hostile section of the overall bureaucratic structure. A riskier option is to capture an existing apparatus and force a change in its priorities. An example of this strategy was the recent attempt by President Reagan to shift the focus of the Department of Justice's Civil Rights Division from essentially Type III functions, direct intervention in matters such as school racial integration, to Type I functions, enforcing basically universal rights of access and action regardless of race. The results of this takeover were mixed. On the one hand the Reagan Administration was able to placate its southern white conservative constituency by demonstrating its acceptance of demands for scaled-down government intervention. However, this change in priorities faced significant opposition from within the apparatus, from civil rights lawyers who appealed directly to the media, and from more activist sections of the National Association for the Advancement of Colored People (NAACP). A less controversial option would have been simply to starve the Division of funds. On the other hand, however, by "capturing" this apparatus, the Reagan Administration was able to use its personnel, power, and contacts to establish links with the more conservative elements in black and white communities. The Civil Rights Division has thus been used as a means of furthering the executive's power and influence over what were otherwise hostile client groups. The appointment of conservative blacks to administer the division has reinforced the schism between the priorities of its line workers and its controllers. The result has been twofold: a fundamental shift has occurred in function (Type I instead of Type III) and, paradoxically, control of the apparatus has given political power to the executive.

There are other options and possible strategies that could be pursued in manipulating the state apparatus. For example, the state could shift functions between apparatus, utilizing different administrative expertise and models of implementation. However, from the discussion above, it is also apparent that each apparatus carries with it a set of agenda that may or may not be consistent with the overall objectives of its political masters at any point in time. For reasons of inertia and constituency-building related to its specific functions (Type I, II or III), state apparatus tend to be hierarchically (vertically) organized, and to focus on specific outcomes and constituents. Horizontal coordination is full of problems and inherently leads to conflicts over the order of functions, which can have far reaching consequences in the political arena.

In summary, our analysis of the state apparatus has enabled us to map the changing complexity of the state during this current phase of "late capitalism." Contemporary capitalist society is characterized by an increased centralization both of economic power and political power. Class struggle has been institutionalized to a far greater extent than hitherto experienced. The state now experiences a high degree of relative autonomy, and the relations of production and reproduction in capitalism have become increasingly socialized. In tandem with these trends, the state apparatus has become more extensive and more finely tuned to accommodate the task of crisis management in an era of consumption-based politics. As class relations become institutionalized in the state apparatus, intra-apparatus conflict concentrates tension and dispute within the apparatus, rather than between social groups. Most recently, as political priorities change, closures and conflicting objectives impact upon the various sub-apparatus, and increase the probability of unpredictable and contradictory outcomes. The contemporary state is under attack: to save itself, it needs to reassert its legitimacy and primacy; to do this, it needs to communicate more effectively and hear its constituencies more clearly.

4 State apparatus and everyday life

Statization of everyday life

Human relations in any social formation are governed by a complex range of motives such as profit, altruism, love, survival and so on. Many of the consequent social contracts are governed by custom, trust or mutual obligation; others require a more formal set of public and private contracts together with agencies and institutions designed to regulate them. The state intervenes to regulate those elements of the social contract which cannot be guaranteed by "normal" contractual arrangements. In particular, the state acts to regulate those contracts which are crucial in the protection and survival of the social aggregate, those contracts which are especially fractious, or those contracts which might otherwise be ignored by individuals in society (for example, national defense).

Once established, a primary goal of any agency, public or private, becomes its own survival. Agencies tend to develop a life and interest of their own, in which questions of status and reproduction dominate. The process of "statization" is the most effective guarantor of the reproduction of a state apparatus. This process may take two forms. First, the apparatus may expand by absorbing other components of the state apparatus, or, more interestingly, by absorption of hitherto independent, private regulatory functions within its own rubric. Secondly, an apparatus may attempt to penetrate the interstices of the social contract, thereby extending the domain of state control into diverse social arrangements. Hence, any apparatus founded in response to a particular need depends for its survival and growth on its ability for self-reproduction, and its successful penetration into the fabric of social contracts.

Statization occurs because society is composed of a heterogeneous social structure which is regulated by a diverse state apparatus with a varying capacity to regulate the lives of individuals. The integration of class or individual interests with these diverse apparatus is the first step in the statization of everyday life. It does not seem likely that such integration is achieved by a passive imposition of central state power – implying an immediate absorption of a particular agency within the state apparatus. Instead, we envisage a progressive identification of common interests among an increasingly tightly knit network of fragmented political powers and class agents. At any specific time, alliances based on this identity of interests may be tactical or temporary. Integration within the state apparatus is achieved ultimately by the crossing of an often ill defined threshold in a *sequence* of alliances. The evolution of the state apparatus is conceived, then, as a constant reassembling of institutions and agencies to perform continually redefined functions. As each new agency inserts itself into the interstices of the existing apparatus, it is transformed and begins its own process of adjustment. Such transformations imply not a simple engulfment of the new apparatus, but a significant reconstitution of the overall framework within which political power operates.

Given this concept, it is easy to understand why the definition of the state apparatus is such an elusive task. It will prove almost impossible to identify the limits of a particular apparatus, and often difficult even to define certain institutions as part of the state apparatus (for example, trade unions, notwithstanding Althusser; see Ch. 3). Moreover, there will exist no simple formula for providing a precise reading of any sector (say, health care or culture) onto the state. Instead, what we should anticipate in analyzing the state apparatus is a constant contest over any territory which intersects with a specific apparatus's or class's field of interest. Capitalist society is composed of a heterogeneous social space which is characterized by continuous conflict over the ambiguities and freedoms which occur in the interstices between different power blocks and apparatus. It is precisely this competition between the various alliances that characterizes the operation of power in capitalist societies, including the power mediated through the state apparatus.

Looking ahead to the empirical study of the state apparatus, we conclude that there is little to be gained by searching for those responsible in the final instance for a particular social contract or political arrangement. It seems far more important to search for specific categories and sites of intervention, and their connection with the prevailing logic of politics and class conflict. These so-called "surfaces of emergence" represent the structure of opportunities for statization – where the potential for alliances is recognized and the further penetration of the state apparatus possible (see Castel 1976, Castel *et al.* 1982, Miller 1980, 1981). The constant adjustment in these surfaces of emergence is a consequence of the structure of power relations in capitalism and of the overarching requirement for the reproduction of the social formation.

Reproduction in the social formation

Society devotes large energies toward reproducing itself. Marx noted that "every social process of production is, at the same time, a process of reproduction" (Marx 1971, vol. 1, p. 531). Any production process must not only produce material objects, but also reproduce continually the production relations and the corresponding distribution relations (Marx 1971, vol. 3, p. 857). Reproduction implies much more than the mere repetition of existing production processes. A theory of reproduction implies a triple continuity: first, a link between individual capitalists, or economic subjects; secondly, a link among the different levels of the social structure, including the noneconomic conditions of the production process; and thirdly, a link between successive historical production processes (Althusser & Balibar 1970, pp. 258–9). Hence, reproduction is the vital method by which the total social "ensemble," including the state and the modes of circulation, distribution and consumption, is protected and repeated through time. The necessity for reproduction may be regarded as the primary motivation for the agents of the state apparatus (see Giddens 1981).

Given the theoretical significance of the concept, it is important to determine exactly how the reproduction of social relations is secured. Traditionally, the answer has been sought in the functioning of the "legal–political and ideological superstructure" (Althusser 1971, p. 148). Historically important elements of this superstructure have been the church and the educational establishment. The rôle of the family in the reproduction of social relations has also been stressed (Engels 1972, pp. 71–2). More than any other relationship, capitalism requires that class structuration be maintained over time.

The existence of differential market capacities (based on ownership of property in the means of production, on educational or technical skills, or on manual labor power) is the source of class structuration. Two factors are important in the structuration of class relations: the mediate and the proximate (Giddens 1973, Ch. 6). The mediate factors are governed by *market capacities* and the *distribution of mobility* chances in society, since the greater the limits on mobility, the more likely are identifiable classes to form. The lack of intergenerational movement reproduces common life experiences, and such homogenizing of experience is reinforced by limitations on an individual's mobility within the labor market. The effect of "closure" generated by the mediate structures is accentuated by the proximate factors of class structuration, according to which the basic within- and between-class structures are intensified and further differentiated. These more "derivative" characteristics are generated by the need to preserve the processes of capital generation (Harvey 1975). There are three groups of proximate factors. First, there is the *division of labor* within capitalism which is both a force for consolidation and for fragmentation of class relationships. It favors the formation of classes to the extent that it creates homogeneous groupings. On the other hand, the profit-motivated drive for modernization and efficiency often implies a specialization of labor functions and hence, a fragmentation within an otherwise homogeneous group. *Authority relations* are a second force for class structuration. These may occur as a hierarchy of command within the productive enterprise, although as Harvey (1975, p. 359) emphasizes, it is equally important that the nonmarket elements in society be so ordered that they sustain the system of production, circulation and distribution. The third source of the proximate structuration of classes, *distributive groupings,* is an aspect of consumption rather than production. Distributive groupings are those relationships (and their concomitant status implications) which involve common patterns of consumption of goods. They act to reinforce the separations initiated by differential market capacity, but "The most significant distributive groupings . . . are those formed through the tendency towards community or neighborhood segregation" (Giddens 1973, p. 109). This tendency is based on many factors, including income and access to the mortgage market, and ultimately gives rise to distinct "working-class" or "middle-class" neighborhoods. It is at this level that the spatial dimension of the social class structuration process is manifest.

The simple precepts of class structuration tend to lead to the creation of relatively homogeneous environments in terms of social status. Such symbolic differentiation of urban space reflects choice in associates and opportunities for interaction in a class-differentiated society. In his analysis of inequality and poverty, Peet (1975) has developed the formal links between social and spatial theory. Central to his thesis is Hägestrand's notion of a "daily-life environment," composed of residence and/or workplace, and defined by the physical friction of distance and the social distance of class. Each social group operates within a typical daily "prism," which, for the disadvantaged closes into a "prison" of space and resources (Peet 1975, p. 568). Deficiencies in the environment – limitations on mobility, and the density and quality of social resources – must clearly limit an individual's potential, or market capacity; similarly, low income limits access to more favorable environments. A self-reinforcing process thus sets in, and it is easy to understand how an individual can carry an imprint of a given environment, and how the daily-life environment can act to transmit inequality. In reproducing the ensemble of sociospatial inequality and poverty, capitalism normally produces a class-differentiated society each stratum of which is allowed to reproduce itself, using varying proportions of its income to raise the next generation. Since the amount of money spent by each stratum varies, unequal resource environments, which perpetuate the class system, are produced. The city is thus composed of a differentiated hierarchy of resource environments which reflect the different hierarchical labor demands of the capitalist economy (Peet 1975, p. 569). The social and the

64 STATE APPARATUS AND EVERYDAY LIFE

spatial dimensions of reproduction are, therefore, inextricably fused.

In this chapter, we shall be addressing the status and reproduction of noneconomic agents in society. These include, for example, the mentally ill and the mental health professionals; the status of neither group can be explained simply by reference to their control over the means of production. As we shall see, their situation is at once more subtle and more complex. In marxist analysis, the traditional point of departure has been the mode of production, which has been defined as a ". . . combination of relations and forces of production structured by the dominance of the relations of production" (Hindess & Hirst 1975, p. 9). Out of this economic base, or foundation, a whole superstructure of legal, administrative and political machinery develops in order to facilitate the productive and reproductive functions of society. The totality of this social order, consisting of the economic, ideological and political, is commonly termed the "social formation" (Hindess & Hirst 1975, p. 13). The precise character of the social formation has historically been viewed as being determined and dominated by the economy. Hence, the existence of a particular mode of production and social formation is dependent upon a particular form of material production. However, more recently, a fundamental critique of these traditional concepts has been prepared by Hindess, Hirst and their associates. They have suggested that over-concentration on modes of production has restricted analysis to a limited range of economically determined class relations, with the consequent neglect of the more complex social relations. For instance, the simple necessity for economic existence is clearly insufficient to explain the noneconomic forces of class structuration. Cutler et al. (1977, vol. 1, p. 314) argue for the "displacement of mode of production as a primary object of marxist conceptualization in favor of social formation conceived as a definite set of relations of production together with the economic, political, legal, and cultural forms in which their conditions of existence are secured." It is obvious from this that the structure of social relations cannot solely be conceived as a relation between "direct producers" and their "exploiters" (those appropriating the surplus product from the direct producer). The analysis of class in the social formation requires a fuller clarification of the division of social labor into distinct branches producing specialized product categories (Hindess & Hirst 1977, p. 67). Such a requirement is taken as the theoretical base of the remainder of this essay. In what follows, we are guided by three assumptions: first, that the reproduction process is determined by the structure of the social formation, which is a complex aggregate of production relations and evolving sociopolitical, legal and cultural apparatus; secondly, that noneconomic forces in the social formation may significantly condition the structure of power within the state apparatus; and thirdly, that the social processes defining the relationships among various actors and apparatus are necessarily mediated by, and constituted through, space.

The social structuration of class relations

The class relation between the mental health professional and the client is determined by two dimensions. First, there is a clearly defined authority relation separating the two. Secondly, there is some form of "exploitative dependence," where exploitation is defined as a socially conditioned form of production of asymmetric market capacities (Giddens 1973, pp. 92, 130). Notice that there is a mutual dependency in this relationship; the client needs professional care, but the professional also needs a client to serve. However, the asymmetry is clear, in that the professional has a much greater power over the individual client's life chance than *vice versa*. The structural requirements for the reproduction of the professional and client classes are defined by this exploitative, authority relationship. Hence, it is worth outlining in more detail.

Consider first the client. Either by choice or by persuasion (including referral), the client agrees to seek psychiatric help. This is the first source of asymmetry in the relationship between professional and client. In accepting the "sick rôle," the client has been labelled as mentally ill, and has implicitly or explicitly given up certain civil rights or freedoms (even if it is only the right to privacy which is surrendered). There seems little consensus on what physical, social, or emotional problems may be appropriately labelled "mental illness." For the present, however, it is more important to emphasize that the labelling process identifies the client as socially separate, with some form of "illness" which can presumably be "cured." In short, the client needs help, and has to accept the label of the sick rôle and dependency upon a professional to obtain it. The exploitative, authoritative social relationship is thus established.

The professionals for their part are in the business of providing care or cure. Their objective, simply stated, is "normalization," or resocialization of the client. This involves five tasks (see Foucault 1977, pp. 182–3): first, referring individuals to a normative social model which acts as a basis of comparison; secondly, labelling and thereby differentiating among individuals in the system with respect to the normative model; thirdly, measuring and categorizing the specific defects and potential of the individual; fourthly, establishing the level of conformity which has to be achieved by each individual; and fifthly, defining by these tasks the operational limits of the social model of the abnormal. Hence, the professional service offered compares, labels, categorizes, homogenizes and excludes; that is, it normalizes.

The power of the psychiatric profession over clients derives from its function as a major institution of social control, not necessarily through political power, but by the state's sanctioning of professional authority, and through the "medicalizing" of much of daily living. This has been caused by expansion of areas deemed relevant to the practice of medicine, retention of control over technical procedures including the use of drugs, and exclusive access to the "taboo" areas of the body's organs including the mind (Zola 1977, pp. 51–61). With a judicious use of the term "illness," there seems to be an infinite expansion potential for the healthcare business. It is easy to be persuaded by McKnight (1977, p. 73) who argues that behind the mask of the medical services lies ". . . a business in need of markets, an economy seeking new growth potential, professionals in need of an income." It is important to point out that the mask of service is not a false or conspiratorial mask. The care-givers' motivation in the delivery of care can only rarely be questioned. However, the service relationship within which the professional and the client interact has an independent effect in structuring their interrelationship. This relationship may be characterized via the notion of "need." Clients have needs; professionals meet needs; psychiatric services are designed to bring clients and services together. In a society where service is a major business, McKnight (1977, pp. 74–5) concludes that

> . . . the political reality is that the central "need" is an adequate income for professional servicers and the economic growth they portend . . . the client is less a person in need than a person who is needed . . . The central political issue becomes the servicers' capacity to manufacture needs in order to expand the economy of the servicing system.

If this is the case, then professional power to manufacture needs is unbounded. To see this, consider the professional judgments which are commonly made regarding needs and the meeting of needs (see McKnight 1977, pp. 78–89). Needs are first translated into a deficiency which is located in the individual, and which requires specialized service to meet. In meeting such needs, the professional defines the problem, the treatment, and (usually) the outcome by which intervention will be judged. This process involves complex tools and procedures, both shrouded in a mystical language. The circle of dependency is completed.

Once established, the class relation in a professional/client dependency/relationship is maintained in many ways. For example, the tendency toward increasing inmate dependency upon an institution, as length of stay in the institution is extended, has frequently been noted. The longer the client remains in care, the less likely he or she is to leave. In addition, patients often respond appropriately to professional expectations that they will remain sick (Illich et al. 1977). These and other iatrogenic factors tend to contribute toward the development of "patient careers," as various expectations set off a chain of dependency-inducing events.

In his study of the French penal system, Foucault (1977a) has illustrated a parallel "professional/client" interdependency in the prison. Foucault concludes that through the centuries the supposed failure of the prison is part of its true function; that, in effect, prisons participate in fabricating (or, at the very least, merely manage) the delinquency they are supposed to combat. In penal systems, as in other institutions, loyalty to the profession and its institutions often seems to transcend the needs of the client (see Ignatieff 1978).

If there is an overall political issue surrounding the class relations of the mental health care system, it is simply the growing tendency to "psychiatrize" a wide variety of social, emotional and mental problems. Service providers are a different class from service clients, and have a vested interest in the continuing existence of mental health problems. The psychiatric apparatus has tended to produce disabling effects in a population as a prerequisite for receiving care. It can be argued that the apparatus does not "cure" mental illness; that it "produces" illness in clients and their social networks (especially the family); and that it encourages long-term dependency in those who enter the system. The state is strongly implicated in this system. Illich (1977, p. 16) has argued that professionals have turned the ". . . state into a holding corporation of enterprises which facilitates the operation of their self-certified competencies." The state sanctions and protects professionals' power. Some suggest that, in return, the psychiatrist is a conservative agent of social control and repression. This may be true. (It is certainly evident that psychiatry tends to encourage the individual to adjust *to* society, rather than addressing the social context itself.) What is of greater concern here is the precise nature of the links between the state élite and the professional élite, and how state policy is directed toward the reproduction of social relations. What is certain is that the power to provide treatment has been increasingly deeply inserted into the social system (see Foucault 1977a, pp. 80–2). At issue is whether or not the limits of this system have been appropriately defined.

The spatial structuration of social relations

The history of treatment of the mentally ill is a study of exclusion, confinement and isolation. Care and/or treatment of the mentally ill has always proceeded from fundamental principles of isolation and separation of individuals in space. In penal systems, the most intense architectural manifestation of this principle was Bentham's "Panopticon," which arranged individuals in isolated cells on tiered circles about a central observation area. More generally, the spatial separation of individuals for treatment requires four principles: (1) *enclosure*, the defini-

68 STATE APPARATUS AND EVERYDAY LIFE

tion of a protected place of treatment; (2) *partitioning*, an elementary principle of internal spatial organization in which each unit has its specific place; (3) *functional sites*, in which internal architectural space is coded for several different uses, reflecting for instance, the need for therapeutic, administrative and work areas; and (4) *rank*, the definition of the place one occupies in a classification hierarchy, in which status is not so much defined by place as by position in a network of relations. These principles enable professionals to describe a functional analytic space, and to allocate patients for treatment within that space (see Foucault 1977a, pp. 141–7). Such functional classification of patients today takes place in the context of a hospital. However, this was not always the case. Every historical culture appears to have had its "madness," although this is not always easily distinguishable from other behaviors. Significantly, most cultures also appear to have devised some principles for the spatial isolation of the mentally ill. In classical Greece, Plato advocated that atheists, whose lack of faith derived from ignorance and not from malice, should be confined for five years in a "house of sanity" (Simon 1978, p. 32). In medieval Europe, the mad were driven out of the city enclosures, and forced to roam in distant fields. In addition, two modes of ritual exclusion were developed: the "ship of fools," where the insane were entrusted to sailors of chartered ships, and dropped off in uninhabited places; and pilgrimages to holy places, in the hope of recovery (Kittrie 1973, Ch. 2). In the Renaissance period, the previous exclusionary practices were replaced by a philosophy of confinement or separation. The "great confinement" of indigent, old, and physically and mentally disabled began in mid-17th century Paris (Foucault 1965). The purposes of the great "hospitals" of Salpetrière and Bicêtre were economic, social and moral. They were intended to increase manufactures, to provide productive work, and to end unemployment; to punish idleness, restore public order, and remove beggars; and to relieve the needy, ill and suffering while providing Christian instruction (Rosen 1968, pp. 162–3).

The true birth of the asylum occurred toward the end of the 18th century when the distinctive qualities of madness led to a call for separate institutions for the insane. At Bicêtre, for example, the reformer Philippe Pinel began the classification of patients and institutional space to calculate needs, observe symptoms and establish treatment (Castel 1976). In England, the principles of "moral treatment" led to further classification and isolation of patients, with concomitant change in hospital asylum architecture (Thompson & Goldin 1975). During the 19th century, there was a large-scale expansion of asylums throughout Europe and North America, representing a decisive assumption of direct state responsibility for mental health care (Rothman 1978, Scull 1977, p. 31). This expansion often took the form of a massive hospital structure situated on an extensive rural campus. Once again, a spatial

THE SPATIAL STRUCTURATION OF SOCIAL RELATIONS 69

exclusion was being practised, albeit with an entirely defensible rationale for facilitating patient cure.

By the mid-20th century, asylums were overcrowded, and were reduced, in the majority of instances, to purely custodial care. Then, in the 1950s, a revolution in mental health care occurred. This was the time when a strong thrust toward community-based care derived from several sources, more especially the burgeoning evidence of the ill effects of extended hospital confinement on the patient, and the counterbelief that community-based care would aid in the normalization of the mentally ill. At the same time, large advances in chemotherapy enabled the effective treatment and symptomatic management of chronic patients without the need for confinement. These changes in treatment philosophy and capacity were sanctioned at the US Federal level by government intervention, on a cost-sharing basis, to promote a non-asylum based community health care. In both Canada and the United States, the infusion of Federal funds enabled local officials to shift the fiscal burden while simultaneously satisfying contemporary psychiatric and civil rights philosophies. The effect of the shift away from asylums to the community has been profound. In the US, for instance, there were 559 000 patients in State and county hospitals in 1955; this had dropped to 193 000 by 1975. Although the resident hospital census had dropped markedly, the rate of admissions and discharges to hospitals has skyrocketed. Additionally, a majority of patient care episodes now occur in community mental health facilities.

In short, the care of the mentally ill has been shifted into the community. Or has it?

One of the most prominent outcomes of the deinstitutionalization of the mentally ill has been the "ghettoization" of the ex-patients. This is the tendency toward a pronounced spatial clustering of former psychiatric patients, usually in the core area of our inner cities. Ghettoization is a complex phenomenon – a result of a wide range of forces including supply and demand for housing, and formal planning policy. The inner city is the place where there are:

(a)   large properties available for conversion to group homes;
(b)   an established supply of transient rental accommodation; and
(c)   established support networks of both service facilities and personal ties.

Demand for housing and jobs by former psychiatric patients has led to:

(d)   an informal (intra-city) spatial filtering of patients to the core area;
(e)   a significant amount of interregional migration from rural areas to core areas of cities with major psychiatric hospitals; and

70 STATE APPARATUS AND EVERYDAY LIFE

(f) the formal referral of ex-patients to core area housing alternatives.

The "market" forces encouraging ghettoization have been reinforced by
two other factors:

(g) an apparently extensive community opposition which has effec-
     tively excluded ex-patients from most urban residential neighbor-
     hoods, especially in the suburbs; and
(h) the development of formal planning strategies which attempt to
     avoid community conflict over locational decisions by seeking out
     noncontroversial sites for neighborhood mental health facilities
     (these so-called "risk aversion" strategies tend to supersede alter-
     native strategies which cannot guarantee a conflict-free siting
     decision).

The mentally ill have been joined in the ghetto by a host of other de-
institutionalized populations, including the dependent elderly, mentally
retarded, physically disabled, ex-prisoners and addicts. The past decade
has witnessed the development of a "public city," the spatial concentration of service-dependent populations and the agencies and facilities
designated to serve them, on an unprecedented scale. As an urban phenomenon, the public city represents a significant structural change in the
form of Canadian and American cities. As a social psychiatric phenomenon, the ghetto acts as a reservoir of potential clients, and as a primary
reception area for discharged patients. As more ex-patients arrive in the
ghetto, so more services are needed to care for them; the new services
themselves act as a catalyst in attracting further ex-patients, and so the
self-reinforcing cycle is intensified.

In short, the *isolation of clients is still practised, but a new spatial partitioning
has been devised, based in the "community."* The partitioning uses spatial
separation to control the elements in the psychiatric apparatus, so that the
rôles and activities within the larger social environment become
manageable. Thus, the social need for client treatment and differentiation
is translated into a policy of community-based isolationism.

The statization of the psychiatric profession

One of the by-products of the founding of mental hospitals in America in
the 18th and 19th centuries was the birth of the psychiatric profession
(Grob 1973, Ch. IV). Irrespective of claims of its scientific or medical
character, psychiatry reflected the rôle assigned to it by society and
hence mirrored the dominant values of that society. Thus, although
psychiatrists preferred to conceive of the mental hospital as a strictly

THE STATIZATION OF THE PSYCHIATRIC PROFESSION · 71

medical institution, by the 1840s a self-conscious profession, confident of its unique expertise, had emerged within the more general framework of welfare and dependency. The hospitals were managed by super-intendent-psychiatrists, who were frequently lay people or were selected from a corpus of socially concerned physicians. In 1844, a group of 13 of the most distinguished superintendents met in Philadelphia and founded the Association of Medical Superintendents of American Institutions for the Insane (AMSAII, now the American Psychiatric Association).

The AMSAII prepared guidelines to govern the care and treatment of the mentally ill. They argued, among other things, that mental illness ". . . was fundamentally no different from physical illness; it therefore required trained and experienced personnel" (Grob 1973, p. 138). This argument should be regarded as an effort to establish professional prerogative. The status of medicine in contemporary America was rather low, and psychiatrists were more concerned to maintain a separate identity. Hence, they laid emphasis on a broad range of physical, mental and moral factors in the etiology of mental illness (Deutsch 1949). This eclecticism is, of course, quite understandable, given the climate of uncertainty in psychiatric diagnosis and the absence of specifically demonstrable causal etiological links. Moreover, the homogeneous social background and mixed training of the superintendents tended to detract from a purely medical interpretation of mental illness. Hence, clear causal links between illness and the "advance of civilization" were observed, as well as contributory religious, political and educational factors (Grob 1973, pp. 153–9).

The most complex organization problem facing the fledgling AMSAII was its wider relationship with the medical profession generally. Although the superintendents viewed insanity as a "disease," they were highly reluctant to affiliate with the American Medical Association (AMA) which was founded three years later in 1847. An AMSAII motion proposing affiliation was soundly defeated in 1853, and all sub-sequent efforts at amalgamation proved futile. While a major factor in this rejection was psychiatrists' fear that their independence and power would be threatened by affiliation with the AMA, many were also sensitive to the precipitous decline in the status of the American medical profession in the 19th century (Grob 1973, p. 149). The absence of State licensing legislation had caused a proliferation of medical "sects" at the same time as "doctors" were daily demonstrating a manifest inability to deal with disease. The consequent withering of public confidence did nothing to inspire the AMSAII of the virtue of professional affiliation. This antipathy was compounded by the increasingly "administrative" character which the psychiatric profession took upon itself in the 1860s and thereafter. Admission to the profession depended less upon specialized training and more upon actual experience in mental hospitals.

72 STATE APPARATUS AND EVERYDAY LIFE

Assistant physicians, for instance, were not eligible for admission to the AMSAII.

In the second half of the 19th century, several changes allowed for greater penetration of the state into the apparatus of psychiatry, and for a decisive shift in favor of the medical profession. As the network of asylums slowly expanded, a major challenge to the autonomy of psychiatrists appeared from the legislators and public officials charged with the responsibilities for welfare programs. Faced with increasing costs of hospital provision the state authorities slowly gained ascendancy during a program of centralization and rationalization of the public welfare structure. As a consequence, the power and status of the hospital superintendents – and concomitantly, of the AMSAII – declined (Grob 1973, Ch. VII).

Later in the 19th century, the antagonism between the AMSAII and the AMA again flared up. The focus of controversy was the debate over the need for separate facilities for the treatment of the "incurable" mentally ill. As mental hospitals became increasingly overcrowded, and the revitalized medical professions took a fresh interest in the insane, Dr S. D. Willard (secretary of the Medical Society of the State of New York) prepared a report for the New York legislature on the conditions of the insane poor in the State. The report concluded by recommending, among other things, the establishment of a new institution for incurables in order to relieve local welfare institutions. The State legislature concurred with this proposal and, in 1869, the Willard Asylum for the Insane opened for the reception of chronic cases. This action was a direct affront to many mental hospital superintendents, since the legislation was counter to their professional judgment (Grob 1973, pp. 309–19). This conflict of interest caused a split within the AMSAII and generated much inconclusive intraprofessional dispute. It remained one of the most important factors in the AMSAII's continuing refusal to merge with the AMA (Rothman 1971, p. 282).

The continuing struggle for professional dominance may be viewed as an attempt to monopolize a certain service apparatus. The professional group, by dint of its expertise, attempts to gain exclusive control of an apparatus and thus gain concomitant status advantages. In the rise of the psychiatric profession, the identification of a separable client group and the establishment of an appropriate treatment setting (the mental hospital) were essential preconditions for professional growth. Consolidation of professional pre-eminence depended upon the formation of alliances with the various apparatus of state power. These alliances have historically taken other forms in various countries, but all have represented forms of competition between the different agencies concerned with psychiatric care (Miller 1981, p. 116).

It is instructive to compare briefly the experience of American

THE STATIZATION OF THE PSYCHIATRIC PROFESSION 73

psychiatry with the rise of the psychiatric profession in Britain. Scull (1977) has documented the increasing attempts which were made from the mid-18th century to claim insanity as part of the legitimate domain of medicine. This claim was initially based on the most precarious of philosophies since the success of "moral treatment" in Britain diminished the importance of traditional medicine. Moral treatment had been developed by lay people, and the model of William Tuke's lay-run Retreat at York dominated the public imagination (Jones 1972). The problem of how to accommodate moral treatment within the general rubric of medicine caused a spate of books and pamphlets to appear in the early 18th century, often blaming the stories of disrepute in asylums on the absence of physician control in those institutions. In a spirit of compromise, a combination of moral and physical treatment was ultimately advocated, and increasingly accepted. This had the effect of leaving the physician in control of the asylum by dint of his specialist knowledge. By the 1830s almost all public mental hospitals had a resident medical director. One of the first moves to consolidate the internal status arrangements of the new profession was the founding, in 1841, of the Association of Medical Officers of Asylums and Hospitals for the Insane.

From its earliest inception, therefore, the apparatus of British psychiatry had tended to be dominated by the medical profession. These trends, which differed significantly from those in America, were undoubtedly fostered by the strength of the medical profession in Britain. The first College of Physicians of London (later to become the Royal College of Physicians) was founded in 1518. British doctors were active partners in the formation of a new political order, and were not merely subordinate to a pre-existing political logic. It was not until 1971 that a separate Royal College of Psychiatrists was established, giving the profession independence in setting standards for entry to the profession, examinations, and official advisory capacity to the national government. Before 1971, these functions were the responsibility of the Royal College of Physicians (Rosenzweig 1975, Ch. 4).

By the end of the 19th century, American asylums became increasingly custodial and desperately overcrowded, and new philosophies were sought. Rothman (1980) describes this Progressive era in America as a constant struggle between "conscience" and "convenience," with the latter usually winning. Indeed, until the middle of the 20th century, the institution of the asylum dominated the pattern of psychiatric care. This was in spite of a burgeoning "mental hygiene" movement which sought to promote mental health in a noninstitutional setting. Mental health, it was argued, could be achieved through psychiatric hospitals which would seek cures for mental illness, arrangements for post-institutional care, and educational programs. However, as the mental health industry became more complex, it was the asylum which endured (Rothman

74 STATE APPARATUS AND EVERYDAY LIFE

1980, Chs 9, 10; also Magaro *et al.* 1978, Ch. 2). The patterns of 19th-century care continued essentially undisturbed; any innovations usually became supplements to the system, and not replacements. However, the seeds of community-based mental health had taken hold in the mental hygiene movement.

Since 1945, the pace of change in mental health care has accelerated rapidly, so that it is possible to speak of the "revolution" in mental health care which occurred during the third quarter of the 20th century. This is usually referred to as the "community mental health" movement. The impact of these program developments on the pattern of care has been immense. In less than 15 years, the number of patients on the books in Ontario provincial asylums dropped by about 75 percent, while rates of admissions doubled, and those of discharges almost tripled. The proportion of readmissions doubled to form two-thirds of all admissions (Woogh *et al.* 1977). These dramatic changes were made feasible only by strategic alliances with the state apparatus. Provincial laws were altered to enable cost-sharing arrangements with the Federal government to be made. The general hospital was encouraged to develop psychiatric service units, and provincial hospital patients could be transferred to community residential or nursing homes on a cost-sharing basis. In addition, provincial ministries other than Health (such as Housing, and Community and Social Services) would share the burden of costs in certain rehabilitation programs (Lemieux 1977). In a very short time, the level of psychiatric care-giving outside the asylum in psychiatric units of general hospitals and in community-based mental health care has increased dramatically.

This well documented movement toward "deinstitutionalization" has had the effect of extending psychiatric control over new sectors and new populations. The domain of psychiatry is being renegotiated by the profession and the state. This involves a triple process of alteration of institutional form, of criteria for the recognition of professional competence, and of the technologies which operate across such a field (Miller 1981, p. 111). As a consequence, the legitimate domain of psychiatric knowledge and action has grown and diversified to include a new range of mental health "problems" and new dimensions of the state apparatus (such as those formerly controlled by other components of the state apparatus). Parallel events have occurred throughout the history of treatment of the mentally handicapped (see Allderidge 1979). For instance, in their review of the history of asylums for the mentally retarded in Britain, Ryan and Thomas (1980, Ch. 5) have commented on the post-1945 absorption of asylums for the retarded into the apparatus of the welfare state in the form of the National Health Service.

Everyday life and psychiatric services

The client. The person who is or has been mentally ill faces enormous challenges in everyday life. Despite the existence of important factual accounts of these difficulties (see, for instance, Allen 1974), we have little systematic knowledge about them. Part of the personal dilemma of mental illness has been described by Janet and Paul Gotkin (1975) who provide a first-hand account of her "personal triumph over psychiatry." As her history of mental illness unfolds, it is apparent that Janet is at least as worried about her husband's "sadness" and her psychiatrist's "rage" as about her own breakdowns. Her relationship with her parents was also "strained." However, by the time she overcomes her illness, Janet's perception of her schizophrenia becomes radically altered. She writes

> The hallucinations, the delusions, the anxiety state, even the wrist-cutting obsession, and, worst of all, the debilitating vision of myself as helpless and sick – I had learned most of these in my years as a mental patient . . . I had never been sick and I wasn't well now. The whole idea of my illness and my eventual cure were inventions of my psychiatrist (Gotkin 1975, p. 379).

This realization is transformed into a powerful anger against the psychiatric profession:

> We must reject the myth that only doctors and other mental health workers can treat this *illness*; that is incorrect and constitutes a monopoly, helping only the treaters, not the *treated* (Gotkin 1975, p. 384).

Janet's husband Paul confesses that he liked and had depended on her psychiatrist, but ultimately that the doctor never knew her:

> . . . it wasn't even his fault that he clung to her well past the point where he could ever do her any good. I wasn't angry at him, only saddened by the arrogance of a profession that believed it knew so much more about human emotions . . . than it could ever possibly comprehend (Gotkin 1975, p. 352).

If one is caught up in the psychiatric apparatus without the support of a caring family, the problems of coping are only magnified. Many mental patients view the prospect of discharge with sheer terror (Schmidt 1965). They face problems of social isolation, finding a job and a home, severe money problems, and coping with their ongoing psychiatric and social difficulties. In a survey of former psychiatric patients in the downtown core of Hamilton, Ontario, Dear *et al.* (1980 pp. 35–7) found echoes of all

76   STATE APPARATUS AND EVERYDAY LIFE

these difficulties in the expatients' own comments. On isolation: "I don't like going home (to my family) because as soon as I get there, everyone goes out and leaves me there alone;" and on housing: "It's hard to find a place to live – people avoid me." On coping with the apparatus of the psychiatric and social services, the ex-patients were vocal and specific in their opinions: "The psychiatric attention I get is not adequate. I feel funny after medication. They only cut down on medication; they don't explain anything; they keep secrets." . . . "I feel I'm being taken advantage of because of my situation. I took 35 or 40 shock treatments. I cooperated with the doctors when I didn't know what they were doing to me." . . . "I feel that the attention I get is almost excessive at times."

Similar problems are encountered by ex-patients in psychiatric ghettos throughout the country. A recent examination of one Toronto neighborhood (Siggins 1982) indicated that most people lived on welfare cheques of $258 per month (1982); room and board took up 90 percent of this. In this extreme poverty, an individual must fight to cope in the community along with the 14 000 other patients who are discharged annually in Toronto. The ex-patient's response is typically one of "rage at every misfortune that led me here, rage at the doctors, the treatments, the pills. Rage at myself, my weakness, my poverty" (Siggins 1982, p. 10).

Life inside the hospital is no easier. In their study of the politics of mental handicap, Ryan and Thomas (1980) point out the lack of freedom felt by the patients, and their inordinate joy at participating in even minor decision making. The patients quickly learn that they have to be supernormal to succeed, but that even then they are not being provided with skills which would enable them to survive outside the hospital.

The community.   The "community" is placed in a highly ambiguous rôle by the requirements of the apparatus of the psychiatric services. It is required to act as an "accepting host" to the mentally ill and to provide some sort of support network to aid in their resocialization. However, large numbers of communities are simply "rejecting" the mentally ill. Community attitudes are mediated through a complex set of predominantly noneconomic relations in the social formation. These relations are symbolic in character, being organized as a system of signs with its own internal logic. The relationship between community and mentally ill is mediated by this set of symbolic representations, and these interdependent mediations define the situation of class structuration and conflict (see Habermas 1971, Ch. 12).

Little is known about the qualities which make for a good "host" community for a community-based mental health service. It is generally acknowledged, however, that successful resocialization of the mentally ill will require a certain input from the community members. Such support services may include assistance in shopping, or even home visits.

Segal and Aviram (1978) suggest that, for the chronic patient, the social support system offered by an institution may best suit the rehabilitative needs of the client. For others, however, there is a great potential for integrating the client totally into the community. Segal and Aviram have determined three basic components which act to produce a positive integration. In order of their importance, these are:

(1) Community characteristics, including positive response of neighbors;
(2) Resident characteristics, including client satisfaction with living arrangement and therapy, and control over financial arrangements; and
(3) Facility characteristics, including the facility as an ideal psychiatric environment and the integration of clients with residents from the external community.

The success or failure of a community-based mental health care will largely depend upon the community's attitudes toward the mentally ill. Research on attitudes suggest a contradictory mixture of sympathy and rejection. On one hand, we sympathize with the "sick" person in need of care; on the other, we seek to maintain our social distance from the social outcast who manifests deviant behavior. This confusion of motives was evident in a survey of community attitudes toward mental illness (Dear & Taylor 1982). Opinions about mental illness resolved into four attitudinal dimensions: (1) authoritarianism, which implied a view of the mentally ill as an inferior class requiring coercive handling; (2) benevolence, a paternalistic, kindly view of patients, derived from humanistic and religious principles; (3) social restrictiveness, viewing the mentally ill as a threat to society; and (4) a community mental health ideology, representing an anti-institution bias in care of the mentally ill.

Although the Dear and Taylor survey indicated a high degree of community tolerance toward the mentally ill, media reports tend to emphasize the negative responses of host communities. For example, one general practitioner in Toronto observed: "The community is beginning to think that [this neighborhood] has more creeps per acre than any other part of Toronto . . . The community will give and take for its own people just as any other community will. But when everybody sees a bunch of weirdos walking around . . . well, most of them are not weirdos, but they just don't look great" (Siggins 1982, p. 8). Ryan and Thomas (1980) emphasize that people tend to shun the mentally handicapped

Outings reveal how very different the patients are from other people – they dress differently, walk around in a group or even in Indian

78 STATE APPARATUS AND EVERYDAY LIFE

file, stack the crockery in restaurants, shake hands with people they don't know (Ryan & Thomas 1980, p. 80).

Neither are the ex-patients properly cared for in the community. The case of medication is especially problematic.

The more responsible boarding home operators lock up medication and dole it out at appropriate times. But most of them don't have the time for that . . . Over a period of 18 months in one boarding house where there are 60 lodgers, Mary jumped out of the third floor window trying to kill herself; Raymond attempted four times to overdose on pills; Roger slashed his wrists and almost bled to death; Linda died of a drug overdose in the bathtub; and Mike almost hanged himself (the rope broke) (Siggins 1982, p. 8).

On one hand, therefore, the community is being asked to provide a supportive, therapeutic milieu for the network of psychiatric services. On the other hand, this rôle is often perceived by the community as a threat to its "turf." If it is true that a limited environment of social resources has a significant impact on one's life changes, then it is evident that the household has an enormous stake in the local environment (see above – Reproduction in the social formation). Hence the need to protect one's environment from any undesirable negative impact becomes paramount. It seems likely that the entrance of the mentally disabled into a community is perceived as a threat to the environmental resource base of the neighborhood, and hence the market capacities contained within it. Accordingly, the community's power for spatial exclusion is often marshalled to prevent the incursion of the mentally ill.

The mentally ill, like other minority social groups such as the poor, are restricted in their selection of residence, workplace and recreational outlets. Their continued isolation can be interpreted as part of a wider system of sociospatial organization which causes the separation of antagonistic groups. Thus, just as the processes of residential differentiation cause the appearance of class- and ethnically-separated neighborhoods, so similar processes tend to isolate and exclude the mentally ill. The community in opposition to mental health care facilities employs two indirect sources of power to exclude the mentally ill: the power of sociospatial exclusion; and the power of state authority as manifest through planning policy.

The power of sociospatial exclusion operates at two separate levels: individual and group. First, the mentally disabled person is subject to a series of informal and formal exclusionary forces which operate at the individual level. Informally, a mental disability often tends to make the person distinguishable in a social setting. Moreover, people have been observed to make personal behavioral adjustments to exclude the offend-

EVERYDAY LIFE AND PSYCHIATRIC SERVICES 79

ing individual. More formally, organizational exclusion can occur, as when an individual is disciplined for aberrant behavior in the workplace, for example. Secondly, and more important for present purposes, is the set of mechanisms of group exclusion. This refers to the generic ability of communities to exclude undesirable or noxious objects and people from their neighborhoods. In an early study of exclusion of the mentally ill, Aviram and Segal (1973) recognized several strategies used by communities to place "social distance" between them and the mentally ill. These included formal strategies, for example, the use of legal (especially zoning) ordinances, and informal strategies, for example, physical abuse of facility or client.

The community not only uses its own power, but also evokes the powers of the state apparatus to exclude the mentally ill. Urban planners have responded to increasing community opposition by developing locational strategies which minimize conflict over facility siting decisions. As a consequence, the formal mechanism of state planning policy is brought to bear on the exclusion process. While some neighborhoods are excluding the mentally disabled, other neighborhoods (with less political clout) are being saturated by mental health facilities (Dear 1977).

The professional. Professions are powerful. They have a "gatekeeper" function in the distribution of society's material and status resources. They have specialist knowledge which is exercised through a state-sanctioned code of practice usually linked to a service ethic. Professions act to monopolize their position and status, emphasizing the dangers which may arise if their professional skills are misused (Esland 1980a). The links between professions and the state are manifest in many ways. Professions have been described as "servants of power," in that they are agents of the state and large corporations and thus have an implicit political rôle which is masked by the welfare ideology. Esland (1980b, p. 270) quotes one psychiatrist in the prison system who was fully aware of the contradictory nature of his intervention: "By participating in the punishment process, even as a healer, I loaned a certain credibility to the existing correction system." Friedson (1970) has emphasized the inevitable cultural alienation which surrounds the practice of medicine:

> For the medical practitioners, the reality of illness is one which is underwritten by the objectives, experimentation and commitments of science. For the patient, illness is an existential phenomenon bound up with his personal identity, his work, his family relationships, and so on (in Esland, 1980a, p. 247).

What Friedson might also have mentioned is the reality of the increasing

80   STATE APPARATUS AND EVERYDAY LIFE

bureaucratization of the professions. This has been associated with a strengthening of hierarchical control and the routinization of activities. It has also led many professionals to "law-breaking" – practical attempts to overcome heavy caseloads, financial stringency, and bureaucratic principles which if adhered to could make the work much more difficult (Esland 1980b).

Much insight into the world of the hospital-based professional is provided by Ryan and Thomas (1980), who looked at life on the ward of a hospital for the mentally handicapped. They found that the hospital world is divided into two, where "staff dominate the patients and the patients are dependent on the staff for most of their needs" (p. 47). In this world, both staff and patients are subject to the exigencies of a rigid, highly centralized and hierarchical organization. The hospital's social structure tends to reinforce the dependence and incapacity of patients. However, in sympathy for the plight of patients, it is too often forgotten that the system is staffed by "vulnerable individuals" (p. 30). There is, for instance, an insufficient number of nurses, who tend to be obliged to substitute control for care. Discretion in nursing and innovation are frowned upon in this strictly routinized environment; there is too little money to provide such innovations as doors on toilets (p. 41); and the "doctor" reigns supreme and "nobody questioned his actions, only carried out his orders" (p. 46).

Under these circumstances, it is hardly surprising that the staff try to distance themselves from the patients. One of the benefits of promotion is the lessening of contacts with patients (p. 60). More important on a daily basis is the range of formal rules which the hospital employs to place distance between staff and patient, including wearing of uniforms, separate dining arrangements, the sharp division of normal and abnormal people, and so on (pp. 64–7). This distancing is carried over into debates about the future of the hospital system. The debate is frequently carried out in inter-professional terms, that is, which profession controls the patient at the various stages of illness? (pp. 130–8). Staff often feel that the overarching medical and administrative hierarchy (the "intellectuals" as one nurse disparagingly calls them; p. 52) are out of touch with the realities of ward life. In a hospital system, both the professional staff and the patients are subject to the rules of the organization. Writing generally about the future of mentally handicapped, Ryan and Thomas (1980, p. 135) observe

> their lives are administered and financed through the state welfare system in one form or another – [the National Health Service], social service departments, local education authorities, etc. Most of the people who care for or educate them are also state employees, and arguments on the part of those involved in the care of the

SYNTHESIS 81

mentally handicapped tend to reflect their status as professionals or semi-professionals within the welfare state.

However, Ryan and Thomas (1980, p. 151) also perceive an equivalent dilemma for the staff who care for the handicapped:

> Many people in the state institutions are attracted to working with mentally handicapped people for some kind of moral conviction: a desire to help, sympathy with the oppressed, guilt at their own advantages; and from some perception that all is not right with the world. Often the work seems to offer some kind of meaning and satisfaction that is not offered by working in a factory or office. The professional and hierarchical world of the hospital does very little to encourage the ideas and enthusiasm that motivate many of its staff initially, and it often makes life very difficult for staff who do persist with their original perceptions.

Synthesis

The state apparatus has a complex impact on the structure of everyday life. Individual outcomes in psychiatric intervention have been shown to be the result of a helping relationship which has essentially been alienated and reified by an evolving historical process of political conflict and adjustment. The territory of psychiatry has been constantly renegotiated and the mandate for "treatment" has been progressively more deeply inserted into the structure of social relations. Statization of the psychiatric apparatus has progressively occurred as psychiatrists have negotiated to infill the interstices of the social contract under an evolving program of state-sanctioned adjustments.

Everyday life in the psychiatric apparatus is structured by three key social processes. First, the most fundamental is the basic process of reproduction in which (a) professionals attempt to maintain both their professional status and a constant flow of clients; and (b) the community protects its class-constituted "turf" at the same time as it is asked (somewhat contradictorily) to be the host to the contemporary mode of community-based mental health care. Secondly, the key aspect of structuration is the class relation between agents of the psychiatric apparatus and those who are dependent on the apparatus for services. The asymmetric dependence which characterizes this relation allows the psychiatrist to act (however inadvertently) as an agent of social control, and thereby sanction and protect the evolving distribution of political power in capitalism. Thirdly, space plays a key rôle in the structuration of social process. It is a necessary element of the professional's program of isolation and treatment ("normalization"); and it is a primary constitutive element in the creation and perpetuation of geographically separate residential and resource environments – through the symbolic isolation of the mentally ill, the private market process of residential differentiation, and the state-sanctioned practice of exclusionary zoning.

In practical terms, the everyday lives of those individuals who intersect with the psychiatric apparatus appear to be rather strictly circumscribed. The clients are locked in by their need for care. The professionals are jealous of their status and their clients, but similarly subject to a range of alienating regulations and structures. The community sees an unequal burden being placed upon certain neighborhoods, and thus seeks to protect its own turf. In the details of everyday life, there are no villains, only victims. The purpose of this chapter has been to search below these levels of appearance for the underlying forces of structuration. There, we have revealed the progressive penetration of the apparatus of psychiatry into the structures of daily living, and the burgeoning alliance between state and psychiatry which simultaneously acts to reproduce the social formation and the structure of the psychiatric apparatus itself.

5 The language of the state

The nature of political language

The process of politics is construed as the way in which the state apparatus intersects with social groups representative of capital and labor in order to determine and implement collective goals. The common vocabulary, of all parties engaged in politics may be termed political language which then refers simply to the mode of discourse adopted for use in the process of politics. We suggest that listening to political language is the nearest we can get to hearing the state "speak." If we trouble to listen, what do we hear?

A powerful fictional account of one example of political language is described in the appendix to *Nineteen eighty-four*, in which George Orwell sets out the principles of "Newspeak." The purpose of this state-sponsored language was not only to provide expression for a world-view and mental habits proper to a new society, but also to make all other modes of expression impossible. Once Newspeak was adopted, thoughts hostile to the new society would become literally unthinkable, an objective to be achieved by diminishing the range of vocabularies. Newspeak words were divided into three categories, known as the A vocabulary, the B vocabulary and the C vocabulary. Vocabulary A consisted of monosyllabic words necessary for everyday life, solely expressing simple, purposive thoughts and usually involving concrete objects or physical activities (such as dog, house, run). The C vocabulary consisted solely of scientific and technical terms. Separate word lists were constructed for each speciality, and researchers or technicians learnt very few words outside their special fields. There was no word for "science," and no vocabulary for discussing the philosophy of science.

Orwell's B vocabulary was composed of words that were deliberately constructed for political purposes. They not only had a political implication, but were intended also to impose a desirable mental attitude upon the persons using them. The words in the B vocabulary were formally similar, being composed of two or more words usually in a noun-verb combination. For example, *goodthink* meant "orthodoxy." The use of such terms encouraged a staccato and monotonous style of

84 THE LANGUAGE OF THE STATE

speech, deliberately drained of consciousness (*sexcrime* for "sexual immorality;" *joycamp* for "forced-labor camp;" *prolefeed* for the "entertainment of the masses"). Words such as "democracy" and "justice" were excised from the Newspeak vocabulary. In Orwell's vision, the totalitarian state had invented a new language by which reality could be structured.

This brief example illustrates many things about political language. First, that language is used to construct or to reconstruct social reality. Secondly, that language is studded with signs, icons, or symbols, which may carry meanings in excess of the simple word being used. Thirdly, that language may be used in a purposeful manner in order to maintain the cohesion and identity of a group. Fourthly, it does so by the use of multiple "registers" in language (the distinction between formal and informal speech is fundamental) and variations in speech styles (vocabulary, syntax and the like). Finally, the social context of language plays a primary rôle in determining variations in the use of language.

Our argument in this chapter is that the state is actively engaged in the linguistic structuring of political and social reality. The purpose of this chapter is to explain the methods and consequences of this undertaking in a general way. Subsequent chapters are then devoted to examining specific examples of the structures of language of the political legitimacy of the capitalist state. If we are to understand the language of the state, however, then a formal theory of political language is indispensable. As an essential preliminary to such a theory, some fundamental concepts of modern linguistic theory are outlined.

Concepts in linguistic theory

There is an enormous variety of language, and, as might be expected, a corresponding range of alternative paradigms for linguistic analysis. One of the major schools is structural linguistics, which is usually identified as originating with Ferdinand de Saussure (1916). Structural linguistics has been developed by several influential thinkers, including Lévi-Strauss and Foucault, and has spawned a number of imitative studies phrased as statements about language and invoking the authority of structural linguistics. Equally influential is the school of formal linguistic analysis associated with Chomsky. Its emphasis is on the acquisition and knowledge of language and linguistic communication (see Smith & Wilson 1979). A natural extension of these concerns is the study of signs and semiotics which has been drawn even further into fundamental questions of philosophy and theory in the social sciences (see, for example, Hookway & Pettit 1978, Putnam 1981, and Ricoeur 1981). Our

CONCEPTS IN LINGUISTIC THEORY 85

present interests derive largely from the field of sociolinguistics which places emphasis on the social context of language (see Giglioli 1972, Robinson 1972). The fundamental sources in the study of political language are by Edelman (1964, 1977).

The importance of language is attested by Wittgenstein's famous dictum: "the limits of my language mean the limits of my world" (Wittgenstein 1961, paragraph 5.6). This implies that language is a barrier which may be used to confine or to expand our consciousness. Language is never innocent; in either its most formal scientific format or in common everyday speech, language imprisons meaning, and there seems to be no way out of that prison. As Olsson (1980, p. 18e) puts it, after hitting his head against the ceiling of language, ". . . language is a closed door without hinges." The indeterminate relativity of language and its interpretation poses many technical and philosophical problems. As we have indicated, we prefer to set these aside and to concentrate in this analysis on a more functionalist view of language. How does a specific type of language, that is, political language, come about? And how is it used by groups in society to structure the collective view of reality?

One important theme in linguistic theory is the relationship between language and social context. As Kress and Hodge noted (1979, p. 13)

Without immediate and direct relations to the social context, the forms and functions of language are not fully explicable.

However, the exact nature of the link between language and context is the subject of much debate. A fundamental distinction has been made between *langue* and *parole*, which may be interpreted as the difference between language and speech, code and message, or competence and performance (Giglioli 1972, p. 7). The former refers to a relatively homogeneous, consistent and abstract set of grammatical rules shared by all members of a linguistic community. The latter refers to the actual utterances of these individuals, and by extension, their intent and meaning. Different branches of linguistics tend to emphasize either the primacy of the social context in shaping language or the way in which language itself structures thought and thereby influences social constructs as well – a viewpoint associated largely with anthropological linguistics, and advanced most strongly by Whorf (in Kress & Hodge 1979, p. 13).

The approach of sociolinguistics attempts to reconcile the schism between language and speech. This effort is especially associated with Bernstein who noted (1972, p. 158)

The general sociolinguistic thesis attempts to explore how symbolic systems are both realizations and regulators of the structure of social

86 THE LANGUAGE OF THE STATE

relationships. The particular symbolic system is that of speech *not* language.

Here, the assumption is that social relations do not directly influence language, but exert constraints on speech. Then, in turn, the type of speech used reinforces the perception of the speaker, thus shaping the view of social reality (Giglioli 1972, p. 14). According to Bernstein, language may be regarded as an invariant set of rules, but it is capable of generating a large number of speech codes, each a function of culture acting through social relationships in specific contexts. Hence

> Different speech . . . codes symbolize the form of the social relationship, regulate the nature of the speech encounters, and create for the speakers different orders of relevance and relation. The experience of the speakers is then transformed by what is made significant or relevant by the speech form (Bernstein 1972, p. 161).

The emphasis on social context has led to a renewed interest in the "situation" in which interaction, or the speech event, occurs. Three aspects are emphasized: *setting, participants* and *purpose* (Brown & Fraser 1979, p. 34). These refer respectively to differences in the physical setting (for example, football stadium or church), the actors and their relationships (for example, friends or strangers), and the variations in their goals or objectives (for example, profit or prayer). The notion of setting warrants further attention, since the essentially contrived character of the political setting has frequently been noted. Political settings tend to be characterized by massive, ornate structures which emphasize departure from normal routines, the exercise of special privilege, and the heroic quality of the unfolding events (Edelman 1964, p. 96). In order to distinguish this purposeful aspect of setting from the more general incidental placement, Brown and Fraser (1979, p. 44) defined a scene as a setting associated with purpose, to distinguish it from a simple setting as such.

There seems to be little doubt regarding the significance of social context for understanding speech and speech codes. However, if each individual sees things differently and can pattern language differently, how do common speech codes and interpretations arise? How can we explain the stability of perception and speech among diverse individuals and communities? Certainly, there exists a set of common speech *markers* related to social class (see Scherer & Giles 1979). But more important is the notion of an *interpretive community*. In his analysis of literary criticism, Fish pondered an analogous question: how do common interpretations of a single text develop? In his answer, Fish began by observing the total fusion of context and language (1980, p. 284):

THE STRUCTURE OF POLITICAL LANGUAGE 87

A sentence is never not in context. We are never not in a situation. A statute is never not read in the light of some purpose. A set of interpretive assumptions is always in force. A sentence that seems to need no interpretation is already the product of one.

In short, raw data are processed by the reader according to some prior framework of meaning. This explains the stability of interpretive communities, groups which speak and listen according to a single relatively stable code:

> . . . members of the same community necessarily agree because they will see (and by seeing, make) everything in relation to that community's assumed purposes and goals; and conversely, members of different communities will disagree because from each of their respective positions the other "simply" cannot see what is obviously and inescapably there. This, then, is the explanation for the stability of interpretation among different readers (they belong to the same community). It also explains why there are disagreements and why they can be debated in a principled way: not because of a stability in texts, but because of a stability in the makeup of interpretive communities and therefore in the opposing positions they make possible (Fish 1980, p. 15).

If we simply substitute the notions of "politicians" and "political language" for those of "reader" and "text," then we may regard most social groups (politicians as well as workers, capitalists, etc.) as interpretive communities, with far reaching consequences for our understanding of the language of the state.

The structure of political language

Social reality is structured through political language. As Edelman (1977, p. 142) observed

> . . . it is *language* about political events rather than the events themselves that everyone experiences.

Hence, alternative linguistic categorizations can create multiple realities, and people respond largely to the cues of language rather than direct knowledge of "facts" (Edelman 1964, p. 190):

> Language forms and terms reinforce the reassuring perspectives established through other political symbols, subtly interweaving

88 THE LANGUAGE OF THE STATE

with action to help shape values, norms, and assumptions about future possibilities.

In this way, language has the effect of including or excluding various groups and individuals according to their perception of the linguistically created "reality." Virtually every phrase carries a heavy interpretive burden which encourages socially approved conclusions and inhibits the recognition of options which are not culturally condoned. Recall the comment by Syme, one of Orwell's characters in *Nineteen eighty-four* who was working on a new edition of the Newspeak dictionary:

> Don't you see that the whole aim of Newspeak is to narrow the range of thought? In the end we shall make thoughtcrime literally impossible; because there will be no words in which to express it. Every concept that can ever be needed will be expressed in exactly *one* word, with subsidiary meanings rubbed out and forgotten (p. 45).

The linguistic structuring of political reality therefore has the effect of creating poles of identification or alienation in the perceiver (Edelman 1964, Ch. 9). At either end of this dimension, "communities" of observers congregate. For them, the perception of politics is not an effort to understand what is happening, but rather it is an effort to make observation conform to their expectations and assumptions. In short, each of these "interpretive communities" possesses a different linguistic paradigm by which reality is assessed (see Fish 1980). These linguistic paradigms provide a setting, or frame of reference, for political debate. Political actions expressed in a specific manner which appeals to one group gain integrity and legitimacy by being situated in the correct frame of reference. For this group, language is a unifying force. At the same time, countervailing evidence of alternative interpretive communities is excluded and their group members shunned.

Both perceptions of fact and their value connotations depend upon the structure of the language available to an interpretive community. Accuracy is not necessarily the primary concern in political language; more important is the common "code" for appraisal available to members of a group. This includes questions concerning the construction of language, vocabulary, syntax, metaphor, and symbols for various formal and informal purposes, as well as a wider interpretive ability deriving from community and social context. Our view of the structure of political language therefore emphasizes the character of the language itself, in addition to its social context. Hence, the discussion which follows is organized sequentially around these twin concepts.

THE STRUCTURE OF POLITICAL LANGUAGE

The structural characteristics of political language. In general terms, language style will vary with the speech setting and the purpose(s) of the participants (Table 5.1). Hence, at the most fundamental level, a difference in register will tend to occur between a general speech setting and a specific scene (that is, a setting with a purpose). Within each register, variations occur according to the specific purposes of the actors. These registers can be directed, for instance, towards cohesion or identity, rivalry or differentiation, and abstract debate or emotional persuasion. Variation in purpose will tend to lead to the adoption of specific sub-registers, which are bound by definite linguistic modes (Table 5.1). Let us now explore this structure of political language in more detail, emphasizing the important notions of "register" and linguistic rules, the "grammar" of politics.

One of the foremost characteristics of political language is its variety. For instance, Hudson (1978, pp. 35–6 & 120) drew attention to the wide variety between the public and private utterances of politicians. He contrasted the language of party rhetoric with the language of the Nixon tapes, and wondered why ordinary citizens, who do not normally hear the behind-the-scenes infighting, are expected to get excited about the "sanitized" version of public events, later served up by party managers. Of course, this contrast between the private excitement and public dullness of political language is quite powerful. Similarly, Edelman (1964, pp. 122–4) referred to the "restful" dulling of critical faculties associated with speeches designed to reinforce a sense of self-identity among the

Table 5.1   The structure of political language.

Setting
  scene
  setting

Register
  formal   public   formal   cohesion
  informal private   public   rivalry

Sub-register
  hortatory
  legal
  administrative
  bargaining

Linguistic
rules (grammar)
  vocabulary
  syntax – rhetoric and jargon
         – metonymy and metaphor
         – keywords and symbols
         – ambiguity

90 THE LANGUAGE OF THE STATE

uncritical party faithful. This soporific effect is quite different in its intent from the words of the same speaker at election time, when the voting predispositions of party members have to be aroused.

The use of purposefully differentiated language by a single speaker, or group of speakers, draws attention to the variety of speech registers used in politics. The term "register" normally refers to variations in the speech situation. Brown and Fraser (1979, p. 39) follow Bollinger when they observed that

> 'a register is a variety . . . that is tied to the communicative occasion', rather than being identified with any geographically defined speech community.

Hence, political language may be expected to consist of several different registers, according to the specific situation and purpose of the participants. For example, the general distinction between *private* and *public* language registers has already been mentioned. Other common distinctions in register include *formal* and *public*. These somewhat confusingly termed categories refer respectively to a formal language which explicitly calls attention of the user and listener to the separate elements of the proposition under debate, and to a public language where shared norms make it unnecessary to refer to premises and meaning (Edelman 1977, pp. 104–17). Also, the distinction between *intra-party cohesion* and *inter-party rivalry* emphasizes the way in which different registers may be used by the same group, first, in order to maintain self-identity and internal cohesion, and secondly, to score points off an opponent (Hudson 1978, pp. 62 & 116).

We prefer to maintain a simple distinction between *formal* and *informal* registers. The former refers to any essentially contrived use of language which follows set grammatical rules or specific rules of order, for instance, a speech or a press release. The latter refers to the essentially unstructured use of language, as in everyday conversation. An example of the use of both formal and informal registers in a scene context is a speech interrupted by heckling in parliament; and of the formal register in the context of a setting may be a proposal of marriage.

Within each register, specific sub-registers may be identified (Table 5.1). Edelman (1964, Ch. 7) distinguished four "distinctive styles" of political language: hortatory, legal, administrative, and bargaining. *Hortatory* language is the language of appeal, used in many settings to engender support. It is pre-eminently the language directed at the mass public, but is also heard in judicial, legislative and other settings. The language of exhortation is notoriously, but deliberately, unstable and ambiguous. *Legal* language embraces all aspects of judicial decision making. It is a register of conflict resolution characterized most strikingly

THE STRUCTURE OF POLITICAL LANGUAGE   91

by its flexibility as interpretations of the same language can vary according to different authorities, changing social mores, altered conditions, or varying group interests. *Administrative* language resembles the apparent precision of legal language, but it differs in terms of its source of origin and its audience. Administrators are not elected officials, and do not need to appeal constantly for public support; neither are they guardians of concrete legal statutes. They do, however, possess an authority which is directed at the public and junior administrators. The language of administrators is a bureaucratic jargon which mediates the reality they oversee, and which gives them cohesion. In this sense, it is an "anti-language." A large and complex society will always contain subgroups within it. Such groups commonly evolve or create a kind of language which serves to reinforce a sense of identity within the group and to exclude outsiders. Halliday (1976) has called language of this kind an anti-language (see Kress & Hodge 1979, p. 70, Chomsky 1973, Marcuse 1964, Ch. 4). Finally, the language of *bargaining* permeates all aspects of government. Bargaining, like hortatory language, is an effort to win support; however, the bargainer offers a deal as well as an appeal. Bargaining occurs at all levels in the political process, but by its very nature tends to be a private medium and, despite the fact that the conditions for bargaining are often formally constituted (for instance, in wage negotiations), procedures in the informal setting usually dominate the process.

It is important to point out that the various sub-registers of political language are not regarded as exclusive categories. Most political situations will, in fact, tend to employ more than one register at different times. For instance, the significance of the hortatory style may diminish as the specific details of compromise are resolved. In this setting, adoption of the language of appeal is often interpreted as a signal of failure (Edelman 1964, p. 150).

Within each language register, there is a common set of linguistic rules, a grammar of politics which, like all grammars, is a structured sequence of codes which enables the construction of an infinite variety of speech statements. Here our attention is focused on the way these linguistic rules are applied in political language. In one sense, this is a question of *linguistic repertoire*, that is, the totality of language forms regularly employed within the context of politics, and the way in which they are used to formulate messages (Giglioli 1972, p. 15). Debate in politics is severely constrained by the nature of this repertoire. In order to understand this, let us consider the two major categories of *vocabulary* and *syntax* in political language.

When we speak of the "vocabulary" of political language, we refer to the set of labels or names which exist as words descriptive of political categories. This process of classification is the basis of language and thought; Kress & Hodge (1979, pp. 64–5) argued that

THE LANGUAGE OF THE STATE

> Classification is a living process, and language offers not only an existing set of classifications, but also a set of operations to enable the individual to further classify or reclassify . . . reality.

The exercise of classifying or naming is highly significant because it places the named object within a wider taxonomy, thereby suggesting the ways in which it is to be judged or compared (Edelman 1964, p. 131). In addition, the act of classification may also have the effect of legitimizing debate on certain topics. Equally important, the absence or deletion of words from a vocabulary has the effect of severely limiting the prospect of political debate. Such a limiting may also result when a political vocabulary is not fully nor accurately understood, as for instance when appeals to "communism" or "fascism" are 'flaunted' or 'flouted.'

The notion of "syntax" refers to the construction of words and sentences in speech and writing. Syntax is important in that it can evoke a full structure of beliefs in an often very subtle manner (see Edelman 1964, Ch. 7, 1977, p. 17). This evocation is achieved in an infinite variety of ways, using a range of grammatical tools. Four examples demonstrate this range and complexity.

Rhetoric and jargon are employed by most political groups at one stage or another, particularly for hortatory purposes (Hudson 1978, p. 71). Resort to rhetoric and jargon is usually understood to be an expression of loyalty to the values that are dominant in a group (Edelman 1977, p. 98). These expressions often take on a ritualistic format which encourages uncritical acceptance of the viewpoint being promulgated. Hence, trade unions invariably "hold the country to ransom," for example.

Metonymy and metaphor are also used with great frequency in order to evoke "mythic cognitive structures" in the listener's mind (Edelman 1977, pp. 16–17). In the case of metonymy, reference is made to some larger structure of social beliefs within which the classified object must be judged and evaluated. Thus, "job training" programs for the unemployed may imply a whole edifice of beliefs about social welfare in capitalist economies. The use of metaphor is probably more common, and is highly powerful in the evocation of political myths. A good example is the way in which problems of an emotional nature have come to be labelled as "mental illness" which by analogy implies a whole panoply of related concepts such as hospitals, doctors and patients. The power of the medical metaphor, for instance "cancer" or "sickness," is frequently invoked in political philosophy and in economic debate in order to reinforce the call for a rational response, or "prescription," for the observed "symptoms" (Sontag 1978, Chs 8–9). Hudson (1978, Ch. 7) has commented about the degree of self-revelation which occurs in a politician's choice of metaphor. For example, former British Prime Minister Edward Heath's interest in sailing was often demonstrated in his choice of metaphor; the need to keep industry "afloat," and not to let the economy "veer" violently. Sporting metaphors seem to be favored by American political leaders. Margaret Thatcher has a tendency to use housekeeping metaphors.

Keywords and symbols are another rich source of political evocation and are "markers" in political language (Scherer & Giles 1979, Williams 1976). For example, political opponents are frequently characterized as a "mob;" to call someone a "racist" is a major insult; and to label an opponent as "hypocritical" is certain to raise the emotional level of debate (Hudson 1978, pp. 67, 88, 97). Orwell was effective in causing the deletion of many Communist party keywords (for example, jackboot, hydra-headed, flunkey, iron heel, lackey) when he drew attention to their frequency of use (Orwell 1968; see also Hudson 1978, pp. 84–5). Both keywords and symbols have the metonymic effect of evoking some larger structure of beliefs and many speakers attempt to develop these evocations deliberately. The religious component of John F. Kennedy's speeches has frequently been noted (Hudson 1978, p. 49), as well as the popular slogans of politics (for example, Harold Macmillan's "You've never had it so good" and Malcolm Fraser's "Life wasn't meant to be easy"). These tend to take on an iconographic quality symbolic of a leader or a party.

Ambiguity is often used in political language in order to make it easier to justify social and political bias. Alternative or vague categorizations can create multiple realities, and these are often used for deliberate effect, as, for example, in the many mythical structures which typically surround interpretations of offer and counter-offer in industrial salary disputes, or in the obfuscatory balance sheets of the costs and benefits of government investment or fiscal initiatives (see Seley & Wolpert 1977).

Any individual who has learned the grammar of politics may be termed linguistically competent. However, as Chomsky suggests, this is not the same as performance, that is, the actual use of language in concrete situations. Those with a competence grammar and a performance grammar may be regarded as part of the interpretive community of political language (Fish 1980, pp. 246–7). This allows for many significant adjustments to the political debate such as telescoping and abridgment of discourse, often rendering difficult and exclusive any rational thought using critical concepts (Marcuse 1964, pp. 91–5). It also allows for debate to be limited to symbols and not facts, so that people perceive only the language and respond to the cues in that language.

The structural context of political language. We now turn attention to the social context within which language operates. Language and social context interact in a dialectical manner, and thereby mediate the political reality. Hence, in our view, the "pure" structure of political language (Table 5.1) is paralleled by an equivalent structure descriptive of the social context of language (Table 5.2).

Table 5.2 The social context of political language.

Except in the most abstract domain, language does not have a shape independent of context; it may take variable forms as different speech codes, according to differences in the social context. Political language, in particular, is used in the process of politics at many different levels. Most visibly, in the parliamentary scene, a setting-with-a-purpose, formal political acts help demonstrate the integrity and legitimacy of the actions they promulgate, creating a reality from which counter-evidence or dissent is excluded. Without this formal setting general acquiescence in power arrangements is threatened. At another level, political language is vital to informal political activities outside the formal legitimizing institutions such as parliament.

Real power is often said to belong to those who wield political influence outside the formal setting in order to shape beliefs and behavior of others. Whatever the context, each group (the state, capital or labor) which impinges upon the political process acts in a particular mode, reflecting the structure of power. Using elections, political parties, unions, lobbying, and industrial relations, for instance, each group adopts a particular speech code to pursue its objectives.

Effective political language calls the attention of a group with shared interests to aspects of their situation which make a specific policy seem consistent with furthering their interests. This applies both to within-group and to between-group dialogues. Political groups are therefore true interpretive communities. They employ speech codes to develop a common political language in order to persuade like-minded groups of the utility of adopting policies for their collective future. The aspirations, and hence speech codes, of antagonistic interpretive communities are excluded, except insofar as they are needed as symbols of an intransigent opposition.

THE STRUCTURE OF POLITICAL LANGUAGE 95

Our previous analyses have highlighted the rôle of the state as an agent of crisis management. The system of government and politics is viewed as part of the state apparatus whereby crises are anticipated and diversionary tactics may be determined and adopted. Political language, in its broadest sense, is the common vocabulary of the political process. Each group may develop its own speech code but all groups must possess some degree of communicative competence in the language (Giglioli 1972, p. 15, Bernstein 1972, p. 161). The precise degree of competence, and hence the effectiveness of the use of political language, will depend upon a number of factors such as social class, political organization, and so on (see, for instance, Olson 1965, Scherer & Giles 1979). Most important, however, is the ability to control the nature of discourse. Power relations in capitalism facilitate the domination of discourse by a powerful minority which may therefore use its control over language to cement its political hegemony over subordinate classes. In order even to be heard, the subordinated groups must accept the need to use the language of the dominant group (Edelman 1977, pp. 66–8). Hence, at the first level of inquiry into social context, political language must be situated within the wider context of capitalist social relations, and more particularly, within the political process of crisis management. Without this direct link to the social context the forms and functions of language are never fully explicable (see Kress & Hodge 1979).

The survival of political groups depends upon their linguistic competence within the social context of capitalism. This fact of political life emphasizes the significance of the notion of political groups as interpretive communities. Individuals are accepted as part of the community only to the extent that their language usage conforms to the current norms. Even though mastery of language conventions does not necessarily imply a complete substantive knowledge of the information dispersed through the language (Gumperz 1972, p. 227), conformity to the current norms is vital in discourse. The important effect of interpretive communities is that their language subsequently becomes a filter through which reality is processed. Daily experiences are evaluated according to preconceived cognitive structures, and categorization quickly occurs. As Edelman argued (1977, p. 25)

> Political and ideological debate consists very largely of efforts to win acceptance of a particular categorization of an issue in the face of competing efforts on behalf of a different one . . .

Interpretive communities provide the social context in which such competing views of reality can be conveniently codified and absorbed. As Edelman again pointed out (1964, p. 186)

96 THE LANGUAGE OF THE STATE

Observation of politics is not simply an effort to learn what is happening but rather a process of making observations conform to assumptions.

A dominant interpretive community uses language for one primary purpose: to structure other communities' perceptions of the political reality. It is not the political events themselves that are therefore being experienced, but the language about those events. A dominant group may attempt to structure discourse through political language for three broad purposes: interpretation; socialization and identity; and control (Table 5.2). First, political language is used to reinterpret fact. This is done to encourage thought *into* certain modes of evaluation and *out* of other modes. It is especially potent when certain messages are difficult or impossible to understand, or when events go against one's group interests (Pateman 1975, pp. 68–70). Such partisan presentation of factual information is a very effective obfuscatory device in politics and may form part of a systematic effort to distort communication (see Habermas 1976, Hudson 1978, pp. 41–3). However, such reconstruction also helps people in the perception and categorization of social issues, and in their prescription for those issues (Edelman 1977, pp. 26–9 & 37–9).

Secondly, political language is also important in the socialization and identity maintenance of social groups. Socialization is a process whereby the biological human is transformed into a specifically cultural being. In a word, it is a process for making people "safe" (Bernstein 1972, p. 162). Political socialization is vital as a means of ensuring the consent of the governed and as a method of controlling legitimation crises. Such socialization can take many forms, as, for instance, in the acceptance of the language of the dominant group by subordinate groups. It is also important in preserving the cohesion of interpretive communities through cognitive organization and identity maintenance (Giles *et al.* 1979, pp. 352–7).

Finally, linguistic structuring is undertaken to ensure social control. The effect of language is:

(1) To control entry to debate, since if you cannot speak the language you cannot participate in the process of politics.

(2) To limit the nature of debate, because in the absence of certain concepts and categories political discourse surrounding these concepts is limited, or even impossible. The linguistic constriction of perception blurs the recognition of alternative possibilities (Edelman 1977, pp. 145–6). Under these circumstances, what we can "see" is limited by what we can "say" (Kress & Hodge 1979, p. 5).

(3) To condition the judgement of political outcomes, since we tend to

THE LANGUAGE OF THE STATE

view political issues in a separate, linguistically segmented ways (Edelman 1975).

The problems associated with each sector of society are then separately assessed, and appropriate policy outcomes evaluated and implemented. However, actual policy outcomes are rarely assessed, and the political "whole" is infrequently glimpsed. Government outputs tend to be identified by symbols rather than accomplishments, and politicians tend to be judged by goals rather than actual achievements. The docility and acquiescence of political groups as well as the "silent majority" are facilitated by this flawed process of evaluating political output. And the state's task of crisis management is considerably simplified.

The language of the state

Political language is the means of communication between different social groups. It reflects the structure of power in capitalist social relations and is a primary medium through which power relations are constituted. This applies to the fundamental relations between state, capital and labor, as well as to inter- and intra-apparatus relations. In this section, we examine some of the implications of the structure of political language as described in the preceding sections. Since this is a somewhat speculative exercise, we prefer to arrange our observations around four hypotheses: the increasing penetration of state power through language; the importance of language in crisis management; the spatial localization of political discourse; and the formalization of discourse through decentralized electoral politics.

Language policy has played a significant rôle in the process of state formation. This has been equally true of conquering states, which have sought to establish their cultural hegemony through their own language, and centralist administrations, which have sought to consolidate central power by linguistic means. Perhaps the best example of this latter trend is modern France, where language has consistently been used as an expression of the penetration of state power and the formation of a national community. As Achard (1980) has indicated, the politics of language in France was harnessed to a politics of centralization as early as the 16th century. The introduction of standardized French was presented as an egalitarian measure which had the effect of devaluing nonconforming dialects and languages. These tendencies are still in evidence in many countries today, including the suppression of the Celtic fringe languages in Wales and Scotland, Brittany and the Basque country. The fundamental concern in these efforts is *control* of the population by making diverse peoples conform to a centralized ideal of

98 THE LANGUAGE OF THE STATE

language and social order. For instance, Achard (1980, p. 179) pointed out that National French was introduced as the official language of "reason."

Conflict over bilingualism is another manifestation of the control issue, although the emphasis in this case is more on maintaining social *cohesion*. For instance, the threatened secession from the federation of Canada by the Province of Québec has recently been countered by the passage of the Canadian Charter of Rights and Freedoms. Under Part I of the Constitution Act 1982, the English and French languages are afforded equal status in the government of Canada. As in Belgium and similar countries, the governments of Canada have increasingly intervened in everyday affairs in order to guarantee the language rights of all Canadians (see Andrew 1982). However, this has also had the effect of increasing state penetration into their lives; for instance, the Government of Québec has passed swingeing laws prohibiting the use of English in street signs, education and the like.

In a less overt manner, the language of political control has penetrated deeply into the discourse of everyday life. The metaphors of "crisis" are commonplace in media and conversation. The language of the various state apparatus are quickly learnt by those needing access to their services or functions as, for example, in preparation of taxes or medical claims, in applying for welfare, and in negotiating pay claims. And the politicization of everyday life is clearly reflected in the adaptation of political language to personal relationships. Hence, for instance, personal arrangements are constantly phrased in terms of "gain," "obligation," or "negotiation." It is a situation which is crystallized in the common response to a great many human difficulties: "Well, ultimately, this is a political problem. . . ."

Nowhere has state penetration by means of language proceeded more deeply than in the case of crisis management. In its daily mediation of social relations, the state has sought to create and recreate the political reality. Its overwhelmingly important objective in this effort has been to perpetuate the myth of state control over an essentially uncontrolled system. The simplest act of naming and classifying social problems gives the impression that the state somehow understands the problems and can control them through its apparatus. Each problem is separately identified, and thus can be separately prescribed for; often the focus of the problem (for example, crime or mental illness) is situated in the individual or in a community. The system as a whole is rarely considered, and still more rarely is it blamed. The political world is thus segmented and disjointed and it is hardly surprising that many people are content to delegate or surrender their political autonomy to those who present themselves as willing or able to make political decisions (Edelman 1975).

THE LANGUAGE OF THE STATE

Crisis management in capitalism is essentially an exercise in the systematic distortion of communication (see Habermas 1976, Kemp 1980). In any crisis situation the state acts to control the flow of information regarding developments in the crisis. That is, the state is reinterpreting the crisis in a language which characterizes the crisis as something that was anticipated, can be controlled, or perhaps warrants new intervention. The state has an extensive information apparatus which enables it to undertake this linguistic restructuring of reality, including extensive propaganda services, as well as more objective "information" services (Hudson 1978, pp. 141–3). However, it has also the option of extending its control by "politicizing" sectors of social relations (Wilby 1979), for instance, through defining an issue as appropriate for public decision making, and thereby denying personal autonomy in crisis.

Control of information and the politicization of capitalist social relations thus mean that the state is capable of manipulating crises in capitalism through its choice of political language. The recurrence of crises encourages anxiety and the less critical acceptance of state actions which would otherwise be resisted, and a careful rationing of issues maintains the impression of aggression and, by careful choice of crisis, of successful action by government. As Orwell (1968, p. 363) put it, political language is essentially used to "defend the indefensible." The "euphemism, question-begging and sheer cloudy vagueness" of such language is intentional. It is evoked so that one may name things without conjuring up mental pictures of them ("a defensive strike based on a window of opportunity"), or sanitize thinking about the unthinkable (as in the dropping of a "demonstration" nuclear bomb).

In its manipulation of crises the state evokes the full panoply of available political language. For instance, political debate consistently occurs in multiple registers, evoking now a moralistic dimension ("the national good"), and now a direct appeal to a consumption-based politics (for example, the promise of new infrastructure investment following re-election). A primary intention in these different registers is to promote ambiguity and to keep opponents constantly off guard by redefining the significance of topics under debate. For instance, bilingualism is frequently couched in terms of a pedagogic debate concerning education, rather than in simple political terms. In Heller's (1981) terms, politics thus becomes a "subtext" to the debate on pedagogical technique. This has the effect of deflecting the focus of debate, unless of course it later becomes politically profitable to resurrect the subtext once again to a primary focus. The media, in their presentation of these debates, have a particularly powerful impact on the public's perception of the "symbolic goods" of the political process (see Hall 1977).

The objective of linguistic segmentation is achieved by the

localization of political discourse. In general terms, "localization" has been used to refer to the practice of "bounding off" a subset of speech practices to an acceptably limited domain (see Heller 1981, p. 81). In this context, we refer particularly to the geographical bounding of political debate to well defined communities. In this manner, potentially contradictory discourse which may undermine the social order may be contained within a limited spatial jurisdiction. This is a linguistic process analogous to techniques of "regionalizing the crisis" used by the central state to implicate the local state in its genesis, a point analysed in more depth in Chapter 7. Hence, dissent may be contained within isolated regions as in the example of black takeover of the inner-city politics of many American cities.

The localization of discourse becomes a particularly powerful concept if we recognize that the interpretive community so isolated may also become in practice a geographical and/or a political community. The emphasis on consumption-based politics and local autonomy, especially in the US (see our analysis in Chs 7 & 8), tends to establish local political jurisdictions as spatially isolated interpretive communities engaged in a competitive struggle for the benefits of production investment and the distribution of public and private goods. Community-based politics therefore dominate at the local level, and the tendency toward localization of discourse is a powerful force for the genesis of urban social movements.

The geographical–interpretive community has available to it a number of formal and informal linguistic registers. These include the power of vote, exiting, or informal voice through lobbying or pressure group tactics. Unfortunately, these linguistic signals are ambiguous and the dominant linguistic groups frequently constrain the means of discourse. The subordinate groups thus find that they may converse, or "participate," only at the discretion of the dominant groups, as in the case of formal community participation in planning decisions; or they may find that their signals are being deliberately misread by those in power (see Arnstein 1969, Dear & Long 1977). In many instances, it has been observed that the option of input by subordinate groups is permitted solely in order to legitimize the activities of the dominant groups (Rein 1969). Localized vocabularies are often simply inadequate to the tasks which are faced by groups using them (see Mollenkopf 1981).

In short, the localization of discourse makes the community a site for manipulation since local territorial communities become identified as interpretive communities. Local consumption-based politics then set these local communities into competition with each other, for example pitting the central city against the suburbs. Geographical fragmentation becomes an expression or articulation of linguistic segmentation and the objective of social control is facilitated.

THE LANGUAGE OF THE STATE

The localization of discourse carries its own tensions within itself. Communities as geographical entities can represent instruments of inclusion and exclusion. The very meaning of "community" can be used to accommodate some and to exclude others. For example, among many white lower-class residents of US cities, "community" and "neighborhood" are interpreted to mean racial, ethnic, and geographical homogeneity. Given such an interpretation, it is not surprising that the language of political debate over such issues as school busing and integration often includes words such as "neighborhood stability," "cohesion," and "cultural strength." To the extent that political debate over public policies such as busing is premised upon this type of language, others holding different value positions become disenfranchised or excluded. An obvious example has been the movement among some black groups to define community in terms of racial, ethnic and cultural heterogeneity. Through inclusion into the local community, blacks have sought to improve their material wellbeing. But of course their claims for "rightful" inclusion often founder upon a political language that they do not control. In this sense, community meaning has an instrumental quality.

A different kind of crisis, just as susceptible to political manipulation, is presented by elections. In terms of this chapter, electoral politics is best understood as a formally programmed period of dialogue between elected political leaders and other groups in the political process. It is an institutionalized dialogue which legitimizes state activities and is characterized by a peculiar system of language and speech codes. The form of democratic participation creates a belief that the "people" are governing themselves. The vote is the unique form of voice in this process. The language of debate during elections enables us to reconcile beliefs and expectations about government and democracy and the true reality of party governments; language is the medium which enables these two disparate perceptions, however temporarily, to be reconciled (Edelman 1964, pp. 192–3). This *rapprochement* is made possible primarily through a distension of political discourse: through the manifestos, speeches, and propaganda of political parties. Using these modes, political parties restructure debate through language with the effect of stimulating public loyalty to vote in the preferred manner suggested by the discourse.

The decentralized structure of electoral politics is once again functional for the task of linguistic segmentation and control. Local elections provide a clear instance of bounded discourse in which political dissent is directed at the *local* representatives of the state and political power. The whole process of establishing electoral and political boundaries, and their subsequent gerrymandering (see Johnston 1979), can be interpreted as effort to redefine the boundaries of discourse within existing

102 THE LANGUAGE OF THE STATE

geographical–interpretive communities. The apparent separation of local politics and local state from central politics and central state has the effect of obfuscating the channels of responsibility and dissent in social relations. Even though local discourse is bounded by exogenously derived rules which must be conformed to and complied with, the target for local debate is the local state. Thus, the formalization of discourse through electoral politics aids in deflecting dissent away from the more fundamental power relations in society. The channels of discourse established by the state control that discourse. Any language outside the properly constituted register is axiomatically delegitimized.

Our argument is then that the electoral system, and particularly the language of democracy, is an edifice of power relations, that is, a *product* of state structuration. In contrast, much of political science takes the electoral–democratic system as the beginning point for inquiry. It ignores the structured character of political debate and has a theory of the organization of politics based on *ad hoc* notions of the natural basis of human conflict. This fatal flaw is transposed into contemporary political geography; it accepts as the analytical norm a view of electoral politics divorced from a systematic and structured political image of linguistic and political debate. It is little wonder that these analyses of the political system, however well-meaning, ultimately fail to resuscitate political discourse.

Conclusions

In a preliminary manner, we have begun to structure analysis of the state in linguistic terms. All other articulations of the state examined in this book may properly be regarded as aspects of political language. This is not meant to suggest that all questions of state and state apparatus can be dissolved into linguistic issues. However, it does emphasize that the state and its apparatus are constituted in many different dimensions of discourse and any proper analysis must necessarily take into account the variety of structures through which state power is exercised.

We have argued that there are many registers of political language and many interpretive communities in the social relationships of capitalism. The resultant confusion and ambiguity is used purposively by dominant groups to achieve discretion within society's rules. The ultimate objective of these groups is power and control through the coercion and domination which political language permits them. Note that we do not mean to suggest that subordinate groups are stupid enough to accept passively the messages of the dominant language. Most groups, however, seem to concede, or to have been persuaded, that there is a finite number of political options and, hence, a finite number of linguistic

CONCLUSIONS
103

registers. The dynamics of linguistic hegemony therefore imply that various groups will align themselves with the "best" register being offered, reflecting the group's class and power situation with respect to the wider social context.

In this general babel of voice and registers, the state, we have argued, has increasingly penetrated the fabric of social relations through its domination of the linguistic repertoire. Language is a primary agent in the control of crises in capitalism. Space is functional in this discourse in that it permits a localization of bounded discourse and a formalization of discourse through electoral politics. The spatial organization of society is therefore part of the linguistic structuring of political reality, the ultimate objective of which is social control.

6 Law and the state

The enforcement and interpretation of law is a fundamental aspect of state activity. The rule of law is part of the everyday life of all individuals and enterprises. Laws are both intermediary variables between individuals as well as determinants of individual behavior. For example, the laws on contracts both define the process and context of commercial exchange and the degree of interdependence and obligations between entrepreneurs (Horwitz 1977). Laws are formalized outcomes of the political process, but once enacted, they become the rules and standards by which individuals and classes have to act. Duncan Kennedy (1976) defined rules and standards in the following terms: a rule is a formal directive that requires response in a specific manner; standards on the other hand, are generally broader and relate to the objectives of a legal order. For example, good faith, fairness, and equity are standards. The judicial apparatus has the responsibility for interpreting, setting the limits of the applicability of laws and deciding the applicability of rules and standards.

Only Teitz (1978) has attempted to incorporate law into the analysis of spatial structure. His attempt however, was placed squarely within the state-as-regulator tradition, focusing on those laws which explicitly govern the behavior of individuals in specific spatial and legal contexts. But of course the impact of law does not only relate to those laws promulgated to regulate and control social and economic relationships directly. The whole legal system affects individual behavior and the arrangement of relationships and interdependence between individuals and classes. For example, the "new" economics-of-law school of thought essentially argues that the structure of substantive law promotes a certain kind of economic system. According to Posner (1977), the practice of law in the United States is premised upon rules of economic efficiency (see Buchanan 1974, Michelman 1979, and Posner 1979, for more general debate over these issues). Posner (1977) has sought to establish the empirical evidence for this proposition as embedded implicitly in the judgments of the Supreme Court over the past 200 years. Moreover, he has also argued that the structure of substantive law ought to "mimic" the private market, especially in instances of nonmarket clearing and extensive transaction costs that would impair economically efficient outcomes. Thus, he concluded that the American legal system is based upon the requirements for market efficiency. Notice that from this perspective very little is said of equity or justice, other than a claim that individuals should be rewarded and accorded legal recognition on the basis of their marginal product (see Polinsky 1974). While disagreeing with Posner's logical positivist notions of social science and his normative view of the appropriate structure of law, other writers such as Horwitz (1977) and Duncan Kennedy (1976), have also attempted to identify the implicit objectives and ideology of law, particularly with respect to contracts and obligations among classes and enterprises.

In this chapter, substantive law is interpreted first with respect to the notion of individual rights, and secondly, with respect to the spatial integration of the United States. Our argument proceeds by demonstrating that the spatial diversity of the United States has been systematically negated by the judiciary since 1800 and that, as a consequence, space as a social and political concept is virtually denied. State rights and constitutional privileges have been consistently placed second to the national interest. In contrast to the general belief that America is a decentralized representative democracy, it is argued that state political and economic power has become spatially and administratively centralized. The structure of law and subsequent Supreme Court interpretations of the Constitution have encouraged the spatial homogeneity and integration of the United States, and not its diversity.

Two reasons for this interpretation of the objectives and impacts of substantive law will be advanced. First, the language of the Constitution and the judiciary is framed in terms of individualism. In fact, individuals are assumed to be the primary units of society. Conflict between the rights of individuals and the power of group interests, whether spatially or socially derived, have been typically decided in favor of the individual (Cox 1976). For example, discrimination on the basis of race, and attempts by some States to treat their own citizens preferentially have been consistently declared unlawful. The philosophical basis for individualism is obvious, and may be found in the utilitarian movement of Bentham and Locke. However, we also argue that the significance attached to individual rights is, in part, a political argument which is concerned with the origin of rights as such.

Secondly, we also argue, by way of illustration, that spatial integration was consciously sought by the ruling élite. For many merchants and traders at the turn of the 19th century, spatial integration was considered to be a necessary condition for national economic growth. Given the individualistic basis of the framework of law, the state, through the judicial apparatus, used this framework to lay the foundations of an

106   LAW AND THE STATE

integrated national economy. Notice that this second argument is dependent upon the first, which concerns the pre-eminence of individual rights.

Interpreting law and society

The way in which law is defined holds the key for further discussions of state power and individualism. By the action of defining law, the problems of identifying its derivation from and within society are immediately confronted. In the simplest terms, the *Oxford English Dictionary* (1955, p. 1115) defined law as a "... body of rules, whether formally enacted or customary, which a state or community recognizes as binding on its members." For a set of rules to be accorded the status of law, two essential conditions need to be met (Hart 1979). First, laws must be general and all encompassing, social rather than individual, so that they are not idiosyncratically interpreted and acted upon. Secondly, laws must be dependable to the extent that individuals expect others to act in accordance with or in reaction to the accepted body of rules. Of course, expectations of behavior are not quite the same as actual behavior, nor may everyone agree with the rules. In essence, law is a social expression of the rules and standards that bind individuals' actions, obligations and intentions (Morawetz 1980).

Given that laws are socially defined, how then are they derived? The intellectual history of law provides two basic answers. According to the traditional naturalistic doctrine, laws reflect innate moral and philosophical perceptions of the rights of man, as, for example, the notions of liberty and freedom derived, in part, from Rousseau and Hume (Unger 1975). The doctrine of naturalism distinguishes between natural rights and human will, arguing that natural law is beyond individual attempts at defining the correct (normative) course of human social action. Thus, naturalism assumes that law is neutral, in the sense of its distributive impact among individuals or groups in society, and that the arrangement of certain rights and assumptions in society is beyond the intervention of mere mortals. Unfortunately for those believing in the rule of natural rights, it has been virtually impossible to determine the origins of natural law in anything other than authoritarian or religious doctrines (David Kennedy 1980). Furthermore, any attempt allowing the judiciary alone to define what is, or what is not, natural law has been confounded by the values and ideology of those deciding litigation (see Ely 1980).

A second explanation is based upon notions of logical positivism, and in particular, two empirical tests of the existence of law (Dworkin 1977). A rule or standard is defined as a law if it meets some mechanical test defined *a priori*. Also, empirical evidence is used to elucidate the truthfulness of law, that is, whether people actually behave as if it is law. This model has gradually overtaken the naturalist school since the French Revolution. Rights, for the natural school, were accorded the status of moral philosophy. In contrast, positivism views rights as being an outcome of legitimate societal behavior which is formalized in law. These laws then define the correct course of action. This second approach depends upon action as the defining mechanism and, significantly, upon a sharp distinction between law and politics. Law is thought to be neutral, although some liberals recognize that this depends upon the degree of separation between the judiciary and politicians (Galanter 1974).

A further distinction can be made between legal principles and legal policy. A principle is a socially defined right or duty, invariant over all cases. The research question appropriate in this context is: who decides the principle? A legal policy, on the other hand, exists where individuals' rights are infringed for some overriding benefit, as, for example, where an individual has no right to a certain privilege, but because it benefits society it is judged appropriate. The policy question is: how should we weight the relative costs and benefits? Just as the naturalist conception of law had difficulty in identifying the source of moral norms, the positivist model has similar problems, unless it is accepted that legitimate norms are received as "divine revelation."

To examine the implications of these issues, we need only reconsider Teitz's (1978) conception of law in urban and regional processes. In his model, law appears as a predetermined social constraint. It is interpreted as a separate variable which ". . . defines a wide range of permissible behavior." Based upon our discussion of naturalistic and positivist theories of law, two objections to Teitz's formulation could be raised. First, from his model it cannot be shown how law is derived. It is assumed to be outside the processes and relationships being studied. Causality for Teitz runs one way, from law to behavior. Yet we argue that law should also be seen as enabling behavior, setting an implicit or explicit opportunity matrix for individual and group action. Secondly, the legal system is assumed to be an institution separate from society. Although Teitz discussed the impacts of the administration and implementation of statutes, no link was made to the state's objectives, or with how the state apparatus derives legal structures that subsequently bind individual behavior.

A model is needed which integrates individual action with the institutional representation of law as an ongoing dialectical process. Essentially, such a theory of law should have the following attributes. First, it should link the duties and expectations of citizens concerning the enforcement of law with judicial adjudication, legislation by the corpus

108   LAW AND THE STATE

of voters, and the legitimacy of both the judiciary and the legislative apparatus. Secondly, such a model must also place law within the structure of society and its institutions. Marxist analyses of law are typically prefaced upon these two attributes and provide an analytical framework for interpretation of law. Class structure, conflict, and position in regard to the privileges of law, are often invoked as forces determining the impact of law on different classes. Marxist theory typically interprets law instrumentally as a coercive tool of the ruling class or as the "strong arm" of the state itself, and as an ideological screen that distorts reality (see Binns 1980 and Pashukanis 1978). In short, law is controlled by the ruling classes for their own interests.

The conception of law as a social fact, rather than a divine or moral claim, was a notion shared by Bentham, Mill and Marx. Understanding the impact of law then requires understanding the specific interrelationships of society. However, even the classical model suffers from being empirically determined rather than being derived from the structure of the capitalist economy. A model of law and society is required that is structurally determined and at the same time allows for instrumental action by the ruling class.

If a classical model of law were to be accepted as the basis for analysing the relationship between law and society, another more difficult methodological problem has also to be faced: how does one discriminate between alternative and apparently equal or valid interpretations of the impact, and function, of law in society? This problem is inherent in constitutional adjudication since interpretation of law is typically based upon historical precedent (Friedman 1965). One school of thought is that the language and intent of the constitution, as defined by its adoptees, is the sole legitimate source for interpreting the object of law. Brest (1980) defined this approach as "originalism" in that, as in naturalism, one particular interpretation of law is the only legitimate and correct reading of the received constitution. Emphasis, in this particular mode of interpretation, is placed upon correctly understanding the written text in terms of language, meaning and structure of sentences of the adoptees of the constitution (Holmes 1899). Originalism is not as popular now as it was in the past, for the simple reason that 200 years later both the context and purposes of law have changed. In addition, it has become virtually impossible to define adequately the intentions of the fathers of the law (Brest 1980). Vestiges of originalism still exist however in the judicial system, as, for example, when judges continue to search for the intent that a particular clause was originally meant to serve.

Modern legal interpretation combines notions of general intent with the realities of current social and political conditions. For example Chief Justice Warren in *Brown v. Board of Education* 347 US 483 (1954) argued (Bickel 1955, pp. 1–2):

INTERPRETING LAW AND SOCIETY

In approaching this problem (segregation), we cannot turn the clock back to 1868 when the Amendment was adopted, or even to 1886 when *Plessy v. Ferguson* was written. We must consider public education in the light of its full development and its present place in American life throughout the Nation. Only in this way can it be determined if segregation of public schools deprives these plaintiffs of the equal protection of the laws.

While originalism provides one empirical test of the correctness of an interpretation, some researchers have claimed a better understanding of the truth than others (see, for instance, the review of Crosskey 1953, by Hart 1954). Recent modes of interpretation have emphasized the widespread debate over the appropriateness of using alternative empirical tests of interpretive correctness (Duncan Kennedy 1976). This problem is particularly acute when sociopolitical conditions change rapidly; how law is interpreted in one context may be irrelevant through the passage of time and events. Empirical tests of the adequacy of a given interpretation are then subject to constant revision and rearrangement.

One alternative proposed by Ely (1980) is to ignore the outcomes of law and concentrate upon the procedures through which laws are interpreted and adjudicated. The argument here is that since society is continually changing, no one empirical test is ever likely to be satisfactory, but that if the procedures of interpretation are founded on higher-order principles central to the constitution (freedom of speech, equality, and representative democracy) then outcomes will always be "just" despite being diverse. The problem, thus, becomes the definition of those higher-order principles; this is itself a political issue bound by the balance of social forces at any given time (Cox 1981). Hence, the problem of interpretation is a crucial issue for all who attempt to analyze substantive law, whether it is approached from orthodox neoclassical economics (Posner 1979) or the marxian tradition (Horwitz 1977).

In this chapter, the validity of hypotheses concerning law, the state, and American spatial integration, are not tested in an empirical–analytic manner. Rather, the mode of analysis is based upon the hermeneutic method of interpretation (Habermas 1971). This approach is similar to Hart's (1979) hermeneutics of jurisprudence. He noted that understanding law is inherently normative in that the attitudes of the individuals undertaking the interpretation can be understood only by reference to their conceptual frameworks. Inevitably, these conceptual frameworks are socially determined, in that human meaning is only derived through the interrelationships of individuals to society. Analysis of both the social purposes of law and the individual's place within law requires a normative lens; there is no pure theory of law, as proposed by Kant (Hacker 1977).

110 LAW AND THE STATE

Law and the state

In objecting to Teitz's analysis of law and other more conventional modes of inquiry, we have simultaneously outlined a more viable theory of law and society. Three principal assumptions guide our analysis. First, social structure is the product of conflict between classes over the material basis of existence: ownership of property and the means of production. Secondly, inherent in this conflict are alternative visions of how society ought to be organized. Thirdly, these alternative social visions must be reconciled if the interdependent nature of production, material existence and class relations are to be maintained. Interdependence is the result of capitalists' having to depend upon labor for the generation of surplus value and labor's dependence on capitalists for the means of production. In cases other than revolution, conciliation is a necessity because one class cannot function without the other. This proposition depends on the argument in Chapter 3 regarding the state's integration function.

Our initial proposition is that law (as a general set of socially defined rules) has two levels of appearance (see Thompson 1975). The first level depends on expectations and social aspirations, where values and conceptions of the appropriate form of society are given expression through a utopian set of rules and standards. Social aspirations are derived through political conflict, and "utopia" is defined by reaction and negation – against what actually exists, for what could be. Consensus on the appropriateness of a set of laws is determined by the distribution of power between classes and the interdependence between capitalists and workers. This implies that aggregate social aspirations may be reconciled as shifts occur in the balance of power between classes. At this first level of appearance individuals and classes resolve a general set of laws that reflect the best possible alternative to, or accommodation with, the *status quo*. Thus, the present is negated by the definition of an alternative. Democracy or direct political action may be the means of defining this future although it must remain a vision until implemented. Notice that there must also be some tacit or expressed agreement between groups regarding the means of conflict resolution. This does not mean that conflict resolution need be perfect or unbiased; different channels of communication may favor different groups because of prior inequalities of wealth, property or more generally, power (Unger 1975, Gintis 1980).

Secondly, law is also defined at the level of action and interaction between individuals and classes. Put another way, law is continually modified and interpreted by the actions of individuals, classes and the judiciary. Action can be thought of as encompassing two aspects of social life: class struggle and individual relationships. Class struggle results

LAW AND THE STATE

because of the location of individuals with regard to the mode of production and the antagonistic social relations of productive life (Wright 1978). There may also be organized class resistance to capitalist control. Note however, that conscious class identity is not necessarily required for class struggle to exist. Both aspects of social life depend upon the existence of a power differential which is the lever for influencing outcomes in the private and public arenas (that is, individual relationships, and the state and judiciary). It is also assumed that inequality in the distribution of power is related to the distribution of wealth and privilege, defined jointly by inheritance and the rights of property ownership and commodity production.

The existence of law at these two levels prompts consideration of their implications for interpreting law in capitalist society. Since law is jointly determined by social aspirations and expectations, it has inherent legitimacy up to the point where the *practice* of law directly contradicts the first level of appearance. However, substantive outcomes of law may not necessarily bring into question the first level of appearance because its veracity depends very much on the legitimacy of the judicial apparatus. Outcomes reflect directly upon the state apparatus, perhaps more so than the aspiration level of appearance. Redesign and reorientation of the legal apparatus is the most likely outcome.

The second major proposition is then that, in terms of its implementation, interpretation, and enforcement, the locus of law is the state. This proposition implies a further question of the relative autonomy of the judiciary. If judges were to be completely insulated (through lifetime appointments, for instance) from the state's imperatives, then the judiciary itself could presumably exist outside the state. This argument implies that the judiciary's role is not concerned with the representation of those underprivileged and underrepresented groups of the political system. Liberal notions of an activist and interventionist court, according to this logic, are at best naive, at worst irrelevant. There can be no unique guardian of the "public interest," for two reasons. First, the definition of a "pure" public interest is itself problematical. What passes for a general social interest is essentially a contract, determined primarily by the balance of power between classes and their relative independence. In Hart's (1979) terms, the public interest is a social fact which is both normative and nonneutral with respect to outcomes.

The basis for judicial decision making is, thus, derivative of the political structure rather than somehow ethically or independently determined. This argument reflects an implied assumption that the social contract determines the rules of enforcement, decision making, and outcomes. Secondly, the judiciary is also implicated in the state's structure and intent because it depends upon the political system for its power and legitimacy. Formal separation of the judiciary from the state,

112 LAW AND THE STATE

through devices such as life tenure, is irrelevant. Although formal separation may protect judges from incidental interest groups' tampering (as suggested by Landes & Posner 1975), the judiciary's interests are closely tied to the political system precisely because of their separation from direct democratic support. Because judicial power and the areas and limits of its intervention are dependent upon its exercise, the judiciary is also dependent upon the political system for the definition of its arena of judgment; that is, its mandate is a product of legislative intent and the social contract embodied in the constitution.

Implementation of law through the state apparatus may then be quite distinct from the first level of appearance. In fact, given the legitimacy implicit in the structure of laws defined at the first level of appearance, the state's use of regulation can be coercive, repressive and reactionary. The state may systematically use the legal apparatus as an instrument of social domination but draw its legitimacy from a general, tacit acceptance of the intent of law at the first level of appearance. Poulantzas (1978, p. 87) made a similar more general point when he argued that "law itself, . . . the embodiment of the people–nation, becomes the fundamental category of state sovereignty; and judicial–political ideology supplants religious ideology as the predominant form." Note that the state's use of law to repress one group may not directly result in the questioning of the first level of appearance. Principles of law can be separated from everyday policy decisions, and it may be to the advantage of the state to invoke this distinction as a means of maintaining its long-run legitimacy and control.

The third proposition concerns the language of law. In defining utopian vision, the language of law is invoked in reaction to the present and in order to ensure legitimacy. In this reaction, the language of the present defines its antithesis (Unger 1975). Further, the notion of law as a code of rights and social norms may have legitimacy beyond specific values (Sennett 1980). The very idea of "law" may be desired for its own sake. One example of language and legitimacy is the process of labelling in psychiatry. Deviance is defined with respect to an empirically established norm by means of rules and standards. Deviant behavior is defined as that which exists outside legitimate activity (see Ch. 4). Similarly, the state may use law in the realm of action to outlaw certain social behavior. Law can be used to label any action or social activity as being "undemocratic" or "unlawful." The language of law itself is, therefore, a control lever of the state. Edelman (1979) similarly argued that owners control the image of society by reason of its manipulation of that image. The language of law can be invoked to legitimize the coercive and repressive use of law by the state.

Rights as contextual obligations

Based on this conception of law and the state, we now turn to analyzing the rights of individuals and their relationship to society. In utilitarian theory, individuals are constituted as human beings outside the immediate structure of society. Nozick's (1974) theory of the rôle of individuals and institutions is particularly instructive on this point. He asserted that society only has character after an agreement has been reached among free individuals over what they desire. In essence individuals form alliances (communities) based upon overlapping preferences, and these logically form what we would identify as society. These communities are loose associations of individuals protected by a representative and minimalist state. Preferences can of course change, and so can the nature and identity of the individuals that make up alliances. By implication, the state's rôle is severely circumscribed; it basically exists to enforce rights of mutual existence and nonimperialism. Further, with free mobility and choice, a long-run equilibrium should result such that an individual's preferences exactly map his or her chosen community. What should be emphasized here is Nozick's extremely narrow concept of the relationship between individuals and the community. According to this logic, the community is the sum of its individual members. Consequently, rights in Nozick's theory reside with the individual.

Although Rawls (1971) is not enamoured with utilitarianism, his model has some similarities with Nozick's. Rawls' conception of a social contract also requires autonomous choice-oriented individuals who base their decisions for association upon mutual advantage. Calculating whether or not to associate with others is, for Rawls, akin to cost–benefit analysis. And again, individuals make their decisions of social contract outside society. As in Nozick's theory, individuals are fully constituted prior (in logical time) to community association. Of course, Rawls (unlike Nozick) relates his notion to an "original position." This original position is hardly a description of reality, nor is it intended as such; rather it is a reference point for evaluating principles of justice, particularly with respect to those who are least well off. Again, according to Rawls, rights begin with the individual. As society is constructed, the prospect of a clash between individual rights and the community good is then inevitable.

The key problem with both Nozick and Rawls is their separation of the individual from society in their respective original positions. It is not simply that such a notion is unrealistic; the issue is deeper and essentially philosophical. How is it possible to have individuals as separate human beings, and as calculating and emotional actors, constituted *prior* to the social relations that contain them? Our position is that such a separation

114   LAW AND THE STATE

is inconceivable. Individuals only have meaning as human beings to the extent to which they are part of a community. Individuals do not choose to belong to community; in fact there is no choice because it is the social relations that define the individual and not a collection of individuals defining the community. Interdependence rather than independence is the key building-block of what can be termed the community. Our argument can then be distinguished from utilitarian and social contract theories because it conceives of the relationship of individuals to the community in terms of their mutual and contextual obligations which are born out of their social relations.

Thus, the notion of choice with respect to individuals and their possible social association is not the issue. Social relations are assumed to be inherent in the human experience. Similarly, individuals are not considered as independent autonomous agents; rather, individuals are inextricably bound by the mutual bonds of interdependence. This should not be taken as implying that interdependence in any way limits the extent and existence of conflict over the moral principles that guide community policy. There is, and must be, continual conflict over what constitutes the community good, with individual claims regarding their needs and deserts, and their rôles. When Duncan Kennedy (1979) noted the problem of this "fundamental contradiction," he framed it in terms of what the individual has to give up for social association. Complete individual freedom, according to Kennedy, is impossible because we need others – their preferences, wishes, and intimate contact – for human development. While it may be romantic to consider ourselves as outsiders, even this position is taken with reference to society.

In our approach, the analysis of the social obligations of individuals is derived from social interdependence, whereby individuals act in the interests of others and themselves with reference to their social relationships. At the first level of appearance, we have expectations of ourselves and our fellow citizens summarily expressed in the notion of a community. Moral expectations are also expressed as social obligations, or rights, which must be observed and maintained for the reproduction of social relations. Thus, the rights accorded an individual can only be defined contextually, in terms of social relations and expectations of moral concern derived out of a particular social context. This implies two further conditions. First, collective coercion by the community of particular individuals can be legitimized in the name of the interdependence implicit in human relations. Obviously, such a notion requires consent. Social obligations can fall more heavily on one group than on another. However as long as the means by which social decisions are agreed upon – perhaps according to the universality rule, as in Rawls' original position – then sacrifices can be made. Secondly, rather than assume individual rights and the community good to be antithetical, individual rights themselves can only be identified in terms of a particular community. This does not necessarily mean that the community will be protected from adverse effects of individual actions or *vice versa*, but the existence of adverse effects must be related to the social structure of power.

At this point it might be protested that our conception of rights as contextual obligations is to imply an extension of positivist empiricism; because rights are contextual they can only be defined in particular societal frameworks. There are no ultimate moral arbiters of right or wrong, according to this logic, just as there are no original positions independent of social life. In response, it should be noted that social obligations can have a large moral component. Rights as obligations can mean that not only are we concerned with how people act but also with the fact that obligations embody normative values, representing expectations of how individuals ought to act and how the community good ought to be achieved. This aspect is missing from positivist theories of rights. In addition, our contextual model does not presume the existence of rights (social values) outside the community. In essence, the principles that guide social life are endogenously determined. Also, our model does not conceive of unique definitions of justice and individual rights separate from social institutions. The political structure of society must be explicitly recognized and integrated within the adjudication mechanism. When confronting the earlier question of positivist and natural rights advocates – where do rights come from? – the answer must be: out of the social and political obligations that form a community. Further, in terms of the question asked by positivists – how are competing rights adjudicated? – the answer must be: squarely in the political arena.

Now, what if a complicating issue is introduced: economic inequality based upon restricted ownership of the means of production? How would we understand rights in this context? With unequal distribution of economic power, the process of defining social obligations is inevitably biased in favor of the more powerful groups. This occurs even if there is equal access to decision-making mechanisms. Economic inequality implies dependence as well as interdependence. Workers need employers for their livelihood, just as employers need workers for production. The relative levels of dependency are key variables in determining outcomes on two fronts. First, the state apparatus is likely to be caught within the web of inequality because it has no separate means of existence. Consequently, the state is intimately implicated in the adjudication of disputes in the interests of its continued existence. Moreover, if all groups recognize their relative dependency, the actual rights of individuals are likely to be defined in terms of interests of dependent classes. In this context, the definition of class interests is related to outcomes.

116   LAW AND THE STATE

Procedures for ensuring the observance of rights are not the crucial factors because it is the distributive consequences of social obligations that are fundamental.

Moral rights under conditions of economic inequality cannot be separated from the community's economic and political structure, no matter how universal their appearance. As Scanlon (1976) noted, the structure and enforcement of rights are intimately related to their distributive consequences. Contrasting Nozick's analysis of the rôle of the state is a useful means of illustrating this argument. In Nozick's model, association is based upon individual preferences and choice: individuals are economically and socially independent as opposed to interdependent; and the state enforces basic rights equally because it depends upon all members and communities for support. Of course, this premise is only plausible if there is no structural basis for social and economic inequality. If the state is dependent on one group more than another, its neutrality with respect to the definition and enforcement of rights would collapse. Thus, evaluating inequality with respect to the supposed choice between values and institutions should be recognized as a choice between different theories of society.

Individualism as a doctrine of public policy was the result of many factors, not least of which was the reaction of American colonialists to the class-related privileges of the British aristocracy. Horwitz (1977) contended that there was a basic conflict between the new colonial merchant class and the older, feudal and military British ruling class. The structure of privilege and law, according to Horwitz, retained the class inequalities of Britain without allowing economic flexibility and the separate development of the new merchant class. All groups, to some extent, were accorded certain socioeconomic positions through the rule of law, even though the economic and social conditions between post-feudal Britain and America were significantly different (Hurst 1967). However, it should also be noted that, despite tremendous anti-British sentiment, the model of British legal justice was not attacked; instead, conflict focused on the particular laws that defined the places of various groups within society.

The reaction of the Founding Fathers to British class-based prejudice and privilege was the design of a constitution as the normative model of how society ought to be organized. It reflected, and reflects now, an ideal of preserving the dominance of individualism over the interest of groups and spatial units of the nation. Emphasis on the individual as the unit of society accomplished two interrelated goals. First, it negated the inherent class-based privilege of the British legal system, without attacking the property and wealth rights of individuals; and secondly, it promoted social acceptance of the Constitution by demonstrating that no one class or group could control access to privilege. In this sense, emphasis upon the individual was a device that went beyond the interests of any one group or class. This argument suggests two hypotheses. First, any exclusion or discrimination against certain individuals because of location would be unlawful. Secondly, spatial and/or economic exclusion of individuals based upon class, race or any other group affiliation would be similarly unconstitutional.

Notice that those actually participating in the bargaining process were a relatively small group of white, male and propertied or taxed individuals. Slaves, Indians, free and indentured laborers were not allowed to participate, just as women were not allowed to participate, regardless of class. Consequently, those issues that appeared at the bargaining table during the Convention and during State ratification debates reflected more the interests of those participating than of society at large (Beard 1935). The concept of individual rights was itself linked to specific rights and privileges that benefited the propertied class in general. In his *Commentaries on the Laws of England* of 1765–9, Blackstone argued that the rights of individuals were threefold: (1) personal security in life and action; (2) personal liberty in mobility, both with respect to the means and location of movement; and (3) the right of an individual to use, dispose and hold property to the extent determined by the general laws of society (see Berger 1977, Duncan Kennedy 1979, and Posner 1981). Blackstone's principles were enshrined in the US Constitution in Article IV, section 2, the Privileges and Immunities clause (although in marginally different terms). At the same time, it should be recognized, as in *Corfield v. Coryell* 6 Fed. Cas. 546 (No. 3230) (CCED Pa. 1823), that these rights were held to be fundamental and to apply to any citizen of any State.

Our discussion should not be taken to suggest that the constitution changed the class character of society as it was reflected in the uneven distribution of wealth, ownership of property, control of the surplus and the social relations of production. For the merchant class, in particular (although not all members of that class), the constitution opened the way for rapid economic growth and economic advantage. Moreover, the judiciary and state, which were dependent upon this new class for support and economic expansion, actively promoted and interpreted the law in favor of the merchant class. At the level of action, the claims of economic self-interest argued by Beard (1935), and for preserving the Union (noted by Brown 1957 and others), can be seen as subsets of this argument. The state, the judiciary and the merchant classes may well have colluded for mutual gain, but this was dependent upon first reaching agreement on a form of law that was general enough to command the support of society at large.

The social contract that recognized individuals as the primary unit of society also defined a spatial hierarchy of governmental authority and

118 LAW AND THE STATE

community. The nation–state was given pre-eminence over its constituent States as regards trade, revenue, interregional migration, citizenship and judicial review (Tribe 1978). Moreover, the nation–state was given the responsibility of protecting the rights of individuals (as embodied in Article IV) against the encroachment of the separate States and their local municipalities. It could be argued that this decision reflected a mutual distrust among Convention delegates of the likely behavior of any existing State which might have been allocated equivalent powers of pre-emption and dominance. Friedman (1973) and others such as Goebel (1978) have noted that exclusion among and within States was a commom feature of colonial America. The commercial competition between States encouraged tariffs, tolls and significant constraints on personal and commodity mobility. The social contract, thus, defined the appropriate scale of government intervention to foster individual rights, and was a clear reaction to the exclusionary practices that operated in the pre-Revolutionary era.

The negation of spatial diversity and the insignificance of group identity, in general, can be interpreted as a result of defining society in terms of the individual. To the extent that spatial jurisdictions were, and are, a barrier to the fundamental rights of individual freedom and mobility, spatial diversity and uniqueness have been systematically denied by the judiciary. Spatial identity has had only very limited legitimacy or even relevance at the first level of appearance, although significantly, social action (the second level of appearance) takes place within the spatial arena. In large measure, law defined at the first level was conceived in terms of enabling action based upon a particular normative concept of social behavior, rather than prohibiting specific instances of action. However, at the second level of appearance, the balance of competing interests, and their impact on the state and judiciary, dominate the definitions of appropriate action and obligation. Hence, the spatial character of the economy could be recognized, if promoted and argued, up to limits imposed by the first level of appearances.

Judicial apparatus and spatial integration

In order to evaluate the impact of law and individualism upon spatial structure, a choice has to be made over what particular legal statutes should be given significance over others. To structure this choice, the impact of law is interpreted with respect to theoretically identified conditions necessary for economic growth and reproduction. For the most part, the conditions emphasized here relate to the spatial and economic coordination of exchange, output and the factors (labor and capital) of production (see Harvey 1982). We have earlier emphasized other aspects related to the social relations of reproduction (see Ch. 4).

Reproduction is defined here, however, in terms related to the circulation of capital. Simple reproduction occurs when enterprises are replaced, but no capital accumulation occurs and workers and capitalists spend all they receive on consumption goods. The replacement of each enterprise is dependent upon realizing the sale in the market place of all commodities produced by the enterprise. If a profit is derived from realized sales, then the enterprise will continue in production. The problem of reproduction is inherently the problem of maximizing the circulation and production of commodities by individual capitalists in a given market. Extended reproduction includes capital accumulation which may incorporate replacement of existing capital stock. Reproduction thus depends upon a portion of the surplus value created by labor being expropriated by the individual enterprise (Clark 1980a, b).

A first condition of reproduction is simply the existence of money. This allows for the exchange of specialized commodities and the anticipation and manipulation of uncertainty in market conditions. It also ensures the existence of specialized commodity production in different areas or locations of the total spatial system. A second condition is free and rapid circulation of commodities (Young 1976). There are two classes of commodities; those produced by enterprises to be sold (exchanged) in the market for money, and those that serve as inputs to the production process. Inputs include physical capital (machines) and labor. Free and rapid circulation for capitalist spatial economies implies movement across space and trading by the exchange in market places of goods and services. Crises in circulation can take many forms: for example, immobile labor located in depressed regions and high labor demand (and excess wage demands) in areas where labor is in short supply.

Both of these conditions for reproduction are of course based upon more general aspects of the capitalist mode of production – ownership of property, wage labor, control of the production process, the generation of surplus value by capitalists, and the acceptance and enforcement of contracts between enterprises (Horwitz 1977). The state's rôle in guaranteeing these conditions of the capitalist mode of production is quite complex. Theoretically, it provides the general conditions; in reality, it may favor one class or group of capitalists over others (see Ch. 2). We now intend to focus on three legal rules adjudicated by the judicial apparatus which bear directly upon American spatial integration and economic development. Particular attention is paid to those legal reflections of the general conditions for circulation and reproduction identified above, as well as the interplay between individualism and the goal of national growth. An exhaustive review of the spatial ramifica-

120   LAW AND THE STATE

tions of all laws is not intended. Rather, a selected set of significant laws, constitutional statutes, and Supreme Court interpretations is presented.

The Commerce Clause.   Article 1, Section 8, Clause 3 of the United States Constitution states that ". . . The Congress shall have Power . . . To regulate Commerce with foreign Nations, and among the several States, and with the Indian tribes . . ." (Library of Congress 1973). Justice Marshall held, in the seminal case of *Gibbons v. Ogden* 9 Wheat. (22 US) 1 (1824), that only commerce exclusively internal to a State and with no impact on trade in (or between) other State(s) escaped this provision. Initially, commerce was thought to apply only to merchandise; however, the clause rapidly came to apply to the movement of all commodities, labor and even information between and within States (for example, *United States v. South-Eastern Underwriters Association* 322 US 533 (1944)). Business transactions, whether formal through the exchange of money and/or commodities, or implicit as in contract obligations that affected interstate commerce laws, have also become included within the scope of the clause's grant of authority (for example, *Chicago Board of Trade v. Olsen* 262 US 1 (1923)).

The Commerce Clause also gave Congress the right to regulate interstate commerce. This has been interpreted as meaning that Congress can set the standards, conditions, prices and even the rates of commerce (Ribble 1937). Further, the Supreme Court has upheld congressional attempts to regulate intrastate commerce if it affects interstate commerce. For example, in *Houston and Texas Railway v. United States* 234 US 342 (1914), the Supreme Court held that the Interstate Commerce Commission (ICC) could regulate the rates of a railroad company which operated exclusively within Texas, because it competed directly with a railroad that operated between Texas and Louisiana. The mandate to regulate interstate commerce has also been used to regulate competition within industries. For example, the Sherman Antitrust Act of 1890 was based upon notions of restraint of trade and commerce through monopoly power. In this instance, the Commerce Clause was used as a vehicle to regulate business practices deemed injurious to general trade (see the leading case, *United States v. E. C. Knight and Co.* 156 US 1 (1895)).

In a case decided in 1905, *Swift and Co. v. United States* 196 US 375 (1905), the doctrine of the unimpeded and free flow of trade between States was given expression in terms analogous to our more theoretical notions of commodity circulation. Justice Holmes, in handing down the Supreme Court's decision, referred to a "current of commerce," suggesting that actions, although local in origin and character, had spatial repercussions beyond State boundaries. The argument was made that commerce, broadly defined, involves the coordination of activities across space implying expectations, contracts, and exchange. Until the 1930s, the Commerce Clause was interpreted as a constraint on State actions. During the depression, the clause was used and interpreted as a vehicle for the federal government to intervene directly in the economy. However, it is significant that the current of commerce concept was used often to indicate the integrated nature of the space economy (see Pred 1973) and the possibility of intervening to manipulate the "flow of the current" (see Library of Congress 1973).

As earlier writers have shown, the Commerce Clause has, since *Gibbons v. Ogden,* been systematically interpreted by the judiciary as operating to limit State power (see Sholley 1936, Brown 1957, Tribe 1978). The general presumption was summarized in *Champion v. Ames* 188 US 321 (1903): ". . . (the Commerce Clause) was intended to secure equality and freedom in commercial intercourse between the States, not to permit the creation of impediments to such intercourse . . .". Sholley (1936, p. 556) quoted an even more explicit treatment of the place of one State within the spatial system by Justice Cardozo in the case *Baldwin v. Seelig* 294 US 511 (1935). The State of New York had passed a statute that forced producers in other States to sell milk products at the New York producers' prices, thus reducing the competitive edge of producers in other States who were able to sell their products at lower prices. Justice Cardozo argued (quoted in Sholley 1936) that

What is ultimate is the principle that one State in its dealings with another may not place itself in a position of economic isolation. . . . Neither the power to tax nor the police power may be used by the State of destination with the aim and effect of establishing an economic barrier against competition with the products of another State or the labor of its residents.

There is no doubt that the intent of the clause was to eliminate vestiges of economic isolationism that had developed over the decade 1780–90 (Horwitz 1977).

Prior to 1930, the Commerce Clause was interpreted and applied as a principle which secured the rights of individuals to trade and exchange between the States. Only rarely was the Clause invoked by the federal government for explicit policy initiatives. The Sherman anti-trust statutes were one example that were justified on the basis that monopolist practices interfered with the current of commerce. In 1933, the federal government moved to restore national economic prosperity by invoking the Commerce Clause as its mandate (Stern 1934). Through a number of congressional Acts, including the National Industrial Recovery Act of 1933, Roosevelt sought to intervene directly in the economy and to restructure national economic conditions. For example, the Recovery Act established minimum wages, free collective bargaining

122 LAW AND THE STATE

and a maximum number of hours of work per week. Competition was to be severely restricted and prices controlled. These, and related, policy initiatives were unparalleled in the history of the United States and in the history of legal adjudication of cases considered under the Commerce Clause. The power of Congress over interstate trade and the importance of the Commerce Clause depends, to a large extent, on two doctrines: pre-emption, which provides Congress with the power to override State and local action on matters delegated to it in the Constitution; and the supremacy clause of Article IV. This latter doctrine has been interpreted as meaning that even if there is no explicit federal legislation in a specific area, Congress may still have the right to enact laws and regulations that take precedence over other local actions because the intent of the Constitution was that Congress should occupy the field (Tribe 1978). As long as federal statutes are complied with and the intent of legislation does not stray beyond its constitutional limits, the federal principle or policy has precedence over any other State action.

In a vital test case of the Recovery Act, *Schechter Poultry Corp. v. United States* 295 US 495 (1935), the Supreme Court held to a very narrow interpretation of the Commerce Clause. In contrast to earlier Supreme Court decisions, only intrastate activities *directly* affecting interstate commerce were held to be the subject of federal power. The implication was that the balance between federal and State control was to be shifted in favor of individual States. This decision prompted many to hail the emergence of a dual federalism (Stern 1946), with States having significant rights over commerce in principle and in policy. Interpretation of the right of the federal government to claim pre-emption or supremacy ultimately rests with the Supreme Court. Cox (1976) noted that attempts have been made (most recently with respect to racial desegregation in the South) to reverse the order of precedence so that States would have the primary right of defining areas of activity and legislative control. These attempts have never been successful. The National Labor Relations Act of 1935 faced a similarly hostile federal judiciary. However, in 1937, the Supreme Court decided in the case of *Virginia R.R. Co. v. System Federation* 300 US 515 (1937), a test of the Railway Labor Act which had been the model of the NLR Act, in favor of a more liberal interpretation of the Commerce Clause. In effect, the Supreme Court recognized the economic geography of the United States which had been sustained and encouraged by the Court for over 100 years prior to 1935, when it held that (quoted in Stern 1946, p. 680)

When industries organize themselves on a national scale, making their relation to interstate commerce the dominant factor in their activities, how can it be maintained that their industrial labor relations constitute a forbidden field into which Congress may not enter when it is necessary to protect interstate commerce from the paralyzing consequences of industrial war? We have often said that interstate commerce itself is a practical conception. It is equally true that interferences with that commerce must be appraised by a judgment that does not ignore actual experience.

Consequently, the Court allowed a significant increase in the power of Congress to use the Commerce Clause for distinct policy purposes. The rapid shift in the Court's opinion has often been attributed to the re-election of Roosevelt by a tremendous majority. Within two months of the election, Roosevelt proposed that the court itself be restructured by the appointment of six new Justices. This swamped the conservative opinions of the majority of the Justices by forging an alliance with three sympathetic Justices, Brandeis, Stone and Cardozo. The Court's resistance collapsed, and in doing so reaffirmed the importance of the political wing in determining the structure of law at both the first and second levels of appearance. This legacy remains today and, at the same time, was only limited by the due process clause *(United States v. Carolene Products Co.* 304 US 144 (1938)). This episode also drastically changed the scale of federal intervention in the economy. No longer was spatial integration the result of previous enabling judgments (by Marshall and others) and the structure of legal individualism. After 1938, spatial integration became an explicit public policy implemented through economic policies that affected every aspect of production and exchange.

The Commerce Clause, and subsequent Supreme Court interpretations had three effects. First, as noted above, it removed any legal barrier inhibiting the free and rapid circulation of commodities (broadly defined). In essence, it created a free-trade union, the precondition for an integrated economy. Secondly, the Clause demanded uniformity in the application of State and federal regulations concerning the flow of commerce. For example, in *Cooley v. Board of Wardens of Port of Philadelphia* 12 How. (53 US) 290 (1851), the Supreme Court held that commerce must be subject to uniform regulation and control throughout the country. Thus, uniformity in law relating to commerce provided another condition for free and rapid circulation of commodities. Moreover, the interpretation of law subsequently expanded the definition of commerce to include contracts or business obligations. Thus, the conditions for a national integrated economy were set in the first years of the Union itself (Nettels 1962). Thirdly, in the litigation over the NLR Act and related economic recovery Acts of the 1930s, the Court reluctantly established the right of the federal government to intervene directly in the economy to maintain all aspects of production and exchange.

124 LAW AND THE STATE

Money and integration. The model of commodity circulation and spatial integration reviewed above also depends upon exchange and, implicitly, the existence of money. Money can take almost any form, although it must be readily accepted in all areas and have expected value. Clause 5 of Article I, Section 8 of the United States Constitution states that "The Congress shall have Power . . . to coin Money, regulate the Value thereof, and of foreign Coin, and fix the Standard of Weights and Measures . . ." (Library of Congress 1973, p. 305). This clause has been interpreted as applying to virtually all aspects of currency and exchange. (See Hurst (1973) for a general history of law and money in the United States.) The right to issue notes and coin and control the velocity of the currency circulation, the form that currency takes, and the uniform payment of debts, are all powers vested in the Congress. The States have no rights under this clause although negotiable bonds are not included in this definition.

There has been remarkably little litigation before the Supreme Court concerning this clause, probably because of the significance of the first case, *McCulloch v. Maryland* 4 Wheat. (17 US) 316 (1819), tried before Justice Marshall (see Gunther 1969). The genesis of the case was Maryland's attempt to tax the Second Bank of the United States which had been chartered by Congress in 1816. The question initially was whether or not a State had the power to tax a congressionally chartered institution. Thus, the case dealt with the constitutionality of federally chartered banks and the exclusion of States from powers relating to federal regulation. Ultimately, the case was an argument over federalism itself. Justice Marshall decided against Maryland. In doing so (quoted in Gunther 1969, p. 47) he held that

> If the States may tax an instrument, employed by the government in the execution of its powers, they may tax any and every other instrument . . . they may tax all the means employed by the government, to an excess which would defeat all the ends of government. This was not intended by the American people. They did not design to make their government dependent on the States.

This case, and the controversy surrounding it, has become famous as a defense of federalism against the parochial interests of States. It also had the virtue, however, of securing the uniformity of money and the value of currency throughout the Union. Thus, another condition was provided for the spatial integration of the economy.

Article IV and the 14th Amendment. The clauses reviewed above were characterized as providing the structural or macro-spatial context for individual action in the United States. The clauses overlap the two levels of appearance of law because of the altruistic nature of their initial specifications in the Constitution (the negation of groups, spatial or otherwise) and the clear objectives of early judicial interpretations to use these clauses as tools for national economic development. For Chief Justice Marshall and others in the 1830s, the Commerce Clause provided a means of promoting spatial integration beyond that which would normally occur because it overruled the initial specification of State powers relative to federal powers. However, this integration occurred only after the Constitutional Convention, which was more concerned with the rights of individuals against other individuals than with the different levels of government.

Given the macro-context, these individual rights are now explored with reference to the extent and possibilities of spatial exclusion and discrimination. Article IV, Section 2 states that ". . . (t)he Citizens of each State shall be entitled to all Privileges and Immunities of Citizens in the several States" (Library of Congress 1973, p. 830). This is a major constitutional provision dealing with the rights of individuals in relation to spatial jurisdictions. The leading case, *Corfield v. Coryell* 6 Fed. Cas. 546 (No. 3230) (CCED Pa. 1823), concerned the rights of an individual located in one State to engage in commercial activity (fishing) in another State (in that instance, New Jersey). It was decided that all persons, regardless of State citizenship, could travel, trade, own or dispose of property, pay taxes and generally enjoy the freedom common to all citizens of the United States (Library of Congress 1973, p. 835). This argument reflects much of the subsequent litigation concerning interstate privileges and immunities (see, example, *Toomer v. Witsell* 334 US 385 (1948) and Brennan 1977).

It should also be noted that the application of this interpretation has been restricted by the courts on two grounds (Tribe 1978). First, it has come to be accepted that the doctrine forbids any State to discriminate against citizens of other States in favor of its own. In *Paul v. Virginia* 8 Wall. (75 US) 168 (1869), the Supreme Court held that the intent of the section was to place citizens of all States on the same footing within State jurisdictions. Thus, even though State laws may be different in regard to all manner of things, their application to individuals must be uniform regardless of their origin. Secondly, the doctrine has also been limited to the protection of individuals' fundamental rights, and those interests basic to the maintenance of the Union (Tribe 1979, p. 34). For example, it was held in *Baldwin v. Fish and Game Comm. of Montana* 436 US 371 (1978), that equal access for hunting is not a fundamental right. Fundamental rights, since *Corfield v. Coryell,* have been interpreted as relating to property, contracts, taxes, trade, ownership and the like, and these are basically economic rights.

Clearly the Privileges Section of Article IV and the Commerce Clause

126   LAW AND THE STATE

are quite similar in effect. Both protect against spatial discrimination in the pursuit of commerce or trade (broadly defined). The former section applies to individuals and provides for freedom of individual action. The latter clause relates to the structural arrangement of the spatial economy, the context in which individuals act. It should also be noted, however, that the Privileges Section has also been applied more widely, for example, in cases concerning minority, political and racial access to equal treatment within State jurisdictions.

The 14th Amendment and, in particular, Section 1 of the United States Constitution also provides protection for individuals from discriminatory laws enacted by States. In brief, the Section holds that

> . . . no State shall make or enforce any law which shall abridge the privileges and immunities of citizens of the United States; nor shall any State deprive any person of life, liberty or property, without due process of law; nor deny any person within its jurisdiction the equal protection of the laws (Library of Congress 1973, p. 1313).

There are a number of clauses within this section that have been open to interpretation: the Privileges and Immunities Clause, the Due Process Clause, and the Equal Protection Clause.

According to Tribe (1978) and others (see Library of Congress 1973), the Privileges and Immunities Clause was initially promoted as a means of controlling the States' abilities to enact their own legislation. However, in the *Slaughter-House Cases* 16 Wall. (83 US) 36 (1873), the court narrowly defined the applicability of the clause, so that it has been comparatively neglected over the past century. States were limited with respect to the national constitution, in such areas as the right of access to transport routes (especially seaports during the 19th century), navigation, justice and government. The Court extended this list in *Twinging v. New Jersey* 211 US 78 (1908) to include the right to travel freely between States (*Crandall v. Nevada* 6 Wall. (73 US) 35 (1868)) and the right to carry out interstate commerce (see *Crutcher v. Kentucky* 141 US 47 (1891)). In recent times, the Supreme Court has also struck down State statutes defining residency requirements for welfare as an unconstitutional impediment to the right to travel and migrate between States (*Shapiro v. Thompson* 394 US 618 (1969); see also Harvard Law Review Association 1980). Although this clause has been conventionally thought of as quite restricted and narrow in interpretation, it is interesting to note that the areas of application bear directly upon individual rights of commerce and travel similar to those mandated in Article IV of the Constitution. Further, the emphasis upon the unrestricted mobility of labor provides yet another condition for economic growth and capitalist reproduction.

The Due Process Clause has been important in many areas of litigation and individual rights issues (Tribe 1978). As with the first clause of the 14th Amendment, it was initially interpreted very narrowly. For example, in *Munn v. Illinois* 94 US 113 (1877), the Court refused to act against State legislation even though the particular statute under litigation was shown to discriminate against the property rights of a merchant (Library of Congress 1973, p. 1311). However, since 1890, the clause has become a means of controlling State powers over individuals. In a series of cases, *Mulger v. Kansas* 123 US 623 (1887) and *Budd v. New York* 143 US 517 (1892), the Court argued that maximum individual liberty and freedom, defined in terms of *laissez-faire* economics and Spencer's (1882) notions of economic evolution, were fundamental rights with which States could not interfere. The Due Process Clause as a control on States' actions was employed by the Court until the 1930s (see *Nebbia v. New York* 291 US 502 (1934)). Subsequently, the Court has been much more restrained in striking down State statutes; so much so, that the Due Process Clause is now more related to individual rights against the legal process itself (*Williamson v. Lee Optical Co.* 348 US 483 (1955)).

The Equal Protection Clause has not suffered ambiguity and styles of interpretation as have the other two clauses of Section 1 of the 14th Amendment. In essence, the Equal Protection Clause protects citizens of any State from discrimination in the design and application of State laws. Thus, the clause provides for appeal and redress of government actions that compromise the liberty, freedom, property or equality of individuals or groups of individuals within a State (see, for example, *Civil Rights Cases* 109 US 3 (1883); *Terry v. Adams* 345 US 461 (1953); and *Yick Wo v. Hopkins* 118 US 356 (1886)).

Both the 14th Amendment and Article IV provide the basis for individual mobility between and within the States. In many instances, mobility has been interpreted in the context of trade, exchange and property rights. Although many other issues have been important (for example, racial discrimination in the case of the 14th Amendment), it is apparent that these clauses have been systematically interpreted as denying the right of States to discriminate between individuals on the basis of State citizenship and location. Article IV provides for interstate equality and due process. The 14th Amendment also provides a procedural framework for individual action, while Article IV provides a procedural framework through which State actions are designed not to inhibit individual freedom. The judiciary has eschewed geographical diversity in favor of individual liberty and mobility regardless of location.

In two distinct ways individualism, according to this interpretation, is evident as a major premise of the Constitution and its adjudication. First, belief in the individual as the primary unit of society prompted explicit

128 LAW AND THE STATE

attempts to curtail interstate discrimination and exclusion, based upon Blackstone's rights of security, mobility and property; it also prompted a general concern with the practices of group segregation. Secondly, belief in individualism allowed for the Supreme Court to use the existing legal structure as a tool of national economic development and spatial integration. This was only possible because the primacy of individualism opened up the total political system to review.

Conclusions

The primary objective of this chapter was to develop an understanding of law and the state and thereby, in the hermeneutic tradition, to provide an interpretation of how and why the constitution has promoted the spatial integration of the United States. Our secondary objectives were to interpret law in terms of its substantive character, essentially its regulatory intent. Basically, our proposition was that the structure of constitutional law, and its subsequent adjudication, has systematically negated spatial diversity and isolation and has promoted spatial integration of the United States through the dominance of the individual as the primary unit of society. The judicial history of a variety of different clauses of the Constitution was presented as evidence for this interpretation; the Commerce Clause, Article IV, and the Money Clause were regarded as necessary conditions for the spatial reproduction of the capitalist system. Similarly, the 14th Amendment was shown to have important implications for spatial homogeneity between States (see also Ch. 7).

The model presented placed the derivation of law within the social and political structure and depended upon a duality and tension between two levels of appearance: the first level, related to the social aspirations and normative goals of society; and the second level being the realm of action, social conflict and class struggle (see Unger 1983). The first level was argued to be derivative of the existing realm of action. In this interpretation of law and its effects on American spatial integration, it was suggested that individual rights rather than social privilege was the consensual vision of the revolutionaries in their struggle against Britain. Consequently, other group dimensions of society have been systematically negated when found to conflict with fundamental individual rights and freedom. Spatial diversity has been one such dimension. Consequently, spatial integration should be seen as being derivative of the structure of substantive law and the objectives of the judiciary.

This interpretation has parallels with other marxist explanations of the Constitution's form and intent. For example, Beard (1935) claimed that the Constitution reflected an explicit attempt to promote integration in

CONCLUSIONS 129

the interests of the merchant class. In fact, at the time of the Convention many speakers argued that the Commerce Clause in particular, but also Article IV (Privileges and Immunities), would be a useful vehicle for stimulating national economic growth (Solberg 1958). Clearly, the structure and goals of the Constitution did in fact enable spatial integration, although this was in part the product of a particular vision of society (individualism) rather than simply the control of any one group.

The implications of interpreting the spatial structure of the state through the "lens" of substantive interpretations of legal rules and administrative practices are manifold. Two issues in particular can be isolated that illustrate the complexity and significance of the legal apparatus in forming and perpetuating the patterns and structure of the American space economy. First, it is apparent that the Supreme Court has not been overly concerned with the consequences of encouraging national economic development. For example, the Court has not considered important whether or not integration promotes even or uneven spatial economic development. The national interest of maximum economic growth has been thought to be synonymous with maximum individual mobility and spatial access to economic opportunities. Secondly, since individual rights are the fundamental principles upon which judicial review was based, it is clear that the spatial pattern of development has been a very weak criterion for judging the constitutionality of Congressional legislation and State actions. The hierarchy implicit in the vision of post-Revolutionary America has had the effect of stripping localities of their legitimacy when confronted with the national interest.

These implications of the structure of laws for the space economy are recurrent themes in American constitutional history. And they remain vital public issues today. For example, as the North-East and Mid-West regions have economically declined over the past two decades, legislators in the affected States and in Congress have attempted to stem the tide by restricting capital mobility (Bluestone & Harrison 1982). The National Employment Priorities Bills of 1977 and 1979 (HR 5040) proposed by Congressman Ford of Michigan for example, sought to penalize relocating firms in at least four ways. First, it was proposed that runaway firms must give their employees at least one year's severance pay in compensation. Secondly, runaway firms would have been required to pay the community affected at least 85 percent of one year's taxes that such firms would normally pay. Thirdly, firms would have been required to offer those affected jobs at other plants with no cut in salary and with adequate moving expenses. Fourthly, before closing firms would have been required to provide an "employment impact statement" to their employees, their community, and the US Secretary of Labor. Other conditions and even more restrictive proposals have

130 LAW AND THE STATE

been offered in the Senate (Bill S. 1609 proposed by Senator Williams of New Jersey).

Given our discussion of how the Commerce Clause has been applied by the Supreme Court, we can speculate on the likely judgment that the Court would offer if such legislation were passed and constitutionally challenged. We suggest that the Court would rule against Congress and in favor of firms affected by such legislation. Clearly, firms could argue that this type of legislation would place them at a competitive disadvantage with respect to firms who had a more favorable location. Moreover, firms could invoke Justice Holmes' "current of commerce" notion expounded in *Swift v. United States,* by pointing to the Commerce Clause as their defense against undue interference with the flow of trade. The common good or national interest could also be invoked to place such legislation within the context of previous cases (even for example *Champion v. Ames).* One need only consider the Commerce Clause to realize the restrictive intent of "plant runaway" legislation, especially as the clause has been the vehicle for national integration.

A more fundamental objection, however, would invoke Article IV, Section 2, of the Privileges and Immunities Clause. Plant-closing legislation threatens two of the three basic rights of individuals: personal mobility and the right of an individual to use, dispose and hold property. Shareholders and owners could well argue that a National Employment Priorities Bill would unduly restrict their rights of mobility and property. Opponents of their position would have to convince the court that the national interest was coincident with the local community's interest. Without dealing with specifics, it is difficult to envisage such a situation unless we think òn the scale of General Motors leaving Detroit to relocate in Taiwan. Massachusetts and West Virginia have also considered plant-closing legislation. Only in Wisconsin has such a law been passed, although to this date it has not been enforced. One can also speculate on the likely fate of such a law if brought before the Supreme Court. It is clear, for the reasons noted above, that the Court would decide against the State.

7   The local state

Understanding the rôle of the local state in capitalist democracy poses considerable conceptual and analytical challenges. For example, one might question whether or not the local state is simply an apparatus of the nation–state. Similarly, we could also question whether its form and functions are distinguishable from other levels of state organization. And, most importantly, we could ask how autonomous is the local state (that is, from higher tiers of the state)? This issue of autonomy is crucial for two reasons. First, with a large degree of autonomy the potential exists for local political transformation that could threaten the whole state structure. Secondly, the local autonomy issue questions the actual existence of the local state as an independent entity. Without autonomy, the local state would simply exist to carry out the orders of other state apparatus.

Traditionally, theories of local government in North America have tended to favor models of political pluralism, decentralization, and competition among local governments. In keeping with liberal democratic theory and its concern for individual rights, emphasis has been on local control, self-determination and a high degree of horizontal competition between local governments over the delivery of local public goods and services (Ostrom, Tiebout & Warren 1961). Typically, debate within this paradigm has focused on two issues: the optimal mix of public goods provision given an objective function of minimizing taxes; and the efficient allocation of government functions given a variety of size, distance and spacing constraints (Bennett 1980). Less interest has been shown in situating the local government within the wider spatial hierarchy of state apparatus. Perhaps the reason for the neglect of such relationships, at the theoretical level, has been an unquestioned acceptance of the ideology of local autonomy, the American ideal of decentralized democracy.

Although very critical of the Tiebout type of model of pluralist competition, marxist theories of the capitalist state have similarly paid little attention to the rôle of the local state and have certainly neglected the question of local autonomy within the existing state system. Recently however, there have been attempts in urban sociology to resituate the local state within the political and economic fabric of the capitalist

132 THE LOCAL STATE

system. For example, Paris (1983) argued that the notion of locality as a determinant of the form of social relations mistakes the empirical or spatial arrangement of power for underlying processes. His argument is similar to Clark's (1980b), which questioned the many theorists who suggest that regional disparities are a requirement for capitalist reproduction (see Peet 1975). Spatial form or organization should be seen as a structured facet of capitalism, but not as a determinant that has equal footing with the principles of capitalist social relations. Even so, space is more than a stage for action; it is itself structured so as to mold social relations, even if it does not determine their political character in the final analysis.

To extend this analysis into an evaluation of the structure of the local state and its place in the hierarchy of state organizations requires a substantial theoretical and empirical edifice. Both liberal and marxist theories of the state can be accused of simple functionalism, whereby cataloguing action gives theory a specific content. In this context, there is a tendency to reduce the local state simply to an administrative apparatus of the nation–state, thereby pre-empting further analysis. Our approach in this chapter is again state-centered, focusing in particular upon the dimensions of local autonomy, and thereby assessing the significance of the local state as part of the state apparatus. Obviously, if the local state is autonomous then it may have a significant capacity for initiating local, or even State-level change.

In the next chapter, we develop a theoretical understanding of the local state as a political institution situated within the social fabric of society. Through these two chapters, we seek a dual analysis of the local state concentrating first upon a state-centered mode and then a society-centered mode. We argue that the local state is both an instrument or apparatus of the state and a democratic institution in its own right. As a consequence, there is a tension between its functions and its basis in democratic political ideals. In the United States it represents an idealization of the sociopolitical "community," wherein people with like preferences seek to locate (see Nozick 1974). Conversely, its functions and even its form are largely determined outside the local electorate by higher tiers of the state. In this respect, it is an instrument of wider social design. A tension thus exists between the image and reality of the local state; this tension is the object of this chapter and the subsequent chapter on legitimacy.

The local state and capitalism

The materialist view of the state reviewed in the early chapters of this book does not provide a specific explanation of the form and functions of the local state. Why should it be necessary to create a small-scale spatial analogue of the national state? Is the replica equivalent? And what is its relationship to the higher tiers? For our purposes, we define the local state as any government entity having a political and spatial jurisdiction at less than the scale of (for example) a Canadian Province or one of the 50 States of the USA, and having the authority to raise revenues from, and make expenditures on behalf of, its constituents. The local state may therefore take many forms and more than one type of local state may exist. For instance, the United States (US) government is arranged in three tiers: a single nation–state; 50 State governments; and innumerable local or municipal states (counties, towns, cities, and regional governments). By our definition, it is these assorted municipalities that constitute the local state; such a definition is consistent with the historical circumstances of the US. The terms nation–state and State will be used for the national government and for the fifty States of the US confederation respectively.

Based upon our previous discussion of state apparatus in general, we assert that the existence of a local state is predicated upon the need for directed long-term crisis avoidance at the local level. It is only through the local state system that social and ideological control of a spatially extensive and heterogeneous national political system becomes possible. Accordingly, local needs are anticipated and answered, and national state legitimacy ensured. While the existence of a local state is functional for capitalism, it is also in keeping with the principles of local self-determination so important in American democracy (Bowles & Gintis 1978, Wolfe 1977). A highly potent ideological and functional alliance thus buttresses the local state system. Our initial presumption is then that the local state is an apparatus of the higher tiers of state (see Duncan & Goodwin 1982). Once the need for and existence of the local state is conceded, the central theoretical and practical question is to determine the degree of autonomy of the local state as compared with the central state. In this section the theoretical limits of local state autonomy are examined and the functional implications of those limits deduced.

In her study of the local state, Cockburn (1977) argued that the state and its many apparatus serve the interests of capital, and that the local state is simply an administrative apparatus of the national and federal states. This viewpoint is supported by others such as Broadbent (1977, p. 128) who argued that "[t]he whole system of local states . . . is nevertheless part of the national state." Local states are presumed to be dependent upon and controlled by the central and federal States despite clear differences in their nature and form of electoral support. This view is of course favored even by orthodox scholars who often suggest that the local state is the most efficient unit for providing public goods and services (Bennett 1980). Nevertheless, service provision may well be bound by standards of service provision mandated at higher tiers. In this

134 THE LOCAL STATE

respect, few would disagree with Cockburn's (1977) empirical observation; class-related objectives are, however, another issue.

According to Cockburn (1977, pp. 51–2) it is the nation–state that predominantly contributes to capitalist *production* (an argument established in detail in the previous chapter). The local state, Cockburn suggested, essentially contributes to capitalist *reproduction*. The general requirements of social reproduction involve the perpetuation of two key sets of social relations: the means of production, and the relations of production (Althusser 1971). The latter requires the use of ideology, coercion and repression, as well as cultural aspects of reproduction (including school, electoral politics, and the church; see Ch. 4). Cockburn (1977, pp. 158–63) focused analysis upon three particular kinds of reproduction arguing that the local state is: (1) the point of *collective reproduction,* where people are the direct clients of state services; (2) the point of *employment in reproduction,* where we are the workforce of the local state; and (3) the point of *privatized reproduction,* that is, our family life.

By directing or targeting and structuring social consumption through expenditures, the local state may effectively co-opt and thereby control the local population. This view was partly supported by Broadbent (1977) who argued that the local state acts mainly in the social consumption sector, especially as the direct provider of services. He noted three important local state interventions in the local economy, all of which support both the productive and reproductive components of the social formation. These interventions were: (1) employment of labor; (2) purchaser and provider of goods and services; and (3) the source of capital infrastructure. Like Cockburn, Broadbent identifies local functions consistent with more general notions of reproduction, although they disagree on which functions are most important.

There are a number of constraints on the actions of the local state employed by higher tiers of the state. For example, the local state receives an increasing proportion of its funds from higher institutional sources, thus curtailing local discretion and autonomy (Tribe 1976). Even though the local state derives revenues from its own jurisdiction, and is directly responsible to local economic and political pressures, the relationship between the local state and the local economy is vague and tenuous. Openness of local economies to external effects is a well known feature that conditions the relationship between the local state and the private market. The main stabilizing device for both national and local economies is the judicious use of fiscal policy. For local states this often means the injection of nation–state funds, and local states are increasingly in competition with one another and with other levels of the state for scarce financial resources (Shapira 1979).

This geographical competition is itself an important dynamic in the sustenance of capital, and is a potentially important unifying factor linking different levels of state apparatus in a common objective: the maintenance of capitalist social relations. The imperatives of maintaining democratic support and sustaining local economic activity (without any real authority or power) places the local state in a powerful vise – a vise of conformity and support of capital which may not need to return the favor. If O'Connor (1973) is correct that the public debt is a "tightening of the grip of capital on the state," then the increased public debt of local states (in proportion to that of the nation–state) is indirect evidence of the effective political penetration of capital interest below the national level. And, even more significantly, while central state debts are externally owed in the market, the increasing local state debts are largely owed to or guaranteed by higher tiers. Clearly, the local state need not be acting as a conscious apparatus of higher tiers of the state to be responsible to higher-tier priorities.

One effect of these conditions and organizational arrangements is to exacerbate the fiscal crisis of the local state. The genesis of the fiscal crisis of the state, and its particular concentration in urban areas, have been well documented in, respectively, O'Connor (1973) and Alcaly and Mermelstein (1977). In brief, local states have lacked the authority to deal with imbalances in the local economy which derive from the continued dispersal of economic activity beyond their jurisdictions. These imbalances have led to a crisis in local legitimacy and rationality which, according to Habermas (1976), rivals national accumulation crises. The lack of integration between the local economy and local jurisdiction is a major difference between the local state and the nation–state (although this is changing for the nation–state as well). The problem is simply that the economic system operates at a much wider spatial scale than is recognized by conventional political boundaries, so that local states may have little impact upon, or control over, the processes affecting local economies. This mismatch between political authority and the power to regulate the private market generates structural tensions between tiers of the state, the most significant being the recurrent call for reallocation of functions among various geographical levels of the state.

The question of centralizing and decentralizing state apparatus and authority has a long tradition in political theory. North American ideology argues for maximum feasible decentralization of political discretion subject to the needs of efficiency, control, and local self-determination (Ostrom, Tiebout & Warren 1961). More pragmatic-ally, Cockburn (1977) has referred to the constant reallocation of state functions among various state tiers as efforts to unload "knotty problems" to adjacent state tiers (see also Friedland et al. 1977). Thus, one tier of the state may take care to dissociate itself from the unpleasant consequences of its actions by ensuring that another level will "reap the whirlwind." According to Hirsch (1981), this represents a purposeful "conflict-diversification" strategy, which shifts the effects of structural crises to community and local levels. The local state often lacks the authority and jurisdiction to solve local crises, and is controlled by higher tiers in capital's interest. Financial, rationality, and legitimacy crises are thus regionalized. The effect is to remove the burden from higher tiers by implicating the local state.

The tension between higher tiers of the state and the local state is summarized in two trends which are increasingly important in advanced capitalist economies. On the one hand, there is an increasing centralization of technological and managerial skills in both large corporations and state-administered apparatus. On the other hand, there are increasing demands for political decentralization, as the interventionist rôle of the nation–state is rejected and pleas for local autonomy advanced. The net effect of these two trends is a forced and increased "politicization" of the spatial structure of capitalist social relations. As the political and economic spheres in capitalism become more fully integrated, tensions between local and higher tiers become a constant feature of modern life. The consequences are many and varied, including problems of maintaining social order and sustaining the requirements for overall capital accumulation. Conflicts over the organization of the federal system of government are consequently unsurprising.

Given these initial suppositions concerning the rôle of the local state in the capitalist system, what can be said about the nature of local state functions? Most local state functions are directed toward a long-term strategy of crisis avoidance in order to sustain the continued reproduction of capitalist social relations. These strategies place emphasis on system stability instead of on reform. In fact, as a more specific hypothesis, it could be argued that the control of local states through uniform codes and statutes sustains political stability despite the implied threat of political fragmentation and disorder which may result from the spatial decentralization of authority. The issue of stability is crucial for many reasons (see Huntington 1981). How it is accomplished through the local state apparatus is another matter.

According to Roweis (1981), the dominant function of the state in late capitalism is the *pre-politics processing of political information*. This mainly involves preparatory work by complex state apparatus in order to forestall and control disputes, and is typically achieved through citizen participation, commissions of inquiry and the like. The pre-politics processing of information is an important method of control, and is part of the ideological hegemony of the state necessary for the survival of the social order (Boggs 1976). The structuring of political discourse implicates the traditional socializing agencies of the church and education, as well as the family, the helping professions (Lasch 1979) and political culture. In these terms, direct state intervention is only an obvious example of a more insidious process.

The local state is strongly implicated in this structuring of discourse in many ways. Most fundamentally, the decentralization of certain powers to the local level implies that conflict over state outputs (rationality crises) are most likely to be focused at the local level. This may occur irrespective of the actual responsibility for a given state output, because it is at the local level that the output becomes manifest. If state efforts fail to co-opt and control the population through expenditures on social consumption, then the state requires defensive mechanisms to avert conflicts. Hence, in its efforts at crisis avoidance, the local state may develop citizen participation channels in order to reduce uncertainty by learning the demands of its electorate. Local state actions are thereby legitimized and facilitated. An important ancillary benefit of social consumption expenditures is that they tend to isolate social crises in smaller social units: the individual, the family or the community, rather than in the wider social formation (Gaylin et al. 1978). Community action for improvement of social conditions is thus directed not at deficiencies in the mode of production, but at its products. Similarly, problems in urban and regional planning policies are typically blamed on local planning machinery, and not attributed to overall structural contradictions of the wider sociospatial formation.

Two vital functional components in achieving state ideological hegemony are local electoral politics and local state administration. In his thorough review of the literature on electoral politics, Johnston (1979) pointed out its almost exclusive concentration on the patterns of electoral behavior. The social reality underlying these patterns is rarely questioned. Yet, as we have argued (Ch. 5), electoral politics is one of the "bulwarks" of capitalism; the party system and elections themselves are part of the language and logistics by which the state achieves its ideological hegemony. Electoral politics are simultaneously a means of containing and channelling social conflict and of obtaining the consent of the governed. The partition of class-based conflict into conflict based on spatial units (as in urban social movements) both consolidates the rôle of electoral politics and, at the same time, tends to deny more general social tensions (Katznelson 1981).

A second functional component of ideological hegemony is the state bureaucracy or civil service, which may be the most significant co-optive mechanism of contemporary capitalism. It has often been said that "real power" lies with the civil service. Even so, the separation of political (legislative) and administrative (state) powers has been used by some to suggest that the bureaucracy is ultimately limited in what it can do. What does seem consistently important is the *proliferation of responsible state or quasi-state apparatus*. These may be viewed as direct attempts to obfuscate

138   THE LOCAL STATE

the system of authority and control in capitalist social relations, both vertically (between various state tiers), and horizontally (between various local state jurisdictions and different, though ideologically related, apparatus of the political and executive authorities). The local state bureaucracy plays a key supportive rôle in this obfuscation. It is, after all, the most immediate location for public services and welfare. The "public city" is but one expression of this high level of interaction between the state and its citizens (Dear 1981).

In summary, the local state is an integral apparatus of the capitalist state. It has a major rôle to play in crisis management. Functionally, a separate local state is required so as to maintain control over spatially extensive and heterogeneous jurisdictions. Capitalist social relations are obfuscated as the fiscal, rationality and legitimation crises of the state are shuffled up and down the state hierarchy. Resultant tensions between levels are obvious and continuous aspects of the maintenance of the social order. In general terms, the apparatus of the local state is largely devoted to the pre-politics processing of political disputes. Electoral politics and the state bureaucracy are then vital elements of their ideological hegemony. Variations in local state outcomes are likely to find their source in differences in local state functions and local state relations with other tiers.

Our theoretical perspective, based on a state-centered functionalist analysis, suggests that the local state is a purposively constituted apparatus of higher tiers of the state; the local state functions largely to facilitate state actions of crisis management and control. The key empirical issue which derives from this viewpoint is the extent of local state autonomy and its relative significance given the revenue-raising and zoning powers of the local state. As an apparatus, the local state must be both controllable and politically viable. In essence, it must be seen as a separate political structure while it is at the same time being directed. However, it is also clear that local state decision-making discretion and local state outcomes vary. This leads to two questions: How is authority maintained across this variety? And how is local autonomy constrained in order to permit effective political control and the implementation of crisis management? In the remainder of this chapter we shall focus upon the extent of local state autonomy in Massachusetts and a case in Michigan, both of which concern the relationships between higher tiers of the state and the local state.

Legal autonomy of the local state

Much of our analysis of local autonomy is conducted in terms of power and legal structures. The definition of local autonomy will then depend on understanding a couple of distinctions. First, it is important to acknowledge that legal power is composed of two elements. Following Bentham (Hart 1972), we can identify the right or liberty of a person or institution to action, given certain *a priori* specifications of rights and privileges. Bentham termed this as the "power of contrectation," that is, the power to act whatever the circumstances, given prior rights to do so. In terms of individuals, the implications of such power are clear. We may decide to migrate and be perfectly able to do so, given that we are free to choose our location, place of employment, and so on. Our right to move, however, depends on a more general principle. We must also respect others' rights to migrate. Thus, the power of contrectation is essentially permissive, it allows (unspecified) action given initial assumptions.

The second element to legal power is the "power of imperation." According to Hart (1972, p. 805), Bentham conceived this power as that which is active as distinct from passive. Put differently, the power of imperation is the power to review, amend, negate and/or enforce. For an individual, this legal power enables a person to use the state and its apparatus to change the behavior of others. This kind of legal power is legitimately coercive, enforcing the rights and privileges of individuals and thereby sustaining determinant outcomes. Essentially, the power of imperation is active, not permissive.

To translate these two types of powers from individuals to social institutions, a number of assumptions need to be made. First, we assume that institutions such as the local state can be treated as purposeful, goal-oriented actors. Like corporations, government institutions can be conceived as entities, and not simply as conglomerates of individuals. In terms of American law this assumption is quite strong, and perhaps overstated if we were to analyse the existing legal arrangement of powers. Even so, as Frug (1980) has pointed out, there is little stopping such an interpretation. Indeed, public policy often acts as if this were true, even if the underlying structural arrangement of powers is ambiguous. Secondly, we also assume that democracy and democratic procedures do not necessitate a specific or unique form of local government. We analyse social institutions as entities as well as their relationships to one another, but we are not concerned to derive their necessary form; that is, we are not concerned to derive natural conceptions of local autonomy.

From this perspective, two primary principles of local autonomy can be identified: the power of *initiation* and the power of *immunity* (Clark 1984a,b). The first principle (initiative) should be considered equivalent to contrectation and refers to the actions of local governments in carrying out their rightful duties. It is entirely possible that local government powers of initiative can be extraordinarily broad or narrowly circumscribed, depending upon the initial specification of the rights and

140   THE LOCAL STATE

privileges of local government as compared with other higher tiers of the state. For example, if local governments have the powers to regulate and legislate with respect to land use and zoning, then they are also able to initiate plans and designs for the formal spatial configuration of local, even national, economic activities. Similarly, if local governments have the power to legislate in the fields of economic activity and employment, then they could initiate residential hiring quotas, minority employment requirements, perhaps even plant-closing regulations. Inevitably the power of initiation is the power to regulate private individuals. Without any such powers, local government could hardly affect any private activity.

The power of immunity is essentially the power of localities to act without fear of the oversight authority of higher tiers of the state. In this sense immunity allows local governments to act however they wish within the limits imposed by their initiative powers (Sandalow 1964). An example of immunity would be if local governments regulate land use (in accordance with their rights to do so) without any outside review agency. To make the example even more concrete, imagine that State governments allow local governments to legislate in the field of land use, and cannot review or amend local decisions within that field of local power. (This would be equivalent to having no State or Federal Court of Appeal as in the United States, or an Ontario Municipal Board, as in Ontario, Canada.) Without immunity, however, higher tiers of the state would be able to enforce their own standards of legislation, administration, and implementation. Without immunity, local governments could have their every decision reviewed and perhaps amended. In this sense immunity is a principal aspect of local autonomy.

Despite a good deal of rhetoric and liberal theory to the contrary (see McBain 1916), the local state as a legal entity is solely a "creature" of State legislatures (Frug 1980). The structure of constitutional and legislative law in the United States grants to the local state only those initiative powers delegated from States. In most jurisdictions, including Massachusetts, the local state has no separate constitution and exists only at the "pleasure" or discretion of State legislatures; it is simply an extension of the State legislature (Frug 1980). Consequently, the local state has no legal authority to design its own policies and take new powers. The power to make such changes remains at the State level, irrespective of the desires of local constituencies.

There is no right of local government in the structure of the American Constitution. Powers that local states may have are subject to absolute State control and, historically, litigation over the immunity of local states from higher tiers has invariably come down in favor of national and State authority, rather than local state authority. The judgment of the Supreme Court in the leading case of *Hunter v. City of Pittsburgh* 207

US 161 (1907) illustrates the clear control that States have over local autonomy

> The (S)tate . . . at its pleasure may modify or withdraw all local (state) power, may take without compensation (local state) property, hold it itself, or vest it in other agencies . . . repeal the charter and destroy the corporation (local state) . . . (c)onditionally or unconditionally, with or without the consent of the citizens. In all respects the (S)tate is supreme. . . .

Attempts have been made to minimize the liability of local state officials when their actions as officials representing municipal authorities have contravened the rights of ordinary citizens (see for example *Owen v. City of Independence, Mo.* 421 F.Supp. 1100 WD Mo. (1976) and *Monroe v. Pape* 365 US 167 (1961)). Other officials, including federal judges and police officials are to some extent protected. If these attempts had been successful, the effect would have been to provide the local state a degree of autonomy that could have effectively discounted central and State control. However under Title 42, section 1982 of the United States Constitution, the Supreme Court has held in *Monell v. New York City Dept. of Social Services* 98 S.Ct. 2894 (1978) and in *Owen v. City of Independence Mo.*, that there is no basis for such immunity. In fact it has been noted that the local state has been routinely treated as a person for many constitutional and statutory purposes (see *Cowles v. Mercer County* 7 Wall. 118 L.Ed. (1869)). Furthermore, the local state has also been held accountable in similar terms for violations of national and State laws (see for example, *Levy Court v. Coroner* 2 Wall. 501 L.Ed. (1864)). Violations of the obligations of local states to their States can, and have been, brought to court. In recent times, moreover, individuals representing the local state have not only been held accountable, but have also had costs awarded against them for actions undertaken on behalf of local states as in the Massachusetts case of *Kadar Corp. v. Milbury* 549 F2d 230 1st Cir. (1977).

The genesis of much of the post-1850 federal and State control of the local state came from a rule first pronounced by Dillon in *Merriam v. Moody's Executors* 25 Iowa 163 (1868), which set the limits to local state powers. According to Justice Dillon, local states may only take those powers framed expressly by federal and State legislatures in their empowering legislation; those necessary and incident powers expressly granted for carrying out the first-named powers; and those powers absolutely necessary in carrying out the powers named in the legislation. In practice this has meant that the courts have invalidated powers assumed by local states but not mentioned in the enabling legislation (see for example, *Berube v. Selectmen of Edgartown* 331 Mass. 72 (1958)).

142   THE LOCAL STATE

Furthermore, the courts have also declared unconstitutional any State legislation that was broad or vague on the exact nature of local state powers (*McRae v. Selectmen of Concord* 296 Mass. 397 (1940)) thus removing, quite deliberately, any possibility of local discretion or initiative powers.

Prior to 1915, in keeping with the view that municipalities had no inherent right to autonomous government, the Massachusetts Legislature would put a municipality's charter into effect by special Act, which could be modified by subsequent special or general laws. In 1915 there was an attempt to extend local state autonomy by permitting options as to the form of government. However local states still held only those initiative powers expressly granted by the Legislature, and these were narrowly construed by the courts against the municipality. In 1966, Article II of the Massachusetts Constitutional Amendments was further amended by Article 89 which gave ". . . to the people of every city and town the right of self-government in local matters, subject to such standards and requirements as the general court [Legislature] may establish. . . ." The Home Rule Procedures Act was subsequently passed in order to detail procedures under which municipalities could effect this constitutional grant of home rule (Dillon, 1911).

The limitations of this grant were, however, quite severe (as is the case in virtually all States of the Union). First, self government relates only to "local matters" but there has been no adequate definition of local matters. Cases related to this issue in Massachusetts and in other States have supported the narrow view of cities and towns as ". . . political subdivisions created for the convenient administration of government" (*City of Trenton v. State of New Jersey* 262 US 182 (1923)). Secondly, any action of the local state must be consistent with the Constitution or General Laws of the Commonwealth of Massachusetts (and also those laws that may be enacted by the Legislature). Thirdly, the Legislature retains the right to act in regard to cities and towns by general law and special law in certain circumstances. This provision gives the Legislature authority to pass special Acts without local consent. Massachusetts is one of the few States which did not ban or restrict the passing of special legislation, or express the absolute requirement for general, as opposed to particular legislation. The aim appears to have been to vest in the Legislature the ultimate veto power over any municipal action.

The influence of the central state and its legal structure on the local state comes not from a specific provision in the US Constitution detailing central control over the local state activities, but rather from several major sources of national power which are explicit or implied in the Constitution, or have developed as a result of the operation of the judicial system (Tribe 1976). Article VI of the Constitution provides that

LEGAL AUTONOMY OF THE LOCAL STATE

> This Constitution and the Laws of the United States which shall be made in Pursuance thereof . . . shall be the Supreme Law of the Land. . . .

This has meant that if Congress acts within an area delegated to it (or implicit in the Constitution's definition of powers), conflicting State and local state actions are pre-empted. For example, under the Cooley doctrine (*Cooley v. Board of Wardens of the Port of Philadelphia* 12 How. (53 US) 290 (1851)), States are free to regulate those aspects of interstate and foreign commerce so local in character as to require diverse treatment. Congress alone has the power to regulate those aspects so national in character that a single uniform rule or standard is necessary. Again, the definition of local versus national has tended to favor the Congress even though intrastate commerce may only indirectly affect interstate commerce (Tribe 1978).

Further, the Contracts Clause of the Constitution prohibits State legislative impairment of private obligations and contracts. This also applies to local state ordinances and charters. For example, when a city makes a contract for a municipal improvement, it cannot in derogation of its contract impose additional burdens on the grantee or vary the terms and conditions of the contract. There is also a provision in the 14th Amendment that no State shall deny a person within its jurisdiction equal protection of the laws or deprive them of life, liberty or property, without due process of law (see Ch. 6 for more details). This places an open-ended set of limitations on local states. The impact is felt, for example, in:

(1) *voting rights and local representation*, where voter eligibility cannot be limited to certain classes without compelling reasons;
(2) *government employment*, where municipal corporations cannot exclude aliens from civil service employment;
(3) *municipal services*, which must be equally available to all citizens; and
(4) *public housing*, where tenants in federally funded projects cannot be evicted without being informed of specific grievances.

It should be noted that while the nation–state can use its powers under these clauses, cities have been uniformly unsuccessful in attempts to protect themselves (immunity) from the exercise of State power through invoking individual or contract rights provisions (except where the rights of citizens as residents of the city equate with their rights as federal citizens). Generally, municipal corporations have no privileges or immunities, under the United States Constitution, which they may invoke against State legislation (see *Williams v. Baltimore* 289 US 36 (1937)).

144   THE LOCAL STATE

The evidence we have reviewed is unequivocal; the local state has very limited legal autonomy. It depends upon the will of State legislatures for its existence, which in turn are subservient to the national interest. All decisions regarding what constitutes legitimate local functions or initiative powers are taken by the State or are reviewed by the court system. Local immunity is virtually nonexistent. In this sense the local state is not autonomous; it is controlled and organized directly by higher tiers of the state outside the political control of its local constituency.

Fiscal dependence and control

Dillon's doctrine of local state dependence on State legislatures remains intact today (Frug 1980). The administrative power of local states has been systematically limited by higher tiers even though electoral politics continues to be framed in terms of a democratic government. Apart from the constitutional and legal restraints on the local state, other controls, in the form of administrative practices, have also acted so as to contain local autonomy. In this section, we examine the effects of intergovernmental transfer payments on local state autonomy.

Over the course of the 20th century, State and local governments have come to rely upon the nation–state for revenue. In the fiscal year 1975/76, Massachusetts received 27 percent of its total revenue from Federal funds; localities depended on average upon federal money for 10 percent of their revenue and upon Massachusetts for 25 percent of their total revenue (Bureau of the Census 1977). These figures are indicative of a more general pattern across the United States (Nathan 1978). Notice however that two qualifications to this statement should be noted. First, property taxes are very important sources of finance for Massachusetts localities compared to other towns and cities outside Massachusetts. For example in 1976/77 property taxes contributed over 50 percent of Boston's total revenue while in New York property taxes contributed less than 23 percent. Secondly, there are also substantial variations in the importance of intergovernmental (national plus State) transfers; Boston depends upon these transfers for approximately 25 percent of its total revenue, while New York depends upon transfers for some 50 percent of its total revenue (Barabba 1980, Eisenmenger *et al.* 1975). On average in 1967 national plus State grants to city governments accounted for over 26 percent of total local state revenue; by 1977, the proportion had risen to nearly 40 percent and by 1987 such transfers are projected to account for 45 percent of total local revenue (Barabba 1980).

Most significantly, much of national and State financial aid to localities is prefaced by conditions of performance and application. Grants are typically categorical; that is, aid must be spent in certain ways on particular projects or functions. Despite a ruling by the Supreme Court,

FISCAL DEPENDENCE AND CONTROL

in *United States v. Butler* 297 US 1 (1936), that the Congress cannot regulate state and local activities through conditions tied to revenue financing and spending, this practice continues unabated. Tribe (1978) has noted that the use of categorical grants has been as effective in controlling and regulating the activities of State and local states as national directives would have been, if they were constitutional. It is an accepted principle in relations between the different levels of government that the funding body has the right to designate and require certain conditions to be met before funding a particular project (see *North Carolina v. Califano* 98 S.Ct. 159 7 (1978)).

Even in the case of government programs designed explicitly to be noncategorical and to enable greater local discretion (as in the example of Community Development Block Grants), Congressional enforcement of legislative objectives and administrative responsibility for the efficient expenditure of federal funds have severely restricted local control. The extent of administrative dependence of local states upon federal agencies has perpetuated categorical control in practice (Congressional Budget Office 1980). At the same time local states have been severely squeezed by the fiscal crisis since their other revenue-raising powers (for example, property taxes) are also often controlled by State legislatures. Many local states have had to surrender what little power they had left to remain financially solvent; the classic case of course is New York City (see Alcaly & Mermelstein 1977).

The limits on local state autonomy imposed by the category-specific transfer payment system in Cambridge, Massachusetts, are shown in Tables 7.1 and 7.2 (Community Services Administration 1979). For the fiscal year 1978/79, the City of Cambridge received $7.8 million in categorical funding from national sources; this represented 66 percent of the total funds received from this source (Table 7.1). The most important single grant was $6.9 million for employment and training under the Comprehensive Employment Training Act (CETA). Other transfer payments were noncategorical, although they were linked to specific areas of application (for example, libraries). During the same period the City of Cambridge received $10.8 million in categorical funding from the State of Massachusetts, representing 74 percent of the city's total grant from this source (Table 7.2). A large proportion of this finance was allocated to mandatory educational programs. Only one major source of State transfer revenue to Cambridge is noncategorical – the State lottery.

A brief investigation of other US cities and towns confirms that this national–state–local state transfer pattern is typical, although in many instances (for example Buffalo, NY) the degree of central control is more rigid. (See Community Services Administration 1979 and other sources such as the Bureau of the Census 1980 for more details.) The evidence suggests an extensive control by national and State governments

146 THE LOCAL STATE

Table 7.1 Intergovernmental transfers: national government to the city of Cambridge (1978/9).

Federal agency	Program	Payments ($)
Housing and Urban Development	Block Grant	1 516 000
	Urban Development Assistance Grants	55 000★
Department of Transportation	Red Line Extension	80 000★
	Station Art	25 000★
Department of Justice	Crime Control	285 275★
Department of Labor	Comprehensive Employment and Training Act	6 912 000★
National Endowment for the Arts	Public Place Art	80 000★
Standards Review Organization	Hospital Technology	25 000★
Miscellaneous Grants	Medical and Public Employment	299 992★
Revenue Sharing Funds	Youth Resources	123 000
	Libraries	150 000
	Elderly Services	98 000
	Police	250 000
	Schools	525 000
	Finance	100 000
	Recreation	350 000
	Public Works	500 000
	Health	450 000
Total payment		11 824 267

★ Categorical grant.

over a significant proportion of local states' budgetary discretion and actual implementation. At a recent conference on local fiscal management it was noted by many commentators that national and State controls on the actual process of budgetary organization were becoming very important to local managers. To qualify for even noncategorical grants strict and uniform standards of fiscal control have to adhered to, as well as specific methods of auditing and compliance with central regulations. The impact has been to transform local managers into reporting agents (US Department of Housing and Urban Development 1980).

So far, it has been demonstrated that local state autonomy is tightly constrained by constitutional arrangements and by controls over local spending. It is also important to note that as well as receiving revenue

FISCAL DEPENDENCE AND CONTROL 147

Table 7.2 Intergovernmental transfers: State of Massachusetts to the city of Cambridge and vice-versa (1978/9).

Category	Payments ($)
(a) State to city	
roads	341 950★
health and welfare	341 945★
state lottery	3 680 135
civil defence planning	25 500★
arts and humanities	5 000★
law enforcement	214 530★
education-related	845 355★
construction	1 774 715★
Chapter 70 Aid	6 741 075★
community development	496 910★
real estate abatement	161 645
total	14 628 760
(b) City to state†	
education	102 825
Massachusetts Bay Transportation Authority (MBTA) assessment	4 081 230
community development tax rebate	15 105
total	4 199 160

★ Categorical grant.

† An additional sum of $1 001 650 was paid by the city of Cambridge to Middlesex County to cover part of the cost of county operations.

from national and State governments, localities are also assessed by the State. "The Commonwealth of Massachusetts" has maintained its founding philosophy wherein the State is akin to a confederation of municipalities. Because the State serves the towns, these towns are assessed for the costs of running State services. While Massachusetts has broad powers to raise revenues, many services are still financed by charges levied on cities and towns (see Table 7.2 for the Cambridge levies).

Assessments are determined by formula. Three criteria formed the major basis of assessment in 1978/79 in Massachusetts: real property valuation, population, and reimbursement of actual costs. Assessments based on population or related measures totalled $183 million, or 75 percent of all assessments. While various weighting factors are used in conjunction with population, the incidence of these assessments mostly affects the populous towns. Land value assessments at $54 million form another 22 percent of the total. These tend to impact upon the geographically large, as well as the highly valued, suburban areas. Finally, reimbursement of actual costs incurred by the State accounts for

148 THE LOCAL STATE

2 percent of assessments and is paid mostly by major towns with many social service needs.

The formula for revenue transfers is similar to that for assessments, in that the allocation of State funds is based on population and service provision costs. Noticeably absent from the formula are measures of tax contribution. The transfer formula contains provisions for reimbursement of costs, in which the State pays towns for costs incurred on approved projects. Thus, funds are distributed back to towns using a formula based on the same factors that determine the towns' assessments. Notice also that local taxes are approved by Massachusetts, primarily through the Governor's Office. Transfers are intended in part to take into account differences in local need and tax base (see Inman & Rubinfeld 1979).

State control over local state functions and finance is applied by using general rather than specific rules (Dear & Clark 1981). While it may be politically expedient to be able to demonstrate the "neutrality" of State allocations, the fact remains that variations in local state economy and policy have very little impact on the State's functional and financial arrangements. (For the fundamental implications of changing population sizes on the allocation of transfers by formula, as an example of the degree of impact, both positive and negative, that States actually have on local states, see Bureau of the Census 1980). Geographical variations in transfer payments are dominated by the population rule implicit in State formulas; this is a product of the State legislature, and is not derived from the local state.

The autonomy of localities in Massachusetts is severely curtailed by constitutional arrangements and by the tightly defined categorical grant system of that State. Constitutional and legal arrangements establish the local state as a "creature" of State government and, ultimately, the nation–state. Both the existence and functions of local states are subsumed under higher tiers' constitutions. Other forms of administrative practices consolidate the grip of the nation–state: categorical conditions, allocation formulas, implementation and reporting conditions, auditing practices and the like. Categorical grants available as transfer payments from higher tiers effectively limit the quality and quantity of local activities. Although considerable variation in the geographical pattern of transfer payments can be observed, both State levies and assessments are dominated by the distribution of population. This clearly demonstrates the general rather than the specific intent of State action; the extent of central control is seen in the fact that local outcomes tend to be a product of rules and formulas which are, in themselves, independent of the local state.

Local self-determination

The structuration of geographical outcomes that is embodied in the hierarchical arrangement of state power is well illustrated in the recent case of *Poletown Neighborhood v. City of Detroit* Mich. 304. NW 2d 455 (1981). Essentially the City of Detroit through its Economic Development Corporation (EDC) expropriated private property in the Poletown neighborhood of the City and turned it over to General Motors (GM) to build a new automobile assembly plant. The community good was defined by the City in terms of the number of jobs (6000) saved for City residents. Without that parcel of land GM would have moved elsewhere to build a new plant to replace two existing, but older, assembly plants (Clark Avenue was 59 years old and Fisher Body was 62 years old). GM went to the City in mid-1980 and apprised the City Council of its intentions. The company claimed that if a suitable site could be found by the City by May 1, 1981, then it would build in Detroit. It set four conditions of suitability: the site must be rectangular in shape (¾ miles by 1 mile); be approximately 450 to 500 acres in size; and have access to long-haul railway facilities and the interstate freeway system. In return GM promised to build a new plant of 3 million square feet, costing $500 million and employing 6000 workers (a promise which, incidentally, has not been kept).

Eight sites were evaluated and rejected. Only the Poletown neighborhood was considered suitable by the EDC. The City agreed to acquire some 1176 separate parcels of land, relocate 3438 residents, and clear the entire site (including demolition of the abandoned Chrysler Dodge Main Plant). The Michigan Supreme Court (MSC) put the cost of land acquisition and provision according to GM's specifications at $199.7 million. GM was given title to the land in exchange for $8 million with a 12-year tax abatement included. Under the Michigan Economic Development Corporations Act, Detroit's EDC invoked its powers of eminent domain (compulsory purchase) to seize the required property. "Condemnation" was the actual procedure which is conditioned by a clause that holds that private property can only be expropriated for "the public purpose or use." Incidental private benefit is allowed, but it must not be the overriding concern. Under the terms of the Act, the municipality has the authority (that is, initiative power) to define the public purpose. These actions were facilitated by the so-called "quick-take" statute which allows for claims against unlawful acquisition to be made after the initial action of authorities. This statute is procedural and does not confer powers of eminent domain.

The issue of "just" compensation was not the primary claim by residents of Poletown against the City. Rather the basis of their claim was twofold: first, the project violated the EDC Act in that private

150 THE LOCAL STATE

property was condemned for another's private use; and secondly, the project was not evaluated for its social and environmental impacts as required by Michigan environmental laws. In a majority opinion (5 to 2) the MSC ruled against the Poletown residents on both counts. It was found that ". . . the project was 'public purpose' within the meaning of the statute governing economic development corporations" (p. 455). Moreover, it was also argued by the Court that the public purpose dominated any incidental gain that GM may have achieved. This argument was based on a claim that the City of Detroit had shown compelling evidence (in terms of unemployment and economic decline) that expropriation was indeed in the public interest (p. 459). Since the Court also decided that the legislature was the sole legitimate determinator of the public purpose, the MSC felt that it could not intervene.

It is clear that the particular economic conditions of Detroit, the project at hand, and the benefits to the community were the prime considerations of the Court. The actual decision was based on the problem at hand and in part was recognized as such by the Court when it noted that ". . . public use changes with changing conditions of society" (p. 457). One could conclude that individual rights in this instance were not only placed second to the community good (as in conventional parlance) but also treated contextually (Clark 1982). Definition of the community "good" was considered in the terms of the EDC Act. Consequently, the City of Detroit was held to represent the public purpose, not the Poletown neighborhood. Thirdly, the economic power of GM was the key underlying factor that determined whether or not individual rights dominated the community good. With adjudication taken contextually, the power of GM determined the outcome.

This last point was not recognized in the MSC majority decision, but in the minority dissenting opinion. Both Justices Fitzgerald and Ryan agreed with the majority that environmental impacts were not at issue. However, they argued separately that private property was being used for direct private gain. Fitzgerald argued (p. 462):

> It is only through the acquisition and use of the property by GM that the "public purpose" of promoting employment can be achieved. Thus it is the economic benefits of the project that are incidental to the private use of property.

Justice Ryan likewise concluded that "there may never be a clearer case than this of condemning (private) land for a private corporation" (p. 477). The implications of this action for Fitzgerald and Ryan were far reaching. According to them, no private property would be safe because all businesses create some public benefits; localities cannot be trusted to define the community good without political biases; and, above all, individual rights were being evaluated according to policy not principle.

Justice Ryan had no hesitation in identifying GM as the primary mover and beneficiary of the whole proceeding. In graphic detail Ryan described the critical economic conditions of Detroit and the power of GM over the City. Detroit had its back to the wall; if no suitable site could be found GM would leave perhaps initiating a further round of local economic crisis and even default on behalf of the City. Ryan argued that there was a conspiracy of activity and promotion of the venture by City interests against the Poletown neighborhood. And ". . . behind the frenzy of official activity was the unmistakable guiding and sustaining, indeed controlling, hand of the General Motors Corporation" (p. 468). According to Ryan, the unilateral power of GM forestalled the democratic process. The very nature of the economic system became the factor determining whose interests would be followed because of the fundamental character of interdependence as against ownership of the means of production. In essence, the dissenting opinions recognized the reality of local powerlessness and how it affected land-use planning and judicial outcomes. Not only was Detroit caught in an economic vise it could not control, but its power to initiate policy was premised upon State legislation. Furthermore, even its actions were reviewed and adjudicated; local immunity was negligible.

The dissenting opinions argued for a return to principles rather than contextual decision making. Of course this begs the question of how principles themselves are determined and brings us back to the problems of natural and positivist law outlined in Chapter 6. It is apparent that in any similar situation, the power of different actors would be unevenly distributed and it is hard to imagine any other outcome. Thus, to call for principle was to call for "screening" the reality of adjudication.

Although the particular issue was at the heart of adjudication, the majority opinion attempted to obscure its meaning by referring to the provisions of the EDC Act. In particular the Court appealed to the sovereignty of the State legislature as the ultimate determinator of the public purpose. By doing so, the Court subtly invoked a natural rights claim of a "higher order." The democratic caucus (at the State level) was used to legitimize the Court's decision as almost a metaphysical category. This was despite the fact that, in reality, the legislature devolved determination of the public purpose to the City of Detroit, and in essence, attempted to make local decision making responsive to the community.

In this illustration it is clear that the local state had no practical legal autonomy or power. Although liberal theories of local government are often framed in terms of competition between local governments, all important decisions regarding local functions and form are taken by States or subsumed under national constitutional guarantees of individual

152   THE LOCAL STATE

liberty and access. In this sense, local governments are not autonomous but are controlled and organized directly by higher tiers of the state structure, outside the control of any given local political constituency. As spatial integration was enforced among States, spatial political homogeneity has likewise been enforced within States. Consequently the imperatives of spatial integration and homogeneity, identified in the previous chapter as operating to promote uniformity among States, have an important representation at lower spatial scales as well. Thus, reproduction through legislative and judicial encouragement under the mandate of individualism permeates all spatial scales of the United States.

Conclusions

Our theory of the capitalist state derived the form of the state from the stage of development attained by the specific social formation. The state's functions are, in turn, determined by the political repercussions induced by crises in accumulation, and by the need to ensure the reproduction of social relations. The separation of the economic and political spheres of society ensures the consent of the ruled, and emphasizes the need for the ideological and repressive functions of the state. The functions of the local state are to act as an input–output mechanism providing services in response to local demands according to national and State constraints. The local state is an apparatus.

Local autonomy is severely curtailed by State legislatures. The links between the local state and local economy are tenuous, since the main source of stability at the local level is the important and growing injection of higher-tier state funds. This intervention, together with the continuous reallocation of state functions among various tiers of government, has the effect of regionalizing the crises of capitalism. The effect is to implicate the local state in the genesis of crises without providing the autonomy necessary for ameliorative policy. Ideological hegemony of the state is facilitated by local state electoral politics and administrative bureaucracies. The former permits social pathologies to be situated at the level of individual, family or community; the latter permits the anticipation and circumvention of crises through the proliferation of state and quasi-state apparatus for purposes of containing political dissent. We now turn to the political dimensions of local state autonomy, the second part of our analysis of the rôle of the local state.

8 *Democracy and the crisis of legitimacy*

While democracy is the basic organizing principle of the liberal theory of the state, marxists have generally ignored the issue. Marxist theorists have been unequivocal in their rejection of the possibility of a true democracy in capitalism (Poulantzas 1973). It is argued that capitalist democracy is a sham: a means of manipulating and subverting the true aspirations of the people. According to Reich and Edwards (1978), by taking democratic bourgeois politics seriously, attention is diverted from the more significant issues of class exploitation and alienation. While it is accepted that politics is important, many marxist critiques reduce the elements of social and political struggle either to insignificance or to a subset of the class "problem" (Miliband 1977). This collapses the significance of legitimate social and political interests of different segments of society through a claim that all would be solved through the imposition of a classless society.

There are many difficulties with such marxist interpretations of democracy. One consequence of such caricatures has been dismissal of bourgeois politics as irrelevant and facile, leading many theorists to reject all advances of the working class. Thus political actions which have wrought tremendous improvements in working conditions, such as the reduction and regulation of work hours, and improved health and medical benefits, are ridiculed. Further, the neglect of democracy has meant that no serious challenge has been made to the authority of models, such as Tiebout's (1956) which dominate orthodox theory of the spatial structure of government. In this chapter the relationship between democracy and the local state is analysed with respect to the rôle of democracy and the capitalist state. Issues of ideology, legitimation of the state through the democratic process, and the sources of the legitimacy of the local state are the issues considered in this chapter.

Democracy and capitalism

Modern political scientists define democracy as a process or procedure. Accordingly, democracy is defined as a political system in which

154 DEMOCRACY AND THE CRISIS OF LEGITIMACY

elections decide the competition for power and policies (Dahl 1956). A set of conditions have to be met for a real liberal democratic caucus (Clark 1981). First, all citizens, regardless of socioeconomic identity or status, must have the right to vote for those who would best express their opinions. Secondly, such votes must be equally weighted, and thirdly, must represent the true opinion of the voter formed in a completely free environment. A free environment in this sense is one where there is no coercion as to the "right" opinion, as well as a full awareness of all possible alternative options. Fourthly, in a collective sense the numerical majority must rule although, fifthly, majority decisions must not limit minority rights.

The modern theory of liberal democracy is not concerned with the socioeconomic structure of society. Rather it is a theory concerned with defining the proper method or means for the resolution of social conflict. By definition, the democratic method is argued to result necessarily in democratic outcomes. This is analogous to Rawls' (1971, p. 80) pure procedural justice concept which "obtains when there is no independent criterion for the right result; instead there is a correct or fair procedure such that the outcome is likewise correct or fair, whatever it is, provided that the procedure has been properly followed." Democracy is argued by many modern theorists to be one such pure procedural method (see Cave 1978). Liberal democracy is not necessarily defined on moral or social grounds, as perhaps commonly supposed; rather democracy is defined in terms of the system of voting.

Dahl (1956) amongst many other orthodox writers on democracy, has argued that as in *laissez-faire* economic markets, votes are market signals. They represent the ultimate test of consumer choice and preference. The choice between competing leaders and élites is argued to be based upon two interrelated criteria: policies and potential outputs. Votes are taken as the true expression of rational self-interest on behalf of the majority of the population (Pateman 1970). Control over leaders and élites is exercised periodically through elections with the ultimate sanction being the loss of elected office.

Dahl (1956) also argued that the theory of democracy is a function of, and implicitly a description of, current political methods. In the tradition of American political science the theory is claimed to be positivistic and value-free. However, as Pateman (1979) has remarked, this claim would appear to be invalid because the process of theory-building is selective of the full range of facts and dimensions of society. Concepts themselves are derivative from the dominant ideology. This intellectual selectivity is itself the cornerstone of normative theory-building. Thus the modern theory of democracy is prescriptive in that a particular type of system is implied, as well as the standards by which democratic practice ought to be judged. Modern theories of democracy are ideological and have a particular view of society.

Three assumptions, which can be identified as being central to liberal democratic theory, illustrate this proposition. First, modern democratic theory is prefaced upon an assumption of equal opportunity or access to power. Access is a precondition for Rawlsian pure procedural justice. Power, however, is rather narrowly defined. MacPherson (1973) noted that the concept of power in such theories is often defined as the right to exercise the vote. Few theorists have been concerned to analyze either the distribution of economic power in society or the assumption that the "ends" of democratic decision making match the "means." In essence modern theorists of democracy ignore the basic inequalities of capitalism.

Secondly, and related to the previous issue, there is the assumption that the distribution of income and class power are assumed to be unimportant. Dahl (1956) goes further by claiming that recognition of such differences would lead to widespread and unjustified instability in the political process. He argued that only certain segments of society participate and typically only for their own narrow self-interest. Consequently economic equality and biased class or group distributions are argued to be separable from the political system.

Thirdly, the process of voting is itself a logical extension of the assumption of rational self-interest and implicitly the principles of utilitarianism. Society is thought to be composed of individual political decision-making units who know their own utility functions; who rationally choose the party or élite that best expresses their utility; and, are able to differentiate between different levels of their own utility (Harsanyi 1977). Although these behavioral assumptions may not hold in all circumstances it is the inherent tendency towards such decision making that is the crucial factor for modern theorists of democracy.

The research agenda for Dahl and others is the product of these assumptions and is more often than not an analysis of the voting process as such. For example, major research themes have been the definition of optimal arrangements of voting; analysis of the so-called equilibrium tendencies of the system; concern for voter apathy and the so-called aberrant or perverse nonoptimizing behavior of some social groups. Geographers have by and large accepted this form of democratic theory as the premise for studying the spatial pattern of voting, elections, and the organization of local government. Many have concentrated upon the veracity of electoral boundaries as well as voting biases that may be a product of location and not rational self-interest. Local government expenditures and functions are often seen as a special case of democratic theory and orthodox public finance economics.

Many writers have designed critiques of the theoretical and empirical foundations of modern democratic theory. Within economics, criticism has often focused upon the notions of utilitarianism implicit in individual choice models such as Downs' (1957). This critique often extends into a full-scale attack on the very foundations of neoclassical economics (Bowles & Gintis 1978). Within sociology, attention has been drawn to the lack of adequate recognition of the socialization processes and group interdynamics inherent in political conflict. Critics from political science have argued that equating political processes to economic systems is totally inadequate. They have argued that the analogy is so stripped of reality as to be completely irrelevant. Worse still, some theorists have argued that the interest of political scientists in elegant theories of democracy has diverted political science from the more significant problems. It is not intended in this chapter to repeat the wide criticisms from these disciplines concerning modern democratic theory. Rather a narrow set of the total possible themes is highlighted and serves to introduce the reader to the more substantive analysis of liberal democracy as regards the spatial organization of the capitalist state.

Downs (1957) was concerned with the implications of uncertainty and inadequate information in affecting rational decision making. The analogy in economics is that less than perfect information can collapse market equilibrium solutions as false trading may occur because of inadequate information of true market prices. In voting, a similar problem is implied. Voters may not know the true policies of competing parties while parties may mistake voter preferences. Barry (1978) provided a detailed analysis of these problems through an analogous examination of the theory of spatial market competition. In the absence of information costs it is argued that competing political parties will tend toward the "center" of the political spectrum (the political spectrum can be thought of as analogous to the straight-line distance between competing retail outlets as in Hotelling's problem). Lack of adequate information could create, however, as in spatial economics, problems of political monopoly and disequilibrium solutions.

At the heart of this analysis is the negation of political ideology as a legitimate, identifiable, and nondivisible political attribute of individuals and groups. Ideology for Downs and others is a problem of inadequate knowledge or of irrationality in decision making. Ideology is seen as a screen or impediment to the expression of true voter preferences and implies less than optimal solutions for the allocation of government outputs according to such preferences. A means of circumventing this problem is to place ideologies on a continuum (presumably left to right) and to assume that ideology is marginally divisible – that is, a voter could move along the continuum, as in fact governments would in their search for the majority of consumer votes. For Downs the problems inherent in ideology could and should disappear as voters come to realize their own self-interests. This theory is, after all, one of individual utility-maximization.

LEGITIMACY IN A DECENTRALIZED DEMOCRACY

The conception of divisible ideologies and revealed true voter preferences is premised upon an implicit assumption of what society is like. Basically there are no classes that have a distinct and mirrored image of themselves both in the political and economic arenas. That is, although economic inequality may exist, it is presumed to be separable from the sharing and distribution of political power. The obvious instrument that may be invoked to support this contention is the one-person, one-vote ballot. However, there is a stronger assumption often unacknowledged in this process. MacPherson (1973) argued that Downs assumed a particular political process whereby the politically important demands of each individual are diverse and are shared with varied and shifting combinations of other individuals although none of the combinations can be expected to be a numerical majority (except perhaps momentarily). Downs then claimed two "conditions." First, that individuals view politics as "a matter of discussion which is conducted from common premises" of evaluation, and secondly, individual preferences are the market signals for government.

It is apparent that individual political preferences exist; however, it is only under very special circumstances that these preferences are likely to swamp class interests as well. MacPherson (1977) argued that class interests are only likely to subside when distributive outcomes are related to ever-expanding (or growing) aggregate welfare. Thus governments of growing economies are able to increase welfare for lower economic groups from a growing "pie," without needing to force a redistribution from a given stock of wealth. Thus the political reality of capitalist economies is two-tiered. At a superficial level it is simply the modern democratic version; at the heart of political reality, however, is some form of class identification – a tension between economic inequality, group identification, and the political expression of one class interest over others. Voters have social and ideological aims which are the result of class identification, workplace or interest-group affiliation.

These arguments raise a fundamental issue and point of disagreement with liberal theories of democracy and government legitimacy. The challenge is to understand capitalism in relation to democracy, both as concrete political institutions and ideology. To do so requires an appreciation of what democracy means in America, and what it represents as a social "ideal." It is this tension between democratic reality and its image that is the basis of our analysis.

Legitimacy in a decentralized democracy

Conflict, inherent in all debates over the interpretation of local and national interests, dominates American federal politics. Each level of the state has attempted to assert its particular vision of federalism, as economic and social forces have attempted to influence the scale and functions of state actions. The result has been unresolved conflicts in interpretation and widespread questioning of the legitimacy of the state at its various spatial scales. On the one hand, each new national administration comes to office with a new plan to reorder intergovernmental relations. Some administrations, like Nixon's, proclaim their objectives in terms such as "the New Federalism." Some administrations are more circumspect, offering a chance to renegotiate national and local responsibilities, rather than impose a new blueprint. President Reagan similarly promised to return many social welfare functions to the States, to reduce federal requirements for local school integration and to curtail revenue sharing, in yet another attempt at rearranging federalism.

Even though what are conceived as local and national responsibilities have varied widely over the last three decades, the language of legitimation has remained associated with local and national interests. As each Administration proclaims a new agenda for decentralization or centralization, it seeks to distort and discredit past versions. Confusion over interpretation allows the state to pose in the rôle of the ultimate interpreter, that is, as a judge of good and bad interpretations. In this manner interpretations are fabricated as distinctive and meaningful.

As the federal government has attempted to refashion federalism, State and local governments have protested loudly about undue interference by the higher levels of government in their affairs. As we saw in the previous chapter, it is hard to escape the conclusion that categorical federalism has made State and local governments handmaidens to the federal bureaucracy. Not only have lower tiers of government become dependent upon the national government for revenue, but also the conditions, character, and even performance criteria of implementation have become major avenues of federal control over local governments. Categorical federalism has meant that uniform rules of quantity and quality have been applied to a diverse set of State and local governments. Claims of local autonomy have been greeted with increasing skepticism in that the major functions and structure of the local state are controlled by higher tiers of the state.

These debates and attempts at redefining the proper character of local and national interests are well known. An important underlying theme of American politics has always been the question of federalism and democratic decentralization. The debate between Jefferson and Madison over the geographical separation of powers could well be cast in these terms (Huntington 1959). Equally important, however, is the fact that these issues are interwoven with what recent commentators, including Freedman (1978), have termed the crisis of legitimacy of American politics. Huntington (1981, pp. 11–12) argued that "the history of American politics is the repetition of new beginnings and flawed outcomes, promise and disillusion, reform and reaction . . . This gap between promise and performance has created an inherent disharmony, at times latent, at times manifest, in American society."

What is meant when a national leader, whether President or Congressional representative, claims that it is in the "national interest" for a certain policy or proposal to be implemented? Clearly some sacrifice is being asked for, by all or part of the national community so that a certain goal can be attained. The implicit promise is, of course, that all members of the society will be served by advancing the national interest (however indirectly). Thus one way of understanding exhortations of the national interest is through cost–benefit analysis: will sacrifice today be more than matched by a better tomorrow? Assuming that the political process can be likened to an interest-group strategic game, cost–benefit analysis might be used to identify who sacrifices and who gains as a result of the national interest. In a society dominated by conflicts over distribution, a marxist theory of the state does not have to be invoked to understand how the national interest can be used as an instrument of domination in interest-group conflict. However, in a spatially decentralized democracy it is less clear how this type of model can be extended to conflicts between national and local interests.

It is true that local and national interests of community and societal interests are treated synonymously. The parts (geographical and social) are conceived in terms of the whole (as organic entities), and it is their relationship to one another that provides evidence of analogous meaning. But, although local versus national interests are intensely argued, we rarely seriously entertain questions of group versus national interests. This is not to say that groups do not compete for influence and power in setting national priorities. On the contrary, this is an extremely important aspect of contemporary politics. However there is a qualitative, ideological difference attached to the significance of local as opposed to group claims; for whatever reason, local claims have greater legitimacy.

The problem with cost–benefit analyses of antonyms such as local versus national interests is that it reduces everything to dollars and cents (or some similar *numéraire* measure). It ignores the subtleties of meaning and of interpretation, and provides no clue for understanding the underlying structure of political legitimacy. Some times local interests are legitimated rather than the national interests; in other instances the reverse holds true. We have to understand the values implicit in each interpretation of local and national interests, their origins and, most importantly, how the process of legitimation utilizes these underlying values.

160   DEMOCRACY AND THE CRISIS OF LEGITIMACY

Taking American values seriously

Common to many interpretations of American democracy is an assumption that Lockean principles of liberalism are the cornerstones of the Constitution. It is this assumption that immediately sets apart the intellectual histories of England and the United States prior to and after the War of Independence. Hart (1976) has noted that the critique of utilitarianism espoused by Bentham has had little force in American debates on the moral bases of justice. The continued currency of Lockean liberalism is to some extent surprising! Bentham was a most ardent critic of Lockean liberalism, as have been both English and American philosophers, from a variety of perspectives. The natural rights thesis, central to Locke's notions of individualism and justice, are given a central position in the Constitution's Articles, Amendments, and Sections. As Bailyn (1967), Berger (1977), Wood (1969), and many others have noted, debates over rights during the Revolutionary era typically began with an affirmation of an individual's natural rights of life, liberty and property.

For those accustomed to believing that the American Constitution was the first statement of these principles, any textual reading of the pre-Revolutionary period will quickly dispel such a myth (see Bailyn 1967, in particular). Wood (1969) noted that many of that era saw the implementation of rights as highly arbitrary and influenced by the monarchy. This view had a great deal of force, since the colonists were clearly unable to represent their views directly in the political process and at the same time were intimately affected by decisions taken in England without their consent. Essentially, the debate was over the functioning of the administration of justice and civil rights, and very rarely over the actual legal doctrine.

Time and again, early critiques of English administration focused on the powerlessness of the colonists within a legal system that supposedly guaranteed freedom. Access to channels of representation and redress were blocked; the colonists believed that they were systematically excluded from participation in the political process (although they did not use this more recent form of political jargon!). There were two dimensions to this issue. First, as Wood (1969) noted, colonists considered themselves to be a minority within the larger British empire. Secondly, the legal system was considered to be a means of repression and control; an institution separate from the will, conditions, and aspirations of the people (however defined). Tyranny was given a legal image and was legitimized in the name of the majority. The legal system was seen as arbitrary and despotic.

That the American colonists were very conscious of the Machiavellian theory of politics has been amply demonstrated by Pocock (1975). For the colonists, the evils of English repression were stylized and identified with the actions of particular Ministers of the Crown (essentially Machiavellian characters or actors). However, the issue was more than personal corruption and the lust for power. Americans, according to Pocock (1975), believed the whole English political system to be corrupt, riddled with opportunism, and morally groundless. And it is clear that English political philosophers (including Bentham; see Hart 1976) saw social theory as being in action rather than moral philosophy. For the colonists however, who sought to avoid the excesses of "politics as action," a moral structure inextricably grounded in civil society was essential.

It is also apparent that the image embodied in the first level of appearance idealized, but did not change, reality. This issue is complex and has two parts. On the one hand, the object of rewriting the constitutional order was to guarantee American legal and political rights of representation and justice against the threat of English repression. In doing so, a consensus was established wherein American society saw itself as a single whole in relation to the threat posed by the monarchy. For all, the central question in relation to the English system was guaranteeing the procedures of justice. However, on the other hand, once written and guaranteed, it is now obvious that these procedures did not change the orders and class-based privileges of the emerging capitalist America. Despite the Lockean rhetoric of equality of man, the procedures of equality of treatment and representation did not, and cannot even now, guarantee equality of outcomes (Horwitz 1979). Unchanged was the structure of economic privilege. The reality of differential economic power was that consensus could only be achieved for the broad principle of equality of opportunity, not equality of outcomes.

The familiarity of many of these concepts should not come as a surprise; after all, an interpretation of the past has been offered in the language of the present (see especially Ch. 6). Concepts such as individual rights are readily acceptable to the reader, and are hardly controversial. However, what is now accepted automatically was the touchstone of the Revolution. Individual freedom was not automatic; the need for social order (stability) had an extremely important intellectual tradition, if not an immediate power to persuade during that era. But it is also remarkable that the principles of American liberalism, especially natural rights theory as embodied in Locke, can be so readily found in the struggle for justice in an earlier era. Arguments for a minimalist state, for individual rights, and procedural justice recently posed by Nozick (1974) are actually restatements of the values of an earlier time. According to Hart (1976) it is this resilience of natural rights theory in American political philosophy that distinguishes the American tradition from English political philosophy. This latter intellectual tradition is more a product of Bentham and the utilitarians than of Locke.

162   DEMOCRACY AND THE CRISIS OF LEGITIMACY

A "good" government according to the American model is one that protects the rights of all individuals to go about their business free from the constraints and intimidation of others. It is also a government that maintains the veracity of the procedures of conflict resolution while at the same time remaining completely neutral with respect to the outcomes implicit in any choice between procedures and clients. Where the state protects against inter-community (local) imperialism, it acts on behalf of the rights of all. To that extent, the legitimacy of the state is a product of its ability to maintain its neutrality with respect to specific interests. At the local level, the state is obviously a direct product of the preferences of its members. To the extent that preferences overlap around specific issues, the local state exists to implement the goals of the community. At this level, the legitimacy of the state is solely a function of the community and its ability to provide community needs. Inherently, the local state is a conduit or a means to an end, while the national state in this model is more specifically an institution that ensures the justice of civil society.

The American (liberal) conception of the state has then two general features. First, the state is *derived* from society in the sense that it exists solely to serve community and national interests. At the same time, however, society is simply the sum of its individuals and, most importantly, the state cannot have a legitimate interest in substantive questions of justice (Michelman 1977). Secondly, although individuals have quite specific and often competing interests, the rôle of the state in this vision of society is to maintain the avenues of conflict resolution and enforce the underlying conception of rights. Consequently, there must be a consensus on the structure of rights prior to civil society, and the rules of conflict resolution must conform, or at least be compatible with these *nonnegotiable* background values.

The American solution to the problem of state autonomy was to institute a system of checks and balances within the very institutional fabric of the state. This doctrine of the separation of powers remains a fundamental organizing principle of American contemporary political thought (Huntington 1981). Presidential power can be curtailed by Congress, as Congress itself can be forestalled by Presidential veto. Separate elections for the executive branch, and appointed cabinet members, distinguish its political constituency from that of the Congress. And even within Congress, the Senate was conceived to be a representative of States' interests, a check upon the national ambitions of the House of Representatives and the Executive. The institution of the Supreme Court was similarly designed as a separate court of appeal, capable of assessing the constitutionality of State and federal actions. In terms of current political theory, the Supreme Court was envisaged as a procedural policeman, an institution designed to monitor the rules of society (Choper 1980).

The notion of institutional checks and balances does not readily mesh with liberal political philosophy. For Nozick (1974) and others, the ultimate constraint on the actions of government is the will of the people. Given that legitimacy is derived out of the collective preferences of all individuals, it is theoretically difficult to integrate institutional limits on state power with the notion that the true (legitimate) constraint is individual will. This conception remains an important strand of constitutional thought, particularly with regard to the so-called "problem" of the Supreme Court. There have been periodic debates over the responsiveness of the court to popular sentiment, but there has been no ready resolution because the élites have not trusted society to adjudicate conflicts equitably. To be undemocratic is to be vulnerable to socially derived movements of impeachment (although in terms of Lockean liberalism, it would be theoretically legitimate). Basically, there is no direct public control over the actions of the court; it is undemocratic compared with other institutions. This was anathema to Jefferson and still is to some constitutional scholars today (Ely 1980).

On the other hand it must also be recognized that the doctrine of the separation of powers has had enormous appeal. Tyranny according to Adams and Madison was a function of the concentration of coercive power in one institution. Implied in this was a fear of the capacity of the state to maintain itself separate from the consent or will of the people. In contemporary terms the issue is quite simply the relative autonomy of the state. This fear among American constitutionalists had a very real image in the tyranny of the English monarchy which was nominally thought to be constitutionally bound to Parliament. Thus the reality of political power prompted a doctrine of separation of powers for two quite distinct reasons: functional efficiency, and distrust of government. The first version can be easily subsumed within liberal theory; the second is not so easily meshed with liberalism. Consent as the ultimate check against government action was considered by Madison to be functionally inadequate, however theoretically desirable, in the face of the reality of institutional power.

The case for federalism, argued by Madison, emphasized the usefulness of a spatial division of powers in fostering the fragmentation of power and, at the same time, the integration of the nation. Writing in *The Federalist* (No. 10), Madison noted the incredible diversity of the emerging nation, and the inevitable problems of scale when trying to adapt national policy to disparate communities. The tyranny of an unresponsive central government was an ever present threat. But for integration and for reasons of individual freedom, centralization of some functions would ensure a wider vision, a freedom from the entrapment of a smaller community. The entire country was divided spatially, institutionally, within and against itself.

164   DEMOCRACY AND THE CRISIS OF LEGITIMACY

Jefferson's doctrine of the separation of powers also held that the more clearly articulated the will of the people, the more decentralized the functions of government. Spatial decentralization in particular was thought by Jefferson to be the ideal way of enabling the participation of the people. It comes as no surprise then that liberal theorists of many persuasions have maintained the virtues of citizen participation and spatial decentralization. Verba and Nie (1972), in a study of contemporary American citizen participation, concluded that the greater the level of citizen participation, the more responsive the local government. For those authors, decentralization is a function of the imperatives of size. Depending upon the scale necessary for efficient administration, local governments were to be primary units of administration. Jefferson articulated a practical conception of America that Nozick (1974) and others have elevated to the status of theory. Of course, Jefferson's image was also a romantic notion of an agrarian village type of society, eschewing urban life for rural republicanism. This image has been subject, then and now, to quite trenchant critiques regarding its impossibility in a modern capitalist economy.

Spatial organization of the state

There are three key issues here that relate to the structure of liberal political philosophy and legitimacy. First the notion of consent, as the ultimate moral constraint on governmental actions, is fundamental at the theoretical level. To the extent that the procedures for expressing individual consent are efficient, governments will be representative of the will of the people. Participatory democracy is then a crucial mechanism for indicating the will of individuals. Secondly, state legitimacy is, in consequence, a function of the consent of all individuals. Inevitably, if avenues for free expression are curtailed then, according to this model, legitimacy itself collapses. Thirdly, there are obviously many ways of facilitating the expression of consent or disagreement with the actions of the state. One option is to decentralize the structure of government, thereby improving democratic access and responsiveness. The extent of decentralization, once agreed upon, is conditional upon the types of functions that can be efficiently carried out locally and, most importantly, the degree to which local control might compromise other avenues (spatial levels) of free expression and democracy. In summary, local government is a means of facilitating the will of individuals; this is its source of political legitimacy.

Given that consent determines the legitimacy of the state, the key issue for liberal political theorists is to show how consent is evidenced. That is, how are the opinions and views of society's members regarding actions

SPATIAL ORGANIZATION OF THE STATE

of the state given concrete expression? Obviously direct polling, voting (voice), and direct representation are ways of establishing consent. However in many instances these strategies are too clumsy and/or complex given the myriad of issues to be evaluated. At the local level, a common solution is to invoke tacit consent, as shown by residency in a given jurisdiction. From Locke through to Nozick (1974), tacit consent has been the means of dealing with questions of implied obligations, immunities and ultimately local legitimacy. Tacit consent is typically inferred and depends on determining empirically what constitutes consent as opposed to simple indifference. In this context, leaving a jurisdiction (exit) represents the actions of those who do not consent. Thus those who reside in a particular area presumably agree to the actions of the local state and are then obliged to be loyal.

Residence as tacit consent depends upon two conditions if it is to be taken at all seriously. First, there must be a choice of localities available for potential residence. After all, we can only leave if there is an alternative place to live. Moreover, it is not enough that there be a choice between places of the same characteristics. Having a choice implies differentiation and heterogeneity particularly with respect to the actions and regulations of any given locality. Choice must be multifaceted; tacit consent is only possible through residence if the actions of individuals are voluntary. Secondly, there must also be free mobility between communities. Otherwise exit will not be possible even though the first condition may be met. To the extent that there is exclusion or any barrier to mobility, tacit consent will be fundamentally compromised. The theories of Nozick and Locke depend upon these two conditions for the legitimacy of their nonoverlapping communities. Because rights are centered upon individuals, it is incumbent upon the state to ensure that all options (exit, voice, and loyalty) are available for all individuals.

Exit is essentially mobility, and this latter concept has a significant place in the history of American development and the ideology of equality. Hartz (1955) noted that it was the option of exit that distinguished American social history from European social history. Exit has been the means of escape, of transforming the individual if not the originating society. It is no surprise then that legal scholars seriously entertain the notion of a "right of mobility." Broadly, there is such a right embodied in the Constitution, especially with regard to the actions of States regarding their treatment of their own citizens and outsiders (see *Shapiro v. Thompson*, 394 US 618 (1969)).

As in all aspects of liberal theory, it is the actions of individuals that indicate the existence of consent. Any restraint on free will or individual action will necessarily be understood in terms of coercion. Consequently it is a relatively straightforward judicial issue to adjudicate. However, less clear and harder to distinguish are instances of nonconsent despite

166 DEMOCRACY AND THE CRISIS OF LEGITIMACY

residency. Does the fact that a person resides in a jurisdiction necessarily imply consent to all actions of the local state? Clearly some actions are more important than others. For example failure to clean streets is perhaps less serious than failure to provide street lights. Does continued residence condone both? The answer is unclear. The problem is that differentiating between actions, or ordering them in terms of importance, requires another theory, whether of fair play or justice itself. And, because liberal theory is foremost concerned with procedures not outcomes, there can be no clear rule or "proper" criterion for distinguishing between small and large issues. The theory is most comfortable with the simple rules of exit and loyalty, and least comfortable with standards of fair play and justice.

Notice that in all this discussion there is a presumption that the "rules of the game," the procedures whereby choices are made, are uniform between jurisdictions. We can hardly migrate between two places if the destination requires an entry fee. Or to take another example, potential choices must be evaluated on a common basis, otherwise rational choice would be impossible. The implication of this requirement is far reaching. It presupposes universal agreement on the rules of choice, and implicitly on the underlying order of the society. As we have seen, Lockean liberal theorists assume the underlying order to be based on natural rights. But in practice, specific institutional forms are required to give these rights concrete expression. However, these forms are often outside political discourse. They are background "variables" which order the processes of conflict resolution (and action). Like divine reason, the justification for the existence of these institutions has to be in terms of a higher order, otherwise the very structure of order would be subject to negotiation.

To maintain inter-community comparability, the procedures of choice and of mobility must be ensured. Nozick (1974) invoked, as we have seen, a higher-level state to guarantee or enforce the rules of the game. Implicitly this means that local state legitimacy is conditional. Not only must local states have the tacit consent of their residents, they must also conform to a wider set of procedures. This is a fundamental result of Nozick's model (and liberal theory in general) because it defines the relationship between local and national interests. Moreover, it provides evidence of a hierarchy of legitimacy, both with respect to the proper spatial distribution of state functions and, most importantly, the spatial distribution of state powers. Local governments, according to this theory, maintain their legitimacy up to the point where they lose either the tacit loyalty of their residents or the protection of the national state.

The obvious question is then: whence does the national state draw its legitimacy? Exit is clearly less practical and, with exceptions, less realistic at this level. Voice remains a crucial means of indicating consent, but at the national level this option is clearly more problematic. Not only are size and complexity an issue, but the competing visions of society embodied in its constituent communities complicate the question of what are important values. Loyalty is even more difficult to evaluate. With fewer real options for exit, there is greater potential for mistaking indifference, or real dissatisfaction, for loyalty. Liberal political philosophy solves this problem by arguing that since rights rest with individuals, regardless of residence, the protection and facilitation of rights will guarantee loyalty (and consent) from all sections of society, and, to the extent that the national state can remain as an impartial umpire between competing values or images of society, it will similarly gain general support from all communities. Of course the only way of maintaining impartiality in such a world is to eschew outcomes in favor of procedures.

The previous discussion concerning consent and legitimacy provides an obvious means of interpreting current public finance assumptions. In particular it is readily apparent how and why public goods are provided. At the national level, public goods are subject to the two provisos, noted above, concerning the legitimacy of the national state. First, public goods must be generally, as opposed to selectively, provided. Loyalty for collective public goods (like defense) is obviously easier to sustain than loyalty (and hence legitimacy) for particular outcomes. Secondly, public goods that facilitate individual choice in general are clearly preferable (in terms of maintaining legitimacy) to public goods directed at particular communities or groups. Here we have one explanation for the distinction, noted at the outset of this chapter, between national and group interests. On one hand, the national interest is served by general as opposed to particular (targeted to groups) public goods. Legitimacy and the national interest are hence mirror images of each other. Group interests on the other hand are almost inevitably illegitimate because they involve outcomes, favoritism, and inequality. Implicit in this is a denial of the rights of individuals to equality of options, or equality of treatment.

Liberal political philosophy also has an answer to the question of scale of government. Local public goods are provided by local governments according to the preferences of local residents. By providing for local preferences, local governments maintain the loyalty and consent of their residents. The parochial character of such activities is a product of the initial assumption made about the "goodness" of governmental responsiveness. Notice that the necessary goodness (or efficiency) of such responsiveness varies with the function provided. In some instances public goods may be national as opposed to local depending on the character of the good. Consequently, communities that have unique or specific nonoverlapping preferences are best served by the local provision of those goods, if this is at all possible. This solution is not particularly

168 DEMOCRACY AND THE CRISIS OF LEGITIMACY

parochial in any negative sense. It is only when the conditions of exit, voice, and loyalty are broken, where exclusion and mobility rights are threatened, that the local interest can be perceived as clashing with the national interest. In these instances it is clear that the local interest would be illegitimate.

A major issue here is distinguishing between the empirical bases for local government functions and their moral imperatives derived from the preferences of a community. Issues of scale and efficiency in the provision of public goods are inadequate as the principal justifications of local legitimacy. For the most part, efficiency rules are empirical in that as the function changes and scales change so do the rules and scales of provision. Yet the argument made by Nozick (1974) was more than empirical; it concerned the underlying values of society, wherein what individuals do provides the rationale for the particular spatial configuration of local government functions.

Despite the rhetoric regarding the presumed efficiency of the local provision of public goods, it is readily apparent that the legitimacy of local government has some form of moral claim. One must first agree with Locke and Nozick, for instance, that the natural rights of man are life, liberty, and property; and, that rights themselves are individually centered, not socially or otherwise conceived. If these assumptions are not agreed upon, there cannot be agreement on the "goodness" of local public goods or for that matter, the origin of the legitimacy of local and national governments. The question of distinguishing the empirical and moral bases for local government legitimacy is essentially an issue of ordering their relative importance. For Lockean liberals, contextual or empirical rules of legitimacy are anathema to the conception of natural order, since once empirical rules are established there can be no overarching measure of good or bad. Every question of legitimacy would be made relative to a specific set of everchanging empirical rules. The reasons for change in the rules would also have no moral basis.

In the absence of moral order we would have a central place theory of legitimacy. It may be useful to characterize liberal theory in such terms, mostly for reasons of caricature, though this was not the intent of liberal political philosophers. If nothing else, the Lockean tradition has prided itself on its nonrelativist basis; it is not a positivist theory of rights. The legitimacy of local and national governments for liberal theorists like Nozick (1974) is based upon a higher order, a set of principles of individual rights that are noncontextual and nonhistorical.

Crisis of liberalism

There is a crisis of liberalism. The state apparently functions quite differently from its ideological image. Evidence for such a crisis is not

CRISIS OF LIBERALISM

hard to find. Politicians are elected on promises to reduce the size of government, to reassert the will of the people, or to go back to the principles of liberalism. Rhetoric would have that the state is out of control; it is not responsive to the aspirations or desires of its people; and has its own agenda. The contrasts between image and reality have often led commentators to invoke the principles of the Founding Fathers, including responsive government, and distrust of government power. Property owners are in revolt against high property taxes and the burdens of the welfare state. For example, not long ago it was suggested by President Reagan that the only way to control government was to cut its revenue, that is, its source of autonomy.

There is little doubt that the fundamental building block of American liberalism is the local community. Of course there are a variety of utopian strands that have given it ideological sustenance. Jefferson's romantic image of a decentralized agrarian settlement system is one obvious image that receives support even today. More generally, even Madison supported the notion of decentralization for the likely advantages of greater responsiveness of government to the will of the people. Nozick (1974) and the others have given both images some credibility. However, it is Madison's claim that has received greatest attention, principally because it is a procedural issue of facilitating democracy. As we noted previously, the existence of distinctive communities under an umbrella national state provides for a range of preferences and choices for the nation's citizens. Moreover, it is the choice implicit in the existence of such communities that allows for liberal claims of procedural justice in a world where claims for the virtues of direct democracy cannot be practically sustained.

The problem with this image is its reality. It could be contended that it fails on at least three counts. Basically, choice between communities is rare and a privilege of the rich; exclusion is an endemic feature of local politics. Choice of community is at best problematic, at worst simply rhetoric. Few individuals are capable of putting choice into action; most operate within a set of financial and work-related constraints that essentially create bounded choices. It is not only that differential prices and incomes make choice difficult; for all intents and purposes, choice is often irrelevant. Moreover, the particular geography of cities, the specialization of land-use activities in terms of jobs, and associated attributes of income and class effectively places severe constraints on the character of choice. For many individuals, choice is possible only within a narrow set of options, and by virtue of the stratification of incomes and prices, choice is between quite homogeneous locations.

Exclusion and segregation are a problem of choice but also a problem of mobility. Localities in America often utilize land-use ordinances, building codes, and construction restrictions effectively to exclude potential residents. The obvious example is that of racial segregation, of exclusion and of constraints on mobility that, regardless of income, operate so as to narrow the options of different ethnic and racial groups. Evidence of segregation, contained in court cases and academic inquiry, is overwhelming. The best summary of the legal evidence on segregation and exclusion is Haar and Liebman's (1977). On the geography of segregation Johnston's (1982) recent book and Smith's (1977) monograph on the geography of welfare are useful references.

Lack of choice and mobility constraints are of course procedural issues, regardless of the substantive issues of justice also involved. Their implications for liberal theory and local legitimacy are far reaching. In the absence of explicit voice support of local government, residence is inevitably taken as tacit consent. However, residence in a world of few choices and exclusion can hardly be used to indicate consent; it is more likely that residence will indicate coercion. With no ability to move, and few avenues to voice opposition, many residents are captured by their local government. By this reasoning, liberal theory cannot provide the basis for local government claims of legitimacy – in fact, quite the contrary, because liberal theory implies dissonance.

It was argued above that because of the relative immobility of much of the population, local states can be relatively politically autonomous from their immediate constituents. We also contend (Ch. 7) that there are significant forces of homogeneity between local governments. The well known fact that "local governments are the creatures of the State," (Frug 1980), implies two fundamental constraints on local state autonomy. First, there is the obvious problem of the functions and policies of any one local state being determined by higher tiers of state, and not by local constituencies. There is an increasing appreciation of the importance of these intergovernmental constraints on local responsiveness. Secondly, States treat their local governments by way of uniform rules of application that lead to homogeneity not diversity. There are often good reasons for uniform application. Most State constitutions exclude the possibility of separate treatment. For example, the Constitution of the Commonwealth of Massachusetts explicitly excludes the possibility that local governments can be treated separately in legislation.

One factor which has wrought massive changes on the character of local government has been the evolution of the spatial economic system. In particular, the scale of the economy has shifted from local to State, to national, and even to international dimensions. Of course this has meant that the ability of any one local government to regulate its local economy has drastically shrunk. Local economic growth and decline respond to forces outside the immediate area. Also, by virtue of this expansion in scale, local governments have become direct competitors in the sense that their abilities to attract and hold industry have come to depend upon

CRISIS OF LIBERALISM

their comparative policies and inducements. While not all localities compete, and some localities have clearly more advantages than others in encouraging growth, the potential choices of local governments have been successively narrowed and homogenized according to constraints set outside their control. Policies are increasingly set in reaction to the requirements of private (and global) capital. The imperatives of competition have encouraged homogeneity, but in doing so have also narrowed the diversity of local government choice. Consequently, the bases for liberal legitimacy have been seriously eroded.

The federal grant systems, revenue sharing, categorical transfers and the like, have all contributed to a greater dependency of local governments on higher tiers of government. Many commentators have argued that, in consequence, local governments have become less responsive to the aspirations of their residents. It is certainly true that by going outside their immediate locality for revenue and support, local governments have been able to circumvent their own populations and have created "costless" constituents and supporters.

In this regard the consumption–orientated politics of local governments takes on a new significance. It represents the breakdown of legitimacy, and the moral claims for support that the local state should be able to command. There is no reason why other forms of democracy, even communism, should not be able to perform the same functions. Local consent, whether voiced or tacit, has not been sought or required by local states wishing to extend their range of services and power. By providing greater levels of public goods and services, attempts have been made to fragment the local electorate and induce greater support by the beneficiary groups of local actions. The politics of self–interest has been played out at the local level precisely because legitimacy has been so ephemeral. Notice of course that by acting in this manner, local governments have redrawn the dimensions of legitimacy; instead of democracy being the organizing rationale, local government operates like a firm dispensing services and rewards to client groups.

The participation of the national state in these schemes is crucial. However, the existence of restrictions on local autonomy is not necessarily the most fundamental criticism of liberal theory. Liberalism has only a poor rationale for the appropriate scale of the provision of public goods. While it is taken to be "good" that governments are decentralized in terms of function and performance, the actual provision of public goods is often determined by empirical rules of efficiency and scale. For example, police services may be best provided locally (for reasons of cost, implementation, responsiveness to needs), but defense is best provided nationally. It may well be that similar rationales can be invoked to support the participation of local governments in federal categorical programs. Basically, a public good is being provided

172   DEMOCRACY AND THE CRISIS OF LEGITIMACY

according to general standards of quality by a decentralized apparatus of the state.

There is however another side of fiscal federalism that may seriously compromise the spatial structure of democratic legitimacy. Essentially fiscal federalism can also be interpreted as a device for ensuring the legitimacy of higher tiers of the state at the expense of the local state. In the first instance, it is clear that the nation–state depends for its own legitimacy on the general support of all residents, regardless of their location. To be identified as a representative of factional or sectional interests is an ever present danger because its legitimacy rests on claims that all constituents are served by its actions. Otherwise, lower tiers of the state which legitimately represent particular (spatial) segments of society could claim equal standing.

In a perfect world the federal government might well represent all people. However, reality intrudes in two ways. First, the power of the federal government is in large part a function of its size; and secondly, in order to grow it must encourage and develop certain sectors of the economy and society since ownership of property is itself unequal. Association with special interests can compromise the federal government morally and fiscally. The former issue is quite obvious in that liberal theory claims a rôle for the nation–state which is beyond group interests; it is the arbiter. Trust and security in the mediating rôle of the nation–state would be severely shaken by direct association. The latter issue is also important in that if the nation–state is unable to sustain its moral legitimacy the only other alternative is to provide consumption goods to many groups.

Thus, the national state must maintain two façades: it must appear to represent the interests of the whole of society for legitimacy, and it must also facilitate the power of certain groups of society for its own growth and power. It simultaneously represents all classes, and supports one class. In this context, our analysis has certain parallels with the critiques mounted by writers such as O'Connor (1973) of the welfare state. The welfare state absorbs the factional interests of the society and in doing so becomes paralyzed because of the inherent conflicts between functions. Consumptionism, although providing a logic and means of legitimacy, carries with it the seeds of destruction for the state. In the long run it has to assert its basic interests, at the same time as restricting consumption.

So far the crisis of legitimacy has been considered in terms of liberal theory and its implications for different levels of the state. It is also appropriate to analyze the legitimacy of the national government on its own terms. The fundamental flaw of American constitutionalism, at least in terms of liberal theory, has been the separation of the judiciary from the democratic caucus (Choper 1980). If the *raison d'être* of the national state is its neutral enforcement of the rules of the game on behalf

CRISIS OF LIBERALISM

of all individuals, then there must be a mechanism for distinguishing the rules of the game from ordinary "background" issues.

Traditionally, the procedures of adjudication have been derived from the liberal consensus that rights reside with individuals. Thus, the degree to which those rights are facilitated will indicate the appropriateness of different forms of adjudication. At first sight then, the selection of procedures is an empirical question, determined by the initial assumptions regarding individual rights. Moreover, liberal theory presumes that outcomes that result from such legitimate procedures should not matter. That is, once we are agreed on the procedures, compensation for "bad" outcomes need not be considered. In consequence a necessary step is to establish ways of categorizing problems of adjudication separate from their substantive outcomes. Ely (1980), for example, argued that the best way to accomplish this task is to use neutral rules of evaluation which follow from a basic consensus on rights. Thus, the use of procedures as rules of adjudication enables observance of rights and, at the same time, legitimacy derived from consensus.

This solution is confounded, however, by the fact that the judiciary is independent of democratic politics. And, because values are so important in interpreting competing claims of individual rights, many commentators have feared that the process of adjudication does not reflect the democratic consensus on the appropriateness of different procedures. Notice that the issue here is not strictly the origin of rights, but rather the adjudication of claims where a very small group of people (judges) may have completely different views from society in general of how adjudication should be handled. One must be careful here not to ignore a supposed virtue of such a system. Essentially, by separating the judicial apparatus from the public will, people may be protected from themselves. Reading the debates of the Confederation Conventions it is apparent that the delegates were afraid of the unrestrained claims of the majority (see Maier 1975). This is Choper's (1980) view, enlarged through a critique of the anti-democratic character of a lobby-orientated Congress. Yet it is a strange argument; democracy is saved by being undemocratic. It also smacks of paternalism; children are being protected by their elders.

Liberal theory depends for the reconciliation of such claims on a social consensus born out of mutual regard and survival. The American judicial system, however, does not necessarily reflect any social consensus because it is not democratic. Legitimacy is then at best problematic; at worst, it is impossible because of the structural dissonance between image and reality. Moreover, because lower tiers of government and their residents depend upon this system for resolving conflicts between communities, the legitimacy of the whole must be in doubt.

We should finally recognize that there is a deeper issue here even if accountability of the judiciary can be resolved (see Ely 1980). This deeper issue is at the very heart of American liberal democracy: that rights reside naturally with individuals. Liberalism is ultimately compromised by this assumption because it is essentially undemocratic. Revolutionary theorists through to Nozick (1974) have argued for a set of rights that remain constant regardless of the particular form of society, including its institutional and economic character. By assuming an invariant set of values, such theorists label socially-derived conceptions of justice as illegitimate to the degree that they depart from natural rights. In this respect the liberal conception of rights is undemocratic because the will of the people is constrained *a priori* within a set of external parameters. It might be claimed that such values were originally democratically derived, but that fact should not imply that subsequent generations are unable to express their own image of how society ought to be arranged.

The problem of legitimacy in this context is far broader than simple democratic representation. The conception of the primacy of individual rights is itself a subjective ordering of moral claims of right and wrong. Consequently, the use of liberal theory as a model of what reality should be is in fact the imposition of an ideology. What must be open to debate is the actual definition of rights for each succeeding generation. It is no wonder then that by questioning the foundations of rights and values, radicals are able to question the very legitimacy of society and its institutions. Since the state imposes these rights through an undemocratic judicial system, it too becomes a target for those who question the substantive assumptions of society. The crisis of legitimacy of American liberalism is then a product of its own assumptions: the conception of a natural order which allows no place for local or national politics.

9 Justice and the state

In this final chapter, our concern is with the potential rôle of the capitalist state in initiating social justice. Much of the previous discussion focused upon the realities of the social and economic system dominated and controlled by the capitalist state; we have not considered the state's possible rôle in changing the underlying structure of capitalism and distribution of wealth. Exactly what that potential may be is the focus of this chapter. Again we assume the relative autonomy of the capitalist state and consider the issue of social justice in relation to the state's own objectives of power and reproduction. Similarly, we also reconsider the state's relationships with élites and client groups in this issue. Given our previous discussion of relative state autonomy it would come as a surprise to the reader if we were to argue that the state was powerless to create a certain pattern of social justice. In fact, we believe that the state can play a significant rôle, even if it is caught within the tentacles of capitalist élites.

These issues are explored via a set of competing propositions that in a sense summarize the opinions of many social activists. On the one hand, it is held that the state is solely the preserve of the ruling classes and thus must be smashed if social and emancipatory change is to take place. On the other hand, it is also argued that, to the extent that the state is autonomous, then it must be captured and used to alter the underlying structure of power. This latter strategy is sometimes conceived as appropriate for implementation at the local level, that is, grass-roots citizen activism aimed at capturing the local state in particular. Thus, the overall concern here is with the limits of state autonomy and the conditions under which the state could deny the rights and privileges of élites in the interests of greater social equality.

Many of the lessons of previous chapters regarding the nature and structure of the capitalist state are applied to understanding these competing notions. However, we are also concerned with a more general problem in this chapter, that of the proper rôle of the state. We depart from the state-centered mode of analysis to consider this rôle in relation to society in general. Instead of focusing exclusively upon the state in capitalism, our interest expands to consider the most general of issues: what is the proper rôle of *any* state with regard to sustaining

176 JUSTICE AND THE STATE

social justice? This normative agenda derives from our previous analysis of the crisis of legitimacy. It was argued in Chapter 8 that the capitalist state, both at the local and national levels, is continually threatened by social classes that question its very rationale. One example of this ongoing turmoil is the fiscal crisis; another is represented by the attempts of the state apparatus to shift the burdens of sustaining legitimacy spatially while simultaneously attempting to localize support.

This analysis, although empirically sound, begged the more general question of the theoretical grounds for state legitimacy. If we are not to return to the inadequate consumption-based rules of public finance, consistent criteria must be established to understand the bases of state legitimacy. Here, sustenance of social justice is emphasized as the crucial linchpin of state legitimacy, although we shall invoke a particular theory of justice.

Two arguments about radical transformation

There are two essentially contradictory positions taken in the literature concerning whether or not the state can initiate social change which is more egalitarian than the political system would propose. Wilson (1978) for example, has suggested that parts of the state apparatus are very conservative, being concerned primarily with maintaining their power in relation to other competing parts. Consequently state agencies are very hesitant in risking radical departures from the *status quo* because of their inherent vulnerability (a point made more recently by Crozier 1982, regarding the French state bureaucracy). On the other hand, Wilson has also suggested that state apparatus with strong and consistent rationales or tasks can be very difficult to control or to dislodge from their perceived goals and modes of operation. The implication is that political vulnerability coupled with bureaucratic inertia can make the state a formidable but conservative force in society.

This argument is not dissimilar from the view taken by many student radicals during the Vietnam war era. The rhetoric of the time often implied that the state protects the interests of the ruling class and that for any radical transformation of society, the state would have to be smashed. The conservative instincts of the state were thought to be fundamental impediments to changing the underlying structure of capitalist power relations: greater state-induced social equality is, in these terms, inconceivable. However, this argument is not necessarily "radical" despite the intuitive conclusions reached by the leaders of the student movement. As Wilson has shown, through careful investigation of specific state apparatus, there are good institutionally based reasons for the state's conservatism.

TWO ARGUMENTS ABOUT RADICAL TRANSFORMATION 177

The principal alternative argument claims that the state is in fact quite capable of radically transforming society. This argument has been made by Berger (1977) who complained that the judicial apparatus of the state has significantly altered and transformed American society. For Berger, the judiciary no longer reviews policy in terms of principles; instead, it initiates policy and has usurped the rôle of the Congress. By doing so, Berger argued that the Supreme Court has drastically altered American society, in a way in which the fathers of the Constitution had not intended. Berger argued that the Court (under Chief Justice Warren in particular) deliberately altered the substantive and original meanings of voting rights, equality before the law, and segregation. For many American conservatives, intervention by the Court in social issues and social justice has gone far beyond its legitimate rôle despite the recent return to conservatism. The Supreme Court is a special institution in American politics, not least because of its isolation from direct democratic control. And, precisely because of its insulation from direct political intervention, there has been a great deal of argument over the socially transformative potential of the judicial apparatus, both from the conservative (Choper 1980) and liberal (Ely 1980) perspectives.

The court system is much like other state apparatus since "administrators" are not elected and have few direct democratic checks on their actions (see Ch. 6). For example, the Reagan Administration had some difficulty in forcing the Civil Rights Division of the Justice Department to change its enforcement and support of the Voting Rights Act. President Nixon continually railed against the supposedly liberal Warren Court, as Reagan has attacked the independent spirit of some state apparatus. The notion that the state is a potentially active agent of social change had a great deal of support in some factions of the radical movement of the late 1960s. The rhetoric of the time implied (as conservatives fear) that the state could be captured, its objectives transformed, and its power used as a means of social revolution.

In recent years this latter position, a tactical strategy termed "capturing the state", has been employed by the right and the left in the US. Rather than attacking the nation–state directly, both groups have sought to develop grass-roots support, and through a strategy of capturing the local state apparatus or its representatives, control of the state has been sought from within. The very fragmentation of the state has given political groups the opportunities for penetration of state agencies.

There are then two essentially contradictory positions concerning the potential of the state as an agent or source of emancipating social change. Neither position is exclusively radical nor conservative, and neither position is entirely consistent. For example, from the radical perspective it is difficult to understand how the state can both be the means of ruling class hegemony and yet have the potential to be captured. And from the

178   JUSTICE AND THE STATE

conservative perspective it is similarly difficult to understand how the state can be politically isolated but at the same time capable of innovative social policies. In the subsequent sections of this chapter we attempt to provide a means of understanding these apparent conflicts. In particular we reconsider issues of state autonomy, democratic politics, and the basis of state legitimacy in social justice.

State autonomy reconsidered

In previous chapters the case was made for two distinct spheres of power: the political and the economic. From this perspective, a case was made for the relative autonomy of the state from the direct control of client classes and even from the democratic process. The consequent separation of state authority and political control may weaken the practice of democracy. The lack of adequate devices to influence the state apparatus directly raises the prospect of arbitrary political and economic repression. Under these circumstances it is no longer clear how control over elected representatives and those who exercise delegated authority can be maintained (Arrow 1974).

The relative separation of democratic political control and its institutional representation (the state) has a number of consequences. In the first place, it creates an illusion of control. Although the dominant ideology may be expressed in terms of the rules of democracy, its actual organization may fall short in practice. The illusion of a political process directed by the electorate in direct control of the state is also buttressed by the state itself, using such tactics as citizen participation and involvement. Not only does this allow for the autonomy of the capitalist state in pursuit of its own interests, but it also allows these interests to be represented as the actions of the democratic process. Secondly, whatever the power of the electorate to control parliamentary representatives, Congress itself may be relatively powerless to control the state's apparatus. The reasons for this are to be found in the separation of bureaucratic control from Congressional responsibility and in the powers of the bureaucracy which exist by virtue of their institutional authority. It is not simply the individual bureaucrat who is at issue; rather it is the power vested in the capitalist state by the praxis of democracy. As a consequence of democratic ideology, the legislature is presumed to be in control; yet if the state were to act against the elected majority the government might be seriously compromised. This would leave the state intact and diffuse revolt through the democratic process. Thirdly, inherent in the notions of separability is the possibility of the converse; it is not clear that the state could stop one party or group from identifying itself with a specific state apparatus. In fact, it may be in the interest of a political party to appear as synonymous with the state. Consequently, the state could be drawn into the political arena and identified with a particular party or social group against its own interests. The issue is, again, the degree of the state's relative autonomy.

State-centered analysis implies a theory of the state as an institution. With the exception of neoclassical economic models of individual rationality within organizations, most theories of the state, including ours, are based upon notions of power and control. For example, Wilson (1978) applied essentially Weberian concepts of authority and rationalization to describe how state apparatus are controlled by rules and procedures and by the hierarchical separation of responsibility from implementation. In this type of model, state apparatus are goal-oriented organizations that seek to maximize their power and minimize their dependence upon other state and nonstate organizations. Wilson argued, of course, that state apparatus often deal in a hostile environment with competition from other agencies, interference from political managers, and demanding client groups. In order to maintain their coherence, their control and autonomy, state apparatus seek to rationalize and differentiate their tasks in relation to threats from outside the agency or from the state structure in general. Internal coherence can be achieved by concentrating the power of task definition and by diffusing internal responsibility. On the other hand, external coherence can be achieved by gaining control over financial and political resources in order to sustain autonomy.

Autonomy is, of course, relative and refers principally to the extent to which an agency is able to define and carry out its own tasks free from the review of other agencies. State apparatus, and the state in general, nevertheless require legitimacy; that is, a justifiable claim for their continued existence. To the extent that state agencies provide needed functions to classes and interest groups, these groups can be conceived as client supporters and, if necessary, political contributors in case of attack by other agencies. (Under these circumstances, the apparatus does not require legitimating moral principles.) For example, the Civil Rights Division (CRD) of the Department of Justice developed strong links over the years with black civil rights groups, the National Association for the Advancement of Colored People (NAACP), and the Urban League. President Reagan's attack on the CRD and its activist stance concerning segregation and voting rights was countered by many of these client groups through direct attacks on the President. While the President might prevail in the long run, the CRD will likely retain greater autonomy than might have been the case without the support of its client groups.

Another strategy that state apparatus can use is to identify their tasks with conservative majoritarian value positions like "adequate police protection," or "upholding the law." The advantage of such a strategy is

180   JUSTICE AND THE STATE

that specific client groups may not be needed, as the agency itself can utilize the dominant ideology to propagandize its own importance. Even so, there are two risks associated with the majoritarian stance. For instance, a change in social values may leave the related state apparatus in a vulnerable position since shifts in social opinions can expose the extent of state autonomy. Hence, in the early phases of President Roosevelt's Administration the Supreme Court declared many of the New Deal policies to be unconstitutional. The court reflected views of an earlier generation, being possibly 50 years out of date. Roosevelt threatened the court's autonomy through a proposal to change its composition by adding more Justices. The court had to give in; to do otherwise would have threatened the entire judiciary. Even though an apparatus may promote a majoritarian stance, its tasks (say, for example, navigation on inland waterways) may have a low priority. Because institutional power is in part a function of resources, a low-priority apparatus may have little power compared with other agencies (this is especially the case for newer agencies such as the US Department of Energy). There are then some incentives for state agencies to be more adventurous and activist, as opposed to being simply conservative. Being allied with majoritarian values may mean limited power, while being allied with strong client groups may mean relatively greater power with lesser security.

How might these ideas help us understand the potential of the state for initiating social change? State apparatus characterized by a great deal of autonomy and power (whether a function of "clientism" or "majoritarian conservatism") are unlikely to initiate social change or even to tolerate indirect challenges to their superiority. A perfect example of this latter phenomenon was the tremendous resistance of the US Department of Defense against the Department of Housing and Urban Development's Urban Impact Assessment (UIA) program, which was initiated in President Carter's Administration. Defense argued that the UIA program compromised their autonomy; it claimed that its mission of protecting the nation was more important than inner-city welfare. In these circumstances there may be some justification in claiming that one sector of the state apparatus impeded social change. However, it is also possible that an ambitious apparatus with some institutional flexibility and versatility could take a lead rôle in initiating social change by creating client groups and external support for their claims for greater resources and institutional power.

Extending this analysis into the realm of the local state, it is apparent that the local state may be more activist in support of its client groups (residents) than other apparatus. The greater the degree of local support which exists for local state actions, the more likely is the leverage of the local state to be used to force a rearrangement of powers at the expense of other higher tiers of authority. Of course, the very strong limits to local power may well have been designed with these issues in mind. The local state has little to lose by associating itself with activist groups. It can easily legitimize its actions by invoking the ideology of decentralized democracy and, if it fails to "deliver the goods," it can always blame higher tiers (or forces outside its control). The local state is in a very vulnerable position. It must respond to the strongest of local pressures, even if it is closely controlled by higher tiers, otherwise the underlying problem of its own legitimacy could become a serious liability. We do not mean to imply altruistic or emancipating motives to activist apparatus, including the local state. Our state-centered theory conceives of the state, its tasks and operational objectives, in terms of power and autonomy.

It is precisely the autonomy implied by state-centered theories that has been a prime motivating force behind normatively conceived, society-centered theories of the proper rôle of the state. Berger's (1977) argument was a restatement of a central theme of American political philosophy: the state should be directly responsible to the democratic caucus. Rather than the state being outside the democratic life of society (that is, relatively autonomous) as many functionalist and realist descriptions have portrayed, the state should, according to Berger, be a product of the consensus established in the political arena at any given time. This idealist model is based on at least two assumptions regarding the sources of power and the fundamental building blocks of society. First, it is assumed that the basic unit of society is the individual. It is his or her actions that are assumed to provide the legitimacy or constraints on actions of social institutions such as the state. Secondly, power itself is presumed to reside with individuals; they can choose to invest it in representative organizations, or remove their mandate at any time. Separate sources of power and control are, in the idealist model, thought to be either irrelevant or at least outside the normal context of social decision making. In this model, the rôle of the state is to facilitate the free actions of individuals.

As we have seen, this normative model had its origins in the American Revolution and the Lockean political philosophy of the 18th century. For American intellectuals of that era, the autonomy of the state was profoundly evident. According to Wood (1969), it was the vulnerability of the colonists to arbitrary and capricious rule that informed and structured political debate during the period leading up to the Constitutional Conventions. Arbitrary rule was a fact of life despite a veneer of English parliamentary democracy. This was also the era of Locke and natural rights theorists. By beginning the analysis of society at the level of the individual, it is axiomatic that the state has no authority except that granted to it by "the people." Moreover, the state is presumed to be the institutional image of the preferences of its constituents. The result of joining the Lockean and Machiavellian traditions were thought to be

JUSTICE AND THE STATE

threefold (see Ch. 8). First, as society was idealized in the Constitution, the state was similarly idealized as having no autonomy other than that granted to it by the electorate. Secondly, to ensure that the state did not become so powerful as to be able to control its own objectives, it was divided vertically and horizontally. Autonomy was recognized as a central problem; its possibility was explicitly conceived in the construction of a Constitution that divided the state against itself (in the separation of powers). Thirdly, the state was given the responsibility to facilitate the freedom and independence of all individuals. In this way, the emerging American state was forced by the rule of law to subordinate its interests to those of the population in general. By doing so it was hoped that its potential autonomy would be fundamentally constrained.

Thus, the very character of the Constitution recognized the significance and potential dangers of state autonomy, that is, the power of state institutions that exists by virtue of their resources and powers of coercion despite the existence of the electoral process. Berger's argument against an interventionist Supreme Court was then much more than a simple disagreement over policy. He objected to the implied shift of power from the electorate to the state, and argued that Supreme Court actions in overturning legislation and policy constitute a threat to civil society itself.

To this point it has been argued that society-centered theories of the state are blueprints or idealizations of the rôle of the state. It is also true that the structure of government and the doctrine of the separation of powers have operated to fragment state power and to limit autonomy. However, it remains an open question as to whether our reality matches the utopian vision. We have suggested in this book that state autonomy is a fact of life; that for all the attempts to bind the state, it still has remarkable autonomy despite the underlying premises of the society-centered model. This realist view dominates contemporary political discourse. All US Presidents since 1945 have run for office on the argument that the state is too autonomous, in relation to the principles of American democracy. If that is the case, then the state must have a great deal of power to initiate social change. Berger's fears of the state's policy-making powers must have some foundation in reality. The extent of state autonomy and its potential for transforming society is a function of the requirements of authority and control mentioned above. One of the lessons of the previous chapters is that autonomy itself depends upon the degree to which the state can legitimize itself in terms of democratic politics.

Normal and crisis politics

To understand the links between state autonomy and democracy, we must immediately distinguish between the politics of interpretation and the politics of change. Let us focus initially on the former, termed "normal politics," which we define to be the politics of routine administration and implementation. Given a set of rules, values and ideology, much of politics involves justifying actions in terms of those values. The rules and values of society are those embodied in common law, or in the American context, the Constitution. For much of society, the Constitution sets the parameters of social and political life. Normal politics is structured by the institutional fabric of the Constitution and involves all state apparatus. Berger's critique of the Warren Court invoked many of these conceptions at least implicitly. For example, the Court was supposedly bound by its review rôle; the proper place of policy making, according to Berger, is Congress.

Normal politics is also the politics of justification and legitimation. By appeal to an ideological conception of society, institutions and parties justify their actions and place themselves in relation to the mainstream of political thought. The state and its apparatus are actively involved in this process, at least to the extent that they require external validity and coherence. Yet we must be wary of ascribing a "straitjacket" image to this political process. The ideological framework of society is rarely as consistent and unambiguous as the brief description above would have one believe (see Walzer 1983). The crucial issue for all political actors, the state included, is to interpret the meaning of substantive social values and ideology. Despite its appearance of consistency and integrity, the Constitution itself is a less-than-perfect recipe for justice and freedom. And when we extend this issue into the realm of widely held unwritten values and beliefs, the ambiguity of meaning and interpretation becomes more acute and apparent (see Ch. 5). For example, what is meant by equality of justice or due process? Does this mean procedural equality (everyone has equal access to the legal process) or does it mean equality of outcomes (everyone has the right to substantive justice)?

The due process argument is more straightforward than many other similar questions of interpretation in law. The more general point is, however, that social values have many competing interpretations despite their apparent universality. Resolution of conflicting interpretations can take many forms. A popular argument is that the meaning of substantive social values can be found in the original definition of the term(s), whether in law or in legislative and administrative decisions. The problems with this mode of interpretation are well known. How can the original meaning be known if the context in which the rules and/or interpretations were first decided is only poorly understood? Why should

184   JUSTICE AND THE STATE

society be held hostage to old ideas and interpretations that have lost their relevance? Is not the very conception of original meaning undemocratic? Alternatively, meaning could be defined by those given exactly that responsibility, for example the judicial system. But even here, some have questioned the predisposition of justices, primarily in terms of their conservative nature (Ely 1980), but others such as Berger (1977) have been worried about possible liberal biases. Another option is Congressional consensus making, that is, interpretation as an explicitly political act. But even here there are problems related to the issue of minority representation (Choper 1980).

No one method of meaning or interpretation is universally accepted, and in reality there are conflicting methods and even conflicting interpretations based on agreed methods. Because of the existence of this ambiguity and conflict over commonly accepted values, the state has a very powerful rôle to play in civil society (Said 1983). As the final arbiter of questions of interpretation, the Supreme Court in particular can virtually make meaning and legitimize specific and exclusive interpretations of basic social values. This rôle is well known and, although controversial in terms of the implicit political nature of judgments, a well accepted way of adjudicating interpretations. Control of the Supreme Court by the right or left can provide an important means of legitimizing state actions, including those of the legislature.

There are more subtle ways that the state can manufacture dominant interpretations, thereby providing external legitimation based upon given social values. The powers of initiation (in terms of policy design) and implementation should not be underestimated. By designing and writing a policy, alternative interpretations are automatically excluded. The state has only to imply or to introduce explicitly certain key ideological phrases for its policy proposals to have an immediate claim of legitimacy. Of course there are competing interpretations. However, for other groups adequately to counter policies initiated by the state, there must be a forum of appeal and argument. Even where such a forum exists, the state can muster a great deal of force in making its case. First, it can oblige client groups to present their own cases in favor of the state policy and interpretation. Secondly, the state does not have to act on any non-Congressional citizen's view. In short, power is unevenly distributed, often forcing citizen groups to compromise. Moreover, there is a great deal of power embodied in the resources that the state apparatus controls.

The state may capture client groups and turn them into advocates (for example, the relationship between the trucking industry and the Interstate Commerce Commission) because of their dependence upon state resources. The state can also create support by designing policies that compromise its adversaries. For example, ex-Governor King of

NORMAL AND CRISIS POLITICS 185

Massachusetts was able to circumvent critics of his "work-fare" program for welfare dependants by proposing more liberal benefits for selected welfare clients and possible decreases in welfare costs generally.

The language of normal politics reflects the values of society, interpreted and structured in terms of the objectives of the state and contending political groups. The extent to which the state can legitimize policies that advance emancipatory social change depends on its ability to dominate the interpretation of social values. The extent of state power in this context is of course an empirical question. Yet there are good reasons for believing the state to have a great deal of power over the assignation of social meaning (see Ch. 5). Some state apparatus are explicitly designed to deal with this issue (for example, the judiciary); other apparatus are also closely involved, but in subtle and manipulative ways. The state can design its own interpretive communities.

Even in terms of state-centered models of state and society, there are ambiguities of meaning that, translated into the terms of the preceding discussion, represent opportunities for legitimating state actions and policies. Given the parameters of an essentially anti-state ideology, the American state can still use the option of interpretation to its advantage. The extent of social change in this context remains dependent upon the degree to which such change would advance the state's interests and would be consistent with social values (however defined and manipulated).

"Crisis politics," on the other hand, are the politics of social transformation, ideological change and redefinition. Contrasted with normal politics, crisis politics are concerned with the transformation of the parameters that define the social and political order. Inherently, this involves a normative reinterpretation (or idealization) of society's institutions. Such social transformation was the goal of activists during the late 1960s. Although the student movement was to a limited extent involved in the politics of reinterpretation (see Huntington 1981 on radical reinterpretations of equality and freedom), the movement also aimed for a real change in social values. In this context, the rhetoric of "smash the state" and "capture the state" took on a particular meaning perhaps best expressed by the question: can the state radically alter society despite existing social values?

The answer to this question requires an appreciation, once again, of the difference between state-centered and society-centered theories of the state. The latter theory would suppose that the state should not, and perhaps even could not, change society in ways counter to existing social values. The society-centered theories see the state as very much the product of society. Democratic participation theorists, such as Verba and Nie (1972), argue that the state responds to social goals, and even if it attempts to alter society radically, the democratic structure would force

186   JUSTICE AND THE STATE

it back to the *status quo*. More philosophically, society-centered democratic theories deny that a state capable of altering society in this way would in fact be democratic; it would more likely be totalitarian. These theories are generally incapable of analyzing such a possibility and necessarily have to invoke some kind of conspiratorial, anti-democratic collusion to explain the phenomenon. Even radical society-centered theories have some difficulty in explaining the transformation of society by the state. For example, the view of the state as an instrument of the ruling class often denies the existence of the autonomy of the state, insisting that social inequality and unequal distribution of power pervade the state just as in capitalist society as a whole.

Thus the "smash the state" argument is premised upon a theoretical model of the state that extends beyond its realist claims. The degree of autonomy is the crucial variable in providing any direct answer to the question of state-sponsored change – an issue that is largely outside the society-centered theories of the state. Consequently, the search for an answer to this question also implies an *a priori* selection of a particular mode of analyzing the state. Here, and throughout this book, we argue for state autonomy and suggest the more adequate perspective is state-centered, not society-centered. Yet if we take this perspective seriously, the answer to the question posed above is not particularly clear. The state apparatus can obviously manufacture client support, cutting across consensual social values which have a variety of interpretations. While this may make state apparatus vulnerable to attack from the political system and other state agencies, such a possibility is not without precedent. For instance, the Central Intelligence Agency (CIA) for many years conducted clandestine internal and external illegal actions that had the backing of certain corporations, especially those based in Latin America. Although this example is of social repression, a further example, this time a liberating, radical agency, was Volunteers In Service To America (VISTA), notable especially for its mobilizing of poor Appalachian communities against other state agencies and the democratic system in general.

There are few other examples of liberating crisis-oriented state apparatus. Most support the *status quo* and relatively conservative interpretations of substantive social values. Those apparatus with missions and tasks central to the continuity of the political and economic system (like defense, police, and the judiciary) are unlikely to be liberating. Their power derives from the autonomy granted to them by society in general (majoritarian values) and client supporters. These élites and their underlying social values would themselves have to change before institutional resistance could be overcome. It may also be true that a different social system would need functions such as defense, and these types of institutions would have powerful *status quo* positions in any type of social system. Thus it is not necessarily ideology as such that defines whether or not a state apparatus would support social change. The power and autonomy inherent in particular functions define the revolutionary potential of specific state agencies. We should not be surprised, therefore, when peripheral parts of the apparatus become social activists and initiate or try to initiate social changes. Such apparatus have much to gain, and little to lose, through establishing supportive clients and a strong, even if radical, image.

Is the state in general capable of initiating social change which breaches existing social values? It is difficult to imagine circumstances that would be conducive to this kind of social revolution. Only if the economic and political system were in jeopardy, or if the current system were obviously unable to deal with threats to its existence, would the state be likely to initiate radical change. Crisis politics is then an apt term for situations where a central state apparatus establishes a new régime. Examples include the recent histories of Portugal, Spain, and perhaps Poland. The first two examples are of left-wing revolution, the last example is of left-wing counter-revolution. The rôle of the state in these first two examples was quite extraordinary when compared with American and English history. The state in these two countries led social reform, initiated greater equality, and fundamentally changed the underlying social order and even the national constitutions. Support for state actions (especially in Portugal) was not universal nor did open revolt by the population initiate strong response. Rather, the power of the state was used against sections of the ruling élite by groups situated within the state (especially the army).

Crisis situations provide opportunities for the state to initiate social change and revolution in social values. Normal politics also provide opportunities for the state to initiate social change, but within the parameters of dominant interpretations of existing social values. Understanding the particular actions of the state and its apparatus in these two contexts involves understanding its power and autonomy. It may well happen that within normal politics, the state apparatus may have the opportunity to initiate a great deal of social change depending upon the degree of external support that can be generated. In this context capturing the state is a viable option as long as it is acknowledged that the state is ultimately limited by the meanings associated with social values (which, of course, state agencies can engineer). Smashing the state may be necessary if radical social change (a transformation of social values) is desired. However, this option requires a more situation-specific analysis, as there are imperatives of power and autonomy that may actually encourage the state to initiate social revolution.

State and society

Our analysis of the rôle of the state as regards social change and society in general has emphasized its relative autonomy. However, autonomy requires legitimacy, otherwise the state's relative isolation from society could become identified as an immediate threat to society itself. In this section we suggest that this threat warrants careful scrutiny and should not be dismissed out of hand. We also want to suggest a solution to the problem of legitimacy that accommodates relative autonomy, but at the same time does not give the state *carte blanche* to reproduce its own powerful position in society. To develop these arguments, we need to introduce a question and an analogy that will structure the analysis and serve as points of reference in suggesting what the state's rôle in society should be. Thus, the focus of the chapter shifts from social–structural analysis to normative idealism.

Before examining our particular conception of the state's proper rôle in society, it should be recognized that idealism itself has been severely criticized in the radical literature. Not only have state theorists such as Weber been dismissed out of hand because of their idealist methodologies (see Saunders 1983 for a defense of Weber), but some radical theorists have suggested that to take moral values seriously is to fall into the trap of taking seriously only surface appearances (see Johnston 1983). In this context we follow Nozick's (1981, p. 555) definition of idealism: "values exist, but their existence and their character are both somehow dependent upon us, upon our choices, attitudes, commitments, structures, or whatever." In some instances, idealism has been equated with irrelevance (equivalent to tilting at windmills). However, such criticism is unwarranted on at least two counts. First, it is only by defining or constructing a political option that reasoned logic can be brought to bear on both reality and its competing images. Secondly, emphasis on idealism forces us to confront the inherent politics of values and how images themselves are constructed. Of course, some idealistic visions may have little bearing upon reality, and may have little in common with existing conceptions of society. What we intend here is an analysis of the rôle of the state conceived in explicitly emancipatory terms.

To develop our argument we need an analogy. If the state is in fact autonomous, if it can create its own legitimacy through clientism and control of the interpretive organs of society and, if it has its own objectives of reproduction and power, how is it different from organized crime (such as the Mafia)? Functionalist descriptions of the state often dwell on collectivist rôles that presumably cannot be undertaken by society at large. This rationale goes as follows (see Ch. 2). First it is noted

STATE AND SOCIETY 189

that the market system may not be efficient; the costs of pollution, to quote a favorite example, are not adequately priced to ensure that its true costs are accounted for in the costs of production (Coase 1960). The market system may not be able to solve problems of underconsumption, economic crisis, or market coordination. The state's function in these circumstances is to act as the market regulator. Secondly, it is also noted in the public finance literature that the market may be far too cruel in distributing rewards. That is, the market may reinforce inequality, create poverty and disproportionate wealth when compared with social standards of equity and justice. The function of the state in this model is to redistribute wealth in accordance with social goals. Both functions, derived from the conventional public finance literature, assume the state exists only as a social instrument; the theory describes only a limited, society-centered state.

A related functionalist model emphasizes the rôle of the state as being the guarantor of the rules of the game, the procedures that enable social intercourse and individual freedom (again, see Ch. 2). It is argued that people have to be protected from one another, and they must be assured that their commitments to one another are undertaken freely without duress, and can be depended upon in the future. The classic restatement of this model is by Nozick (1974), who emphasized American values of natural order coupled with the theory of the minimalist state. Yet another functionalist model can be derived from the sociological literature on conflict (see Dahrendorf 1959). The state acts as an umpire or arbiter of conflict in this type of model. A more general functionalist description would of course include all these functions plus many others (Johnston 1983). But when this functionalist model of the state is coupled with realist notions of relative state autonomy and hidden objectives of power and continuity, the state becomes a quite ominous institution. Despite nominal democratic control, it becomes difficult to separate the actions of the state from those of any other organization that purposely seeks to maintain its power and at the same time to ensure external support through specific client groups. In these terms, the Mafia and the state have some provocative similarities.

For instance, the state ensures orderly trading in goods and services. The Mafia might do the same, perhaps for a more limited set of goods (drugs such as heroin), but nevertheless for a rationale not so different from that of the state. Orderly trading facilitates the generation of a social surplus; it benefits those who control the production of goods; and it *creates* support for organizations that guarantee the possibility of trade. These organizations garner external support, perhaps even legitimacy, for their actions; they appropriate revenue through taxing the social surplus; and they are able to ensure their power and relative autonomy. Just because the state provides and is sustained by these actions in a

190   JUSTICE AND THE STATE

legally sanctioned market economy does not make it any different in effect from a Mafia that runs illegal markets. At this point, one could object that our characterization of state functions ignores the democratic electoral system. Perhaps so, but it is important to distinguish between the potential of democratic action from its reality. We have suggested throughout this book that it is difficult to sustain the argument that democracy alone determines the actions of the national or local states.

Extending this analogy further, it is also true that the state and the Mafia have supporters outside their institutional membership. These groups are termed interest groups or client groups in the conventional political science literature. We can imagine interest groups that support the actions of the Mafia, such as moneylenders, prostitutes, drug traffickers and addicts. What is the difference between these client groups and ordinary voters? As first sight, it is obvious that they are *often* different people, although even here we should not ignore the close links between organized crime and some sections of government. But, let us assume that they are different people (Anscombe 1981). On closer inspection, it should be obvious that they do have some things in common. They are often consumers of "public" goods; they often depend upon the "state" for their livelihood; and they have a vested interest in the continued existence of the "state," despite the threats and extortion that may be inherent in the relationship. The point is that in all these circumstances, legal and illegal, the relationships between clients and institutions are coercive, based upon power and autonomy, but they nevertheless reward all those involved.

There are many other state functions that could be considered as equivalent to Mafia functions. Policing intergroup conflicts is an obvious function shared by the state and Mafia. Guaranteeing rights and contractual agreements is a similar function for both. Even capital infrastructure, such as road, railways and other physical goods could be provided by the Mafia if such functions contributed to the power and longevity of that organisation. To the extent that social capital goods facilitate maximum economic growth, the state can sustain its own activities by "skimming off" income and at the same time creating external support for its actions through the benefits that accrue to certain privileged groups. More recently the state has become highly involved in creating its own wealth through its ownership of production facilities (such as energy exploration corporations in Canada, gambling casinos in Nevada, and steel mills in Germany). Again, it should be emphasized that organized crime has very similar functions.

The point in exploring this analogy is not to suggest that the state is simply a bandit. Obviously it can be interpreted as such in specific circumstances; more generally, it should be noted that many different types of social institutions could provide its functions. Functionalist,

STATE AND SOCIETY 191

even realist, descriptions of the state describe situations wherein an organization like the state may be necessary. However, the state need not provide marketing boards, for instance; collective capitalist agencies could just as easily function in the same manner (Coase 1974). So if it is not the functions that distinguish the state from other social institutions (legal or illegal), what is the specific characteristic that could provide a unique rationale for the state, and distinguish it from other social institutions? The only plausible answer is one that does not deny the functions of the state but that also provides a reason for action that exists outside the state itself. The only answer that could possibly accommodate these requirements has to be normative and essentially altruistic. So as to distinguish the state from the Mafia, the state must act through its manifold apparatus to provide for the welfare of its citizens, not of itself. And the one goal that would command legitimacy and support from society in general, not just from specific client groups, is social justice (Clark 1983).

Our perspective on the proper rôle of the state assumes that, to paraphrase Hobbes' *Leviathan,* without the direct intervention of the state, "life would be nasty, brutish, and short" (Cooter 1982). A more circumspect way of putting this claim is that "justice is the first virtue of social institutions" (Rawls 1971, p. 3). The legitimacy of governments and their functions must then satisfy the aspirations of its citizens for justice (however defined). The rôle of the state, in Rawls' view, is as a positive agent of social change, a rôle we recognized in Chapter 2 at the center of more liberal conceptions of national policy since the New Deal era. However, it would be insufficient simply to note this model as our preference; the achievement of social justice is actually the *only* true rationale for the state.

For Rawls (1971), a well ordered society is one which is "designed to advance the good of its members and [is] effectively regulated by a public conception of justice" (p. 14). Note that the exact definition of what is good is left open, as are the specific procedures by which the good is to be achieved. The abstractness of this model is evidenced in Rawls' (1971) attempts to conceive of rights that are neutral with respect to the definition of what is *good.* As in Dworkin's (1977) model of rights, however, Rawls is concerned to establish basic conditions and procedures for action. In essence, society is consciously designed, and not consigned to anarchy; and it is given a fundamental moral goal, not consigned to amorality. This well ordered society is democratic in the sense that it is effectively regulated by a public conception of justice, and its institutions are dependent upon society for legitimacy. In consequence, the rôle of the state is to be responsive to public conceptions of justice, and to implement those policies that would achieve goals of justice and fairness. Thus, state intervention is not simply a function of

JUSTICE AND THE STATE

empirical rules of efficiency. The state exists in this model to bring about social transformation. Moral principles guide its action.

Social justice has many definitions and theoretical bases, extending from Rawls' (1971) vision of maximizing the welfare of those worst off through to neoclassical models (such as Buchanan & Tullock's 1962) which conceive of justice in terms of economic ability. The merits of any particular definition are not at issue here, except that it must command the support of the majority. For such a goal-oriented theory of the state to have any meaning, it must be immediately recognized that the normative intent of state functions has to come from outside its own objectives. That is, the definition of social justice has to be derived from society because any other mechanism will invite the state to attempt a definition most compatible with its own objectives. Thus, a requirement for such a system to work is a vital democracy that is capable of responding swiftly to social movements and one that is also capable of redefining its constitutional character endogenously. Appeals to state institutions to adjudicate conflicting interpretations of justice will only perpetuate the state's rôle in defining society in its own interests.

There are many blueprints for a revised model state and society. Our conception, only briefly sketched here, differs fundamentally from the American model. We should remember that the American model basically distrusts the state and, in so doing, seeks to restrict and constrict the avenues of the legitimate exercise of state power. By dividing the state against itself, the object is to ensure its relative weakness and dependence upon society. However, the problem with this solution is that the segmentation of the state has encouraged clientism, in which groups have been captured by the state to sustain its external coherence and legitimacy. The irony is that segmenting the state has allowed the state to cement its hold over dependent and client sections of society. Autonomy from wider social goals has been encouraged and, in a world of inequality and unequal power, relative social advantage has typically been procured through alliance with particular state apparatus. Thus Berger's (1977) model of the fragmented state, a state wracked by internal schisms, may only serve to reinforce state action designed to maintain its power and relative autonomy from the intrusion of other state apparatus and hostile social groups.

The alternative is to legitimize state action according to its degree of involvement in achieving the fundamental goals of social justice and equality. This would provide an external rationalization for state power and autonomy that at the same time would not depend upon clientism and similar manipulative techniques. The state would have a positive rationale for intervention and would need no legitimation other than its involvement in securing an overriding social goal. Rather than dividing the state against itself in terms of power and influence, cohesiveness and

CONCLUSIONS 193

mutual interdependence between apparatus would be encouraged. By ensuring that the definition of social justice is external and capable of swift democratic revision, the political process itself could define the extent to which state functions accomplish social justice. This does not obviate the need for interpretation and political debate. On the contrary, it forces a great deal of responsibility back onto the political process, away from the supposed neutrality of the state.

This model also recognizes the inevitability of power and social structure associated with social institutions. However, unlike the American model, the ability to direct the state is set within the democratic system, and not in a set of values which deny direct agency and which place the responsibility of interpretation within a state apparatus. But there are two important implications of this model. First, the fact that the political and economic system may be changed rapidly in the face of changing majoritarian preferences for justice and equality also means that established privilege is likely to be vulnerable to direct attack by the state as an agent of the democratic process. Secondly, conventional notions of order and stability, which dominate the writings on the state by authors such as Huntington (1981), would be eschewed in favor of responsiveness and justice. In these terms the state could be a major force in facilitating social justice, both in terms of conventional norms or value judgments and in terms of changing social values.

Conclusions

At the outset of this chapter, two contending arguments were discussed regarding the potential of the state for initiating social change. The first view emphasized bureaucratic inertia and the perceived interests of the state in maintaining the *status quo*. We have argued for a qualified rejection of that position. Essentially, within the existing normative structure of society, the state can promote change that may in fact be more liberal than that promoted by the political process. The crucial variables here are state power and autonomy. To the extent that political change advances state interests, the state may encourage and direct political change. Thus, there is some theoretical evidence for the veracity of the second position which argued that the state can be a tool of change. However, once we consider the problem of crisis politics, where social values are challenged and not simply interpreted, the state's rôle is likely to be conservative. This was especially the case where a central state apparatus is closely associated with and protects the ruling élite. Yet it should also be recognized that peripheral state apparatus may have a real stake in transforming society. The key issue here is the relationship between state apparatus and their relative position with respect to the locus of power in society itself.

194 JUSTICE AND THE STATE

Thus the conclusion that the state inhibits radical social change does not have to hold in all situations. It is a historically specific product of American democratic theory and conservative constitutionalism. The idealist 18th century vision that conceived of a shackled and minimalist state need not be the only way of organizing state and society. An alternative vision would make the state a liberating agent of social justice. Legitimacy would be found by the state in its ability to accomplish social equality. Rather than designing the state as an agent of the *status quo*, it is possible to think of a positive, goal-orientated state. Implicit in this discussion is, of course, a marked methodological shift, away from analyzing the state using a state-centered model to a society-centered vision of the rôle of the state with inherent qualities of autonomy and insulation from direct democratic control. This vision of the state is our research agenda for the future.

Bibliography

This bibliography contains some useful supplementary material not referred to in the text.

Achard, P. 1980. History and the politics of language in France *Hist. Work. J.* **10**, 175–83.

Advisory Council on Intergovernmental Relations 1977. *Design and implementation of categorical grants.* Washington, DC: US Government Printing Office.

Alcaly, R. E. and D. Mermelstein (eds) 1977. *The fiscal crisis of American cities.* New York: Vintage Books.

Allderidge, P. 1979. Hospitals, madhouses and asylums: cycles in the care of the insane. *Br. J. Psych.* **134**, 321–34.

Allen, P. 1974. A consumer's view of California's mental health care system. *Psych. Q.* **48**, 1–13.

Alonso, W. 1964. *Location and land use.* Cambridge, Mass.: Harvard University Press.

Althusser, L. 1971. *Lenin and philosophy and other essays.* New York: Monthly Review Press.

Althusser, L. and E. Balibar 1970. *Reading Capital.* London: New Left Books.

Altvater, E. 1978. Some problems of state interventionism. In *State and capital: a marxist debate,* J. Holloway & S. Picciotto (eds). London: Edward Arnold.

Anderson, P. 1974. *Lineages of the absolutist state.* London: New Left Books.

Andrew, E. 1982. Pierre Trudeau on the language of values and the value of languages, *Can. J. Polit. Social Theory* **6**, 143–59.

Anscombe, E. 1981. *Ethics, religion and politics.* Minneapolis: University of Minnesota Press.

Arrow, K. 1974. *The limits of organization.* New York: Norton.

Arnstein, S. 1969. A ladder of citizen participation. *J. Am. Plann. Assoc.* **35**, 216–27.

Aviram, V. and S. P. Segal 1973. Exclusion of the mentally ill. *Arch. Gen. Psych.* **29**, 126–31.

Bailyn, B. 1967. *The ideological origins of the American revolution.* Cambridge, Mass.: Harvard University Press.

Barabba, V. P. 1980. The demographic future of the cities of America. In *Cities and firms,* H. J. Bryce (ed.). Lexington, Mass.: Heath.

Bardach, E. 1977. *The implementation game.* Cambridge, Mass.: MIT Press.

Barry, B. 1978. *Sociologists, economists and democracy,* 2nd edn. Chicago: University of Chicago Press.

Baumol, W. 1965. *Welfare economics and the theory of the state,* 2nd edn. Cambridge, Mass.: Harvard University Press.

Beard, C. A. 1935. *An economic interpretation of the constitution of the United States.* New York: Macmillan.

Bennett, R. J. 1980. *The geography of public finance.* London: Methuen.

Berger, R. 1977. *Government by judiciary: the transformation of the fourteenth amendment.* Cambridge, Mass.: Harvard University Press.

196 BIBLIOGRAPHY

Bernstein, B. 1972. Social class, language and socialization. In *Language and social context*, D. Giglioli (ed.). Harmondsworth: Penguin.

Bickel, A. M. 1955. The original understanding and the segregation decision. *Harvard Law Rev.* **69**, 1–64.

Binns, P. 1980. Review article: law and marxism. *Capital and Class* **10**, 100–13.

Blackstone, W. 1765. *Commentaries on the laws of England.* Oxford: Clarendon Press.

Bluestone, B. and B. Harrison 1982. *The deindustrialization of America.* New York: Basic Books.

Bobbio, N. 1978a. Are there alternatives to representative democracy? *Telos* **35**, 17–30.

Bobbio, N. 1978b. Why democracy? *Telos* **36**, 45–54.

Boggs, C. 1976. *Gramsci's marxism.* London: Pluto Press.

Bowles, S. and H. Gintis 1978. The invisible fist: have capitalism and democracy reached a parting of the ways? *Am. Econ. Rev.: Pap. Proc.* **68**, 358–64.

Brennan, W. J. 1977. State constitutions and the protection of individual rights. *Harvard Law Rev.* **90**, 489–504.

Brest, P. 1980. The misconceived quest for the original understanding. *Boston Univ. Law Rev.* **60**, 204–58.

Brest, P. 1982. Interpretation and interest. *Stanford Law Rev.* **34**, 765–93.

Broadbent, T. A. 1977. *Planning and profit in the urban economy.* London: Methuen.

Brown, E. J. 1957. The open economy: Justice Frankfurter and the position of the judiciary. *Yale Law J.* **67**, 219–39.

Brown, P. and C. Fraser 1979. Speech as a marker of social situation. In *Social markers in speech*, K. R. Scherer & H. Giles (eds). Cambridge/Paris: Cambridge University Press and Editions de la Maison des Sciences de l'Homme.

Buchanan, J. M. 1974. Good economics – bad law. *Virginia Law Rev.* **69**, 483–91.

Buchanan, J. M. and G. Tullock 1962. *The calculus of consent.* Ann Arbor: University of Michigan Press.

Bureau of the Census 1977. *Governmental finances in 1975–76.* Washington, DC: US Department of Commerce.

Bureau of the Census 1980. *Conference on census undercount.* Washington, DC: US Department of Commerce.

Byrne, D. 1982. Class and the local state: *Int. J. Urban Reg. Res.* **6**, 61–92.

Calabresi, G. and A. D. Melamed 1972. Property rules, liability rules, and inalienability: óne view of the cathedral. *Harvard Law Rev.* **85**, 1089–128.

Canada 1982. *The charter rights and freedoms: a guide for Canadians.* Ottawa: Minister of Supply and Services Canada.

Castel, R. 1976. *L'ordre psychiatrique.* Paris: Editions de Minuit.

Castel, R., F. Castel and A. Lovell 1982. *The psychiatric society.* New York: Columbia University Press.

Castells, M. 1976. Theory and ideology in urban sociology. In *Urban sociology critical essays*, C. Pickvance (ed.). London: Tavistock.

Castells, M. 1977. *The urban question: a marxist approach.* London: Edward Arnold.

Cave, N. S. 1978. Participation and policy. *Ethics* **88**, 316–37.

Chomsky, N. A. 1973. *The backroom boys.* London: Fontana/Collins.

Choper, J. H. 1980. *Judicial review and the national political process: a functional reconsideration of the role of the Supreme Court.* Chicago: University of Chicago Press.

BIBLIOGRAPHY

Chorney, H. and P. Hansen 1980. The falling rate of legitimation: the problem of the contemporary capitalist state in Canada. *Stud. Polit. Econ.* **4**, 65–98.

Clark, G. L. 1980a. Urban impact analysis. *Prof. Geogr* **32**, 82–5.

Clark, G. L. 1980b. Capitalism and regional disparities. *Ann. Assoc. Am. Geogs.* **70**, 226–37.

Clark, G. L. 1981a. The employment relation and spatial division of labor: a hypothesis. *Ann. Assoc. Am. Geogs* **71**, 391–412.

Clark, G. L. 1981b. Regional economic systems, spatial interdependence and the role of money. In *Industrial location and regional systems*, J. Rees, G. J. D. Hewings and H. Stafford (eds). New York: Bergin.

Clark, G. L. 1981c. Law, the state, and the spatial integration of the United States. *Environ. Plann. A* **13**, 1197–232.

Clark, G. L. 1981d. Democracy and the capitalist state: towards a critique of the Tiebout hypothesis. In *Political studies from spatial perspectives: Anglo-American essays on political geography*, A. Burnett and P. J. Taylor (eds). New York: Wiley.

Clark, G. L. 1982. Rights, property and community. *Econ. Geog.* **57**, 120–38.

Clark, G. L. 1983. *Interregional migration, national policy, and social justice.* Totowa, NJ: Rowman and Allanheld.

Clark, G. L. 1984a. A theory of local autonomy. *Ann. Assoc. Am. Geogs.* (forthcoming).

Clark, G. L. 1984b. Local autonomy and the spatial structure of political discourse. In *Social relations and spatial structures*, D. Gregory and J. Urry (eds). London: Macmillan.

Clark, G. L. and M. Dear 1981. The state in capitalism and the capitalist state. In *Urbanization and urban planning in capitalist society*, M. Dear and A. J. Scott (eds). London: Methuen.

Clark, R. C. 1981. The four stages of capitalism: reflections on investment management treatises. *Harvard Law Rev.* **94**, 561–82.

Coase, R. 1960. The problem of social cost. *J. Law Econ.* **3**, 1–14.

Coase, R. 1974. The lighthouse in economics. *J. Law Econ.* **17**, 334–42.

Cockburn, C. 1977. *The local state.* London: Pluto Press.

Community Services Administration 1979. *Geographic distribution of federal funds in Massachusetts.* Washington, DC: Office of the President.

Congressional Budget Office 1980. *Community development block grants: reauthorization issues.* Washington, DC: Congress of the United States.

Connerton, P. (ed.) 1976. *Critical sociology.* Harmondsworth: Penguin.

Cooke, J. E. (ed.) 1976. *The Federalist.* Middletown: Wesleyan University Press.

Cooter, R. 1982. The cost of Coase. *J. Legal Stud.* **11**, 1–33.

Corrigan, P. 1979. The local state: the struggle for democracy. *Marxism Today* **23**, 7, 203–9.

Cox, A. 1976. *The role of the Supreme Court in American government.* Oxford: Oxford University Press.

Cox, A. 1981. Review of *Democracy and distrust* by John H. Ely. *Harvard Law Rev.* **94**, 700–16.

Crosskey, W. W. 1953. *Politics and the constitution in the history of the United States.* Chicago: University of Chicago Press.

Crouch, C. 1979. The state, capital and liberal democracy. In *State and economy in contemporary capitalism*, C. Crouch (ed.). London: Croom Helm.

Crozier, M. 1982. *Strategies for change.* Cambridge, Mass.: MIT Press.

CSE State Group 1979. *Struggle over the state: cuts and restructuring in contemporary Britain.* London: CSE Books.

Cutler, A., B. Hindess, P. Hirst and A. Hussain 1977. *Marx's Capital and capitalism today.* London: Routledge and Kegan Paul.

198 BIBLIOGRAPHY

Dahl, R. A. 1956. *Preface to democratic theory*. Chicago: University of Chicago Press.

Dahrendorf, R. 1959. *Class and class conflict in industrial society*. Stanford: Stanford University Press.

Dear, M. 1977. Psychiatric patients and the inner city. *Ann. Assoc. Am. Geogs.* **67**, 588–94.

Dear, M. 1981a. A theory of the local state. In *Political studies from spatial perspectives: Anglo-American essays on political geography*, A. Burnett and P. J. Taylor (eds). New York: Wiley.

Dear, M. 1981b. The state: a research agenda. *Environ. Plann. A* **13**.

Dear, M. 1981c. Social and spatial reproduction of the mentally ill. In *Urbanization and urban planning in capitalist societies*, M. Dear and A. Scott (eds). London: Methuen.

Dear, M. 1981d. The public city. In *Residential mobility and public policy*, W. A. V. Clark and E. Moore (eds). Beverly Hills: Sage.

Dear, M., L. Bayne, G. Boyd, E. Callaghan and E. Goldstein 1980. *Coping in the community: The needs of ex-psychiatric patients*. Hamilton: Canadian Mental Health Association.

Dear, M. and G. L. Clark 1978. The state and geographic process: a critical review. *Environ. Plann. A.* **10**, 173–83.

Dear, M. and G. L. Clark 1981. Dimensions of local state autonomy. *Environ. Plann. A* **13**, 1277–94.

Dear, M., R. Fincher and L. Currie 1977. Measuring the external effects of public programs. *Environ. Plann. A* **9**, 137–47.

Dear, M. and J. Long 1977. Community strategies in locational conflict. In *Urbanization and conflict in market societies*, K. Cox (ed.). Chicago: Maaroufa Press.

Dear, M. and A. J. Scott (eds) 1981. *Urbanization and urban planning in capitalist society*. London: Methuen.

Dear, M. and S. M. Taylor 1982. *Not on our street: community attitudes to mental health care*. London: Pion.

DeLeuze, G. and F. Guattari 1977. *Anti-Oedipus: capitalism and schizophrenia*. New York: Viking Press.

Deutsch, A. 1949. *The mentally ill in America*. New York: Columbia University Press.

Dillon, J. 1911. *Commentaries on the law of municipal corporations*. Boston: Little, Brown.

Donzelot, J. 1979. *The policing of families*. New York: Pantheon.

Downs, A. 1957. *An economic theory of democracy*. New York: Harper & Row.

Duncan, S. S. and M. Goodwin 1982. The local state: functionalism, autonomy and class relations in Cockburn and Saunders. *Polit. Geog. Q.* **1**, 77–96.

Dworkin, R. 1972. Social rules and legal theory. *Yale Law J.* **81**, 855–90.

Dworkin, R. 1977. *Taking rights seriously*. Cambridge, Mass.: Harvard University Press.

Dworkin, R. 1981. What is equality: part I, equality of welfare; part II, equality of resources. *Phil. Public. Affairs* **10**, 185–246, 283–345.

Dye, T. 1972. *Understanding public policy*. Englewood Cliffs, NJ: Prentice-Hall.

Edelman, B. 1979. *Ownership of the image: elements for a Marxist theory of law* (transl. E. Kingdom). Boston: Routledge and Kegan Paul.

Edelman, M. 1964. *The symbolic use of politics*. Urbana: University of Illinois Press.

Edelman, M. 1975. Language, myths and rhetoric. *Society* **12**(5), 14–21.

Edelman, M. 1977. *Political language*. New York: Academic Press.

BIBLIOGRAPHY 199

Eisenmenger, R. W., A. H. Munnell and J. T. Poskanzer 1975. *Options for fiscal structure reform in Massachusetts*. Boston: Federal Reserve Bank of Boston.

Ely, J. 1980. *Democracy and distrust: a theory of judicial review*. Cambridge, Mass.: Harvard University Press.

Engels, F. 1972. *The origin of family, private property and the state*. New York: International Publishers.

Erikson, K. T. 1967. Notes on the sociology of deviance. In *Mental illness and social process*, T. J. Scheff (ed.). New York: Harper & Row.

Esland, G. 1980a. Diagnosis and therapy. In *The politics of work and occupations*, E. Esland and G. Soloman (eds). Toronto: University of Toronto Press.

Esland, G. 1980b. Professions and professionalism. In *The politics of work and occupations*, E. Esland and G. Soloman (eds). Toronto: University of Toronto Press.

Esping-Anderson, G., R. Friedland and E. O. Wright 1976. Modes of class struggle and the capitalist state. *Kapitalstate* 4/5, 186–220.

The Federalist papers 1961. With an introduction by C. Rossiter. New York: Mentor Books.

Ferraresi, F. 1981. *The institutional transformation of post laissez-faire state*. Paper presented at a conference on "Organization, Economy and Society." Brisbane: Griffith University.

Fincher, R. 1979. *The local state and the urban built environment: the case of Boston in late capitalism*. Unpubl. PhD dissertation. Worcester: Department of Geography, Clark University.

Fincher, R. 1981. Locational implementation strategies in the urban built environment. *Environ. Plann. A* **13**, 1233–52.

Fish, S. 1980. *Is there a text in this class? The theory of interpretive communities*. Cambridge, Mass.: Harvard University Press.

Fiss, O. 1982. Objectivity and interpretation. *Stanford Law Rev.* **34**, 739–63.

Foucault, M. 1965. *Madness and civilization: a history of insanity in the age of reason*. New York: Vintage Books.

Foucault, M. 1977a. *Discipline and punishment: the birth of the prison*. New York: Pantheon.

Foucault, M. 1977b. *Language, counter-memory and practice*. D. F. Bouchard (ed.). Ithaca: Cornell University Press.

Frankel, B. 1978. *Marxian theories of the state: a critique of orthodoxy*. Melbourne: Arena Publications Association.

Freedman, J. O. 1978. *Crisis and legitimacy: the administrative process and American government*. Cambridge: Cambridge University Press.

Freeman, J. O. 1978. *Crisis and legitimacy*. Cambridge: Cambridge University Press.

Friedland, R., F. E. Piven and R. R. Alford 1977. Political conflict, urban structure and the fiscal crisis. *Int. J. Urban Reg. Res.* **1**, 447–71.

Friedman, L. M. 1965. Law, rules and the interpretation of written documents. *Univ. Chicago Law Rev.* **59**, 751–80.

Friedman, L. M. 1973. *A history of American law*. New York: Simon and Schuster.

Friedson, E. 1970. *Professional dominance*. Chicago: Aldine.

Frug, G. E. 1980. The city as a legal concept. *Harvard Law Rev.* **93**, 1057–154.

Gabel, D. 1977. Intention and structure in contractual conditions: outline of a method for critical legal theory. *Minnesota Law Rev.* **61**, 601–43.

Galanter, M. 1974. Why the 'haves' come out ahead: speculations on the limits of legal change. *Law and Society* **9**, 95–160.

200   BIBLIOGRAPHY

Galston, W. A. 1980. *Justice and the human good*. Chicago: University of Chicago Press.
Gaylin, W. *et al.* 1978. *Doing good: the limits of benevolence*. New York: Pantheon.
Giddens, A. 1973. *The class structure of the advanced societies*. London: Hutchinson.
Giddens, A. 1981. *A contemporary critique of historical materialism*. Berkeley: University of California Press.
Giglioli, P. 1972. *Language and social context*. Harmondsworth: Penguin.
Giles, H. *et al.* 1979. Speech markers in social interaction. In *Social markers in speech*, K. R. Scherer and H. Giles (eds). Cambridge/Paris: Cambridge University Press and Editions de la Maison des Sciences de l'Homme.
Gintis, H. 1980. Communication and politics: marxism and the problem of liberal democracy. *Socialist Rev.* **10**, 189–232.
Glickman, N. J. (ed.) 1979. *Urban impact analysis*. Baltimore: Johns Hopkins University Press.
Goebel, J. 1978. King's law and local custom in seventeenth century New England. In *American law and the constitutional order*, L. M. Friedman and H. N. Scheiber (eds). Cambridge, Mass.: Harvard University Press.
Gold, D. A., C. Y. H. Lo and E. O. Wright 1975. Recent developments in marxist theories of the capitalist state. *Monthly Rev.* **27(5)**, 29–43, **(6)**, 36–51.
Gotkin, J. and P. Gotkin 1975. *Too much anger, too many tears: A personal triumph over psychiatry*. New York: Quadrangle/New York Times Book Co.
Gough, I. 1979. *The political economy of the welfare state*. London: Macmillan.
Gramsci, A. 1971. *Selections from the prison notebooks*. New York: International Publishers.
Gregory, D. 1978. *Science, ideology and human geography*. London: Hutchinson.
Grob, G. N. 1973. *Mental institutions in America: Social policy to 1875*. New York: Free Press.
Gumperz, J. 1972. The speech community. In *Language and social context*, P. Giglioli (ed.). Harmondsworth: Penguin.
Gunther, G. (ed.) 1969. *John Marshall's defense of McCullock v. Maryland*. Stanford: Stanford University Press.

Haar, C. and L. Liebman 1977. *Property and law*. Boston: Little, Brown.
Habermas, J. 1970. *Toward a rational society*. Boston: Beacon Press.
Habermas, J. 1971. *Knowledge and human interests*. Boston: Beacon Press.
Habermas, J. 1974. *Theory and practice*. Boston: Beacon Press.
Habermas, J. 1975. *Legitimation crisis*. Boston: Beacon Press.
Habermas, J. 1976. Problems of legitimation in late capitalism. In *Critical sociology*, P. Connerton (ed.). Harmondsworth: Penguin.
Habermas, J. 1979. *Communication and the evolution of society* (transl. T. McCarthy). Boston: Beacon Press.
Habermas, J. 1982. A reply to my critics. In *Habermas: critical debates*, J. B. Thompson and D. Held (eds). Cambridge, Mass.: MIT Press.
Hacker, P. 1977. Hart's philosophy of law. In *Law, morality and society*, P. Hacker and J. Raz (eds). Oxford: Clarendon Press.
Hall, S. 1977. Culture, the media and the 'ideological effect'. In *Mass communication and society*, J. Curran *et al.* (eds). London: Edward Arnold.
Halliday, M. A. 1974. *Exploration in the functions of language*. London. Edward Arnold.
Halliday, M. A. 1976. Anti-languages. *UEA Papers in Linguistics* **1**, 15–45.
Hampshire, S. 1977. *Two theories of morality*. Oxford: Oxford University Press.
Harsanyi, J. C. 1977. *Rational behavior and bargaining equilibrium in games and social situations*. Cambridge: Cambridge University Press.

BIBLIOGRAPHY

201

Hart, H. L. A. 1972. Bentham on legal powers. *Yale Law J.* **81**, 799–822.

Hart, H. L. A. 1976. Bentham and the United States of America. *J. Law Econ.* **19**, 547–67.

Hart, H. L. A. 1979. *The concept of law.* Oxford: Oxford University Press.

Hart, H. M. 1954. Professor Crosskey and judicial review. *Harvard Law Rev.* **67**, 1456–86.

Hartz, L. 1955. *The liberal tradition in America.* New York: Harcourt, Brace and World.

Harvard Law Review Association 1976. *A uniform system of citation,* 12th edn. Avon: Lovell Press.

Harvard Law Review Association 1980. The right to travel – residence requirements and former residents: *Fisher v. Reiser. Harvard Law Rev.* **93**, 1585–94.

Harvey, D. 1975. Class structure in capitalist society and the theory of residential differentiation. In *Processes in physical and human geography,* R. Peel, M. Chisholm, and P. Haggett (eds). London: Heinemann.

Harvey, D. 1976. The marxian theory of the state. *Antipode* **8**, 80–98.

Harvey, D. 1982. *The limits to capital.* Chicago: University of Chicago Press.

Harvey, D. and L. Chatterjee 1974. Absolute rent and the structuring of space by governmental and financial institutions. *Antipode* **6**, 22–36.

Held, D. 1980. *Introduction to critical theory.* Berkeley: University of California Press.

Heller, T. C. 1981. *The meanings of bilingualism.* Unpubl. paper. Stanford: Stanford Law School.

Hendel, C. W. 1958. An exploration of the nature of authority. In *Authority,* C. J. Friedrich (ed.). Cambridge, Mass.: Harvard University Press.

Hindess, B. and P. Hirst 1975. *Pre-capitalist modes of production.* London: Routledge and Kegan Paul.

Hindess, B. and P. Hirst 1977. *Modes of production and social formation.* London: Macmillan.

Hirsch, J. 1978. The state apparatus and social reproduction: elements of a theory of the bourgeois state. In *State and capital,* J. Holloway and S. Picciotto (eds). London: Edward Arnold.

Hirsch, J. 1981. The apparatus of the state, the reproduction of capital, and urban conflicts. In *Urbanization and urban planning in capitalist society,* M. Dear and A. J. Scott (eds). London: Methuen.

Hirschman, A. O. 1970. *Exit, voice, and loyalty.* Cambridge, Mass.: Harvard University Press.

Hist. Workshop J. 1980. Editorial: language and history. **10**, 1–5.

Holloway, J. and S. Picciotto (eds) 1978. *State and capital: a marxist debate.* London: Edward Arnold.

Holmes, O. W. 1899. The theory of legal interpretation. *Harvard Law Rev.* **46**, 417–20.

Hookway, C. and P. Pettit (eds) 1978. *Action and interpretation: studies in the philosophy of social sciences.* Cambridge: Cambridge University Press.

Horowitz, I. L. 1983. From the New Deal to the New Federalism: Presidential ideology in the US from 1932 to 1982. *Am. J. Econ. Soc.* **42**, 129–48.

Horwitz, M. J. 1977. *The transformation of American law 1789–1860.* Cambridge, Mass.: Harvard University Press.

Horwitz, M. J. 1979. The jurisprudence of Brown and the dilemmas of liberalism. *Harv. Civil Rights – Civil Lib. Law Rev.* **14**, 598–613.

Hudson, K. 1978. *The language of modern politics.* London: Macmillan.

Huntington, S. 1959. The founding fathers and the division of power. In *Area and power: a theory of local government,* A. Maass (ed.). Glencoe, Ill.: Free Press.

BIBLIOGRAPHY

Huntington, S. 1975. The crisis of democracy: the United States. In *The crisis of democracy*, M. Crozier, S. Huntington and J. Watanuki (eds). New York: New York University Press.

Huntington, S. 1981. *American politics: the promise of disharmony*. Cambridge, Mass.: Harvard University Press.

Hurst, J. W. 1967. *Law and the conditions of freedom in the nineteenth century United States*. Madison: University of Wisconsin Press.

Hurst, J. W. 1973. *A legal history of money in the United States, 1774–1970*. Lincoln: University of Nebraska Press.

Ignatieff, M. 1978. *A just measure of pain: The penitentiary in the industrial revolution, 1750–1850*. New York: Pantheon Books.

Illich, I. *et al.* 1977. *Disabling professions*. London: Marion Boyars.

Inman, R. P. and D. L. Rubinfeld 1979. The judicial pursuit of local fiscal equity. *Harvard Law Rev*. **92**, 1662–750.

Jessop, R. 1977. Recent theories of the capitalist state. *Cambridge J. Econ*. **1**, 353–73.

Jessop, R. 1978. Capitalism and democracy: the best possible political shell. In *Power and the state*, G. Littlejohn, *et al*. (eds). London: Croom Helm.

Jessop, R. 1980. The transformation of the state in postwar Britain. In *The state in western Europe*, R. Scase (ed.). London: Croom Helm.

Jessop, R. 1982. *The capitalist state*. New York: New York University Press.

Johnston, R. J. 1979. *Political, electoral and spatial systems*. Oxford: Clarendon Press.

Johnston, R. J. 1982. *The geography of the United States*. New York: Methuen.

Johnston, R. J. 1983. *Geography and the state*. London: Macmillan.

Jones, K. 1972. *A history of the mental health services*. London: Routledge and Kegan Paul.

Jones, K. and K. Williamson 1979. The birth of the schoolroom. *Ideology and Consciousness* **6**, 59–110.

Katznelson, I. 1981. *City trenches: urban politics and the patterning of class in the United States*. New York: Pantheon.

Kemp, R. 1980. Planning, legitimation and the development of nuclear energy. *Int. J. Urban Reg. Res*. **43**, 350–77.

Kennedy, David 1980. Book review of *How nations behave* by L. Henkin, *Harvard Int. Law J*. **1**, 301–22.

Kennedy, Duncan 1976. Form and substance in private law adjudication. *Harvard Law Rev*. **89**, 1685–778.

Kennedy, Duncan 1979. The structure of Blackstone's commentaries. *Buffalo Law Rev*. **28**, 205–382.

King, L. J. and G. L. Clark 1978. Government policy and regional development. *Prog. Human Geog*. **2**, 1–16.

Kittrie, N. N. 1973. *The right to be different: deviance and enforced therapy*. New York: Penguin.

Kress, G. and R. Hodge 1979. *Language as ideology*. London: Routledge and Kegan Paul.

Laclau, E. 1975. The specificity of the political: the Poulantzas–Miliband debate. *Econ. Soc*. **5**, 87–111.

Landes, W. M. and R. A. Posner 1975. The independent judiciary in an interest group perspective. *J. Law. Econ*. **18**, 875–901.

BIBLIOGRAPHY

Lasch, C. 1979. *Haven in a heartless world: the family besieged*. New York: Harper & Row.

Leder, M. L. 1968. *Liberty and authority: early American political ideology, 1689–1763*. Chicago: Quadrangle Books.

Lefebvre, H. 1976. Reflections on the politics of space. *Antipode* **8**, 30–7.

Lemieux, M. 1977. *One hundred years of mental health law in Ontario*. Unpubl. paper, Hamilton Psychiatric Hospital, Hamilton, Ontario.

Lenin, V. I. 1949. *The state and revolution*. Moscow: Progress.

Levy, F. S., A. J. Meltzner and A. Wildavsky 1974. *Urban outcomes*. Berkeley: University of California Press.

Library of Congress 1973. *Constitution of the United States*. Washington, DC: US Government Printing Office.

Littlejohn, G. *et al.* (eds) 1978. *Power and the state*. London: Croom Helm.

Maass, A. 1959. Division of powers: an areal analysis. In *Area and power: a theory of local government*, A. Maass (ed.). Glencoe Ill.: Free Press.

MacAvoy, P. W. 1979. *The regulated industries and the economy*. New York: Norton.

MacPherson, C. B. 1973. *Democratic theory: essays in retrieval*. Oxford: Oxford University Press.

MacPherson, C. B. 1977. *The life and times of liberal democracy*. New York: Macmillan.

Magaro, P. A., R. Gripp and D. J. McDowell 1978. *The mental health industry: a cultural phenomenon*. New York: Wiley Interscience.

Mahon, R. 1980. Regulatory agencies: capitive agents or hegemonic apparatuses. In *Class, state, ideology and change*, J. P. Grayson (ed.). Toronto: Holt, Reinhart and Winston.

Maier, C. S. 1975. *Recasting bourgeois Europe: stabilization in France, Germany, and Italy in the decade after World War I*. Princeton, NJ: Princeton University Press.

Mandel, E. 1975. *Late capitalism*, transl. and revised edn. London: New Left Books.

Marcuse, H. 1964. *One-dimensional man*. London: Sphere.

Martin, R. M. 1983. Pluralism and the new corporatism. *Polit. Stud.* **31**, 86–102.

Marx, K. 1971 edn. *Capital*, 3 vols. Moscow: Progress.

Marx K. and F. Engels 1967 edn. *The Communist Manifesto*, A. J. P. Taylor (ed.). Harmondsworth: Penguin.

McBain, M. L. 1916. The doctrine of an inherent right of local self government. *Columbia Law Rev.* **16**, 190–299.

McCormick, A. E. 1979. Dominant class interests and the emergence of antitrust legislation. *Contemporary Crises* **3**, 399–417.

McKnight, J. 1977. Professionalized service and disabling help. In *Disabling professions*, I. Illich, I. K. Zola, J. McKnight, J. Coplar and H. Shaikei (eds). London: Marion Boyars.

Michelman, F. I. 1977. Political markets and community self-determination: competing judicial models of local government legitimacy. *Indiana Law J.* **53**, 145–206.

Michelman, F. I. 1979. A comment on 'some uses and abuses of economics.' *Univ. Chicago Law Rev.* **46**, 307–15.

Miliband, R. 1973. *The state in capitalist society*. New York: Basic Books.

Miliband, R. 1977. *Marxism and politics*. Oxford: Oxford University Press.

Miller, P. 1980. The territory of the psychiatrist. *Ideology and Consciousness* **7**, 63–106.

Miller, P. 1981. Psychiatry – the renegotiation of territory. *Ideology and Consciousness* **8**, 97–122.

BIBLIOGRAPHY

Mollenkopf, J. 1981. Community and accumulation. In *Urbanization and urban planning in capitalist society*, M. Dear and A. J. Scott (eds). London: Methuen.

Morawetz, T. 1980. *The philosophy of law*. New York: Macmillan.

Murray, R. 1977. The internalization of capital and the nation–state. *New Left Rev*. **67**, 84–109.

Musgrave, R. A. and P. B. 1980. *Public finance in theory and practice*. New York: McGraw–Hill.

Nathan, R. P. 1978. The outlook for federal grants to cities. In *The fiscal outlook for cities: the implications of a national urban policy*, R. Bahl (ed.). Syracuse: University of Syracuse Press.

The National Times 1980. July 12–18, p. 55. Australia.

Nettels, C. 1962. *The emergence of a national economy, 1775–1815*. New York: Holt, Rinehart and Winston.

Nordlinger, E. A. 1981. *On the autonomy of the democratic state*. Cambridge, Mass.: Harvard University Press.

Nozick, R. 1974. *State, anarchy and utopia*. New York: Basic Books.

Nozick, R. 1981. *Philosophical explanations*. Cambridge, Mass.: Harvard University Press.

Oakland, W. 1979. Discussant on a paper by White and Wittman. In *Essays on the law and economics of local governments*, D. L. Rubinfeld (ed.). Washington, DC: The Urban Institute.

O'Connor, J. 1973. *The fiscal crisis of the state*. New York: St Martin's Press.

Offe, C. 1974. Structural problems of the capitalist state. In *German Polit. Stud.* Vol. 1, K. Von Beyme (ed.). London: Sage.

Offe, C. 1975. The theory of the capitalist state and the problem of policy formation. In *Stress and contradiction in modern capitalism*, L. N. Lindberg, *et al.* (eds). Lexington, Mass.: Heath.

Offe, C. and V. Ronge 1975. Theses on the theory of the state. *New German Crit.* **6**, 137–47.

Offe, C. 1976. Political authority and class structures. In *Critical sociology*, P. Connerton (ed.). Harmondsworth: Penguin.

Olson, M. 1965. *The logic of collective action*. Cambridge, Mass.: Harvard University Press.

Olsson, M. 1980. *Birds in egg, eggs in bird*. London: Pion.

Orwell, G. 1954. *Nineteen eighty-four*. Harmondsworth: Penguin.

Orwell, G. 1968. Politics and the English language. In *Collected essays, journalism and letters of George Orwell, Vol. IV*. London: Secker & Warburg.

Ostrom, V., C. Tiebout and R. Warren 1961. The organization of government in metropolitan areas. *Am. Polit. Sci. Rev.* **55**, 821–42.

The Oxford Universal Dictionary 1955. Oxford: Oxford University Press.

Panitch, L. 1980. Recent theorizations of corporatism. *Br. J. Social.* **31**, 159–87.

Panitch, L. 1981. Trade unions and the state. *New Left Rev*. **125**, 21–44.

Panzor, J. C. 1980. Regulation, deregulation and economic efficiency: the case of CAB. *Am. Econ. Rev.* **70**, 311–15.

Papageorgiou, G. J. 1978. Political aspects of social justice and physical planning in an abstract city. *Geogl Anal.* **10**, 378–85.

Papageorgiou, G. J. 1980. Social values and social justice. *Econ. Geog.* **56**, 110–19.

Paris, C. 1983. The myth of urban politics. *Environ. Plann. D.: Society and Space* **1**, 89–108.

BIBLIOGRAPHY

Paskukanis, E. B. 1978. *Law and marxism*. London: Ink Links.

Pateman, C. 1970. *Participation and democratic theory*. Cambridge: Cambridge University Press.

Pateman, C. 1979. *The problem of political obligation: a critical analysis of liberal theory*. Chichester: Wiley.

Pateman, T. 1975. *Language, truth and politics*. Nottingham: Stroud and Pateman.

Peet, R. 1975. Inequality and poverty: a marxist–geographic inquiry. *Ann. Assoc. Am. Geogs* **65**, 564–71.

Piven, F. and R. Cloward 1971. *Regulating the poor: the functions of public welfare*. New York: Pantheon.

Pocock, J. G. A. 1975. *The machiavellian moment: Florentine political thought and the Atlantic republican tradition*. Princeton: Princeton University Press.

Poggi, G. 1978. *The development of the modern state: a sociological introduction*. London: Hutchinson.

Pole, J. R. 1980. *American individualism and the promise of progress*. Oxford: Clarendon Press.

Polinsky, A. M. 1974. Economic analysis as a potentially defective product: a buyers guide to Posner's *The economics of law. Harvard Law Rev.* **87**, 1655–81.

Portis, E. B. 1983. Max Weber and the unity of normative and empirical theory. *Polit. Stud.* **31**, 25–42.

Posner, R. A. 1976. Blackstone and Bentham. *J. Law Econ.* **19**, 569–606.

Posner, R. A. 1977. *Economic analysis of law*, 2nd edn. Boston: Little, Brown.

Posner, R. A. 1979. Some uses and abuses of economics in law. *Univ. Chicago Law Rev.* **46**, 281–306.

Posner, R. A. 1981. *An economic theory of justice*. Cambridge, Mass.: Harvard University Press.

Poulantzas, N. 1969. The problem of the capitalist state. *New Left Rev.* **58**, 67–78.

Poulantzas, N. 1973a. *Political power and social classes*. London: New Left Books.

Poulantzas, N. 1973b. On social classes. *New Left Rev.* **78**, 27–35, 37–39, 47–50.

Poulantzas, N. 1978. *State, power, socialism*. London: New Left Books.

Pred, A. R. 1973. *Urban growth and the circulation of information; the United States system of cities, 1790–1840*. Cambridge, Mass.: Harvard University Press.

Purcell, E. A. 1973. *The crisis of democratic theory: scientific naturalism and the problem of value*. Lexington: University of Kentucky Press.

Putnam, H. 1981. *Reason, truth and history*. Cambridge: Cambridge University Press.

Rabkin, J. 1972. Opinions about mental illness. *Psychol. Bull.* **77**, 153–71.

Rae, D. *et al.* 1982. *Equalities*. Cambridge, Mass.: Harvard University Press.

Rawls, J. 1971. *A theory of justice*. Cambridge, Mass.: Harvard University Press.

Reich, M. and R. Edwards 1978. Political parties and class conflict in the United States. *Socialist Rev.* **8**, 37–57.

Rein, M. 1969. Social planning: the search for legitimacy. *J. Am. Plann. Assoc.* **35**, 233–44.

Reynolds, G. G. 1928. *The distribution of power to regulate interstate carriers between the nation and the state*. New York: Columbia University Press.

Ribble, F. D. G. 1937. *State and national power over commerce*. New York: Columbia University Press.

Ricoeur, P. 1981. *Hermeneutics and the human society*, J. B. Thompson (ed.). Cambridge/Paris: Cambridge University Press and Editions de la Maison des Sciences de l'Homme.

Robinson, W. P. 1972. *Language and social behavior*. Harmondsworth: Penguin.

BIBLIOGRAPHY

Roemer, J. 1981. *Analytical foundations of marxian economic theory*. Cambridge: Cambridge University Press.

Rosen, G. 1968. *Madness in society*. Chicago: University of Chicago Press.

Rosenzweig, N. 1975. *Community mental health programs in England: an American view*. Detroit: Wayne State University Press.

Rothman, D. J. 1971. *The discovery of the asylum: social order and disorder in the new republic*. Boston, Mass.: Little, Brown.

Rothman, D. J. 1978. The state as parent: social policy in the progressive era. In *Doing good: the limits of benevolence*, W. Gaylin, I. Glasser, S. Moran and J. Rothman (eds). New York: Pantheon.

Rothman, D. J. 1980. *Conscience and convenience: the asylum and its alternatives in progressive America*. Boston: Little, Brown.

Roweis, S. 1981. Urban planning in early and late capitalist society. In *Urbanization and urban planning in capitalist society*, M. Dear and A. J. Scott (eds). London: Methuen.

Ryan, J. and F. Thomas 1980. *The politics of mental handicap*. Harmondsworth: Penguin Books.

Ryan, M. 1982. *Marxism and deconstruction: a critical articulation*. Baltimore: Johns Hopkins University Press.

Said, E. W. 1983. *The world, the text, and the critic*. Cambridge, Mass.: Harvard University Press.

Samuels, W. J. 1971. Interrelationships between legal and economic processes. *J. Law Econ.* **14**, 435–50.

Sandalow, T. 1964. The limits of municipal power under home rule: a rôle for the courts. *Minnesota Law Rev.* **48**, 643–721.

Saunders, P. 1980. *Urban politics: a sociological interpretation*. Harmondsworth: Penguin.

Saunders, P. 1981. *Social theory and the urban question*. London: Hutchinson.

Saunders, P. 1983. On the shoulders of which giant? The case for Weberian political analysis. In *Social process and the city: urban studies yearbook 1*, P. Williams (ed.). Sydney: George Allen & Unwin.

Saussure, F. de 1966. *Course in general linguistics* (transl. from original 1916 edition by W. Baskin). New York: McGraw Hill.

Scanlon, T. 1976. Nozick on rights, liberty and property. *Phil. Public Affairs* **6**, 3–25.

Scase, R. (ed.) 1980. *The state in western Europe*. London: Croom Helm.

Scherer, K. R. and H. Giles (eds) 1979. *Social markers in speech*. Cambridge/Paris: Cambridge University Press and Editions de la Maison des Sciences de l'Homme.

Schmidt, P. 1965. Democracy's scrap heap: the rehabilitation of long-term patients. *Canada's Mental Health*, Supplement 46.

Scott, A. J. 1980. *The urban land nexus and the state*. London: Pion.

Scull, A. T. 1977. *Decarceration: community treatment of the deviant – a radical view*. Englewood Cliffs, NJ: Prentice-Hall.

Scull, A. T. 1979. *Museums of madness: the social organization of insanity in nineteenth-century England*. London: Allen Lane.

Segal, D. 1977. *Urban economics*. Homewood: R. D. Irwin.

Segal, S. P. and U. Aviram 1978. *The mentally ill in community-based sheltered care*. New York: Wiley.

Seley, J. and J. Wolpert 1977. A strategy of ambiguity in locational conflict. In *Locational approaches to power and conflict*, K. R. Cox, D. R. Reynolds and S. Rokkan (eds). New York: Wiley.

BIBLIOGRAPHY

207

Sennett, R. 1980. *Authority*. New York: Knopf.
Shapira, P. 1979. *The uneven economy and the state in Massachusetts*. Unpubl. MCP thesis, Cambridge, Mass.: Department of Urban Studies and Planning, Massachusetts Institute of Technology.
Sholley, J. B. 1936. The negative implications of the commerce clause. *Univ. Chicago Law Rev.* **45**, 556–96.
Siggins, M. 1982. Madness in South Parkdale. *Today Magazine*, March 6, 6–10.
Simon, B. 1978. *Mind and madness in ancient Greece*. Ithaca: Cornell University Press.
Skocpol, T. 1979. *States and social revolutions*. Cambridge: Cambridge University Press.
Smith, C. J. 1976. Residential neighborhoods as humane environments. *Environ. Plann. A* **8**, 311–26.
Smith, D. 1977. *Geography and human welfare*. London: Edward Arnold.
Smith, N. and D. Wilson 1979. *Modern linguistics: the results of Chomsky's revolution*. Harmondsworth: Penguin.
Soja, E. W. 1978. *Topian marxism and spatial praxis: a reconstruction of the political economy of space*. Paper presented at the annual meeting of the Association of American Geographers, New Orleans.
Solberg, W. U. (ed.) 1958. *The federal convention and the formation of the Union of the American States*. New York: Bobbs-Merrill.
Sontag, S. 1978. *Illness as metaphor*. New York: Farrar, Straus and Giroux.
Spencer, H. 1882. *Social statics*. New York: Appleton.
Stepan, A. 1978. *The state and society: Peru in comparative perspective*. Princeton: Princeton University Press.
Stern, R. L. 1934. That commerce which concerns more states than one. *Harvard Law Rev.* **47**, 1335–66.
Stern, R. L. 1946. The commerce clause and the national economy, 1933–1946. *Harvard Law Rev.* **59**, 645–93, 883–947.
Storing, H. J. 1981. *What the Anti-Federalists were for: the political thought of the opponents of the Constitution*. Chicago: Chicago University Press.

Teitz, M. B. 1978. Law as a variable in urban and regional analysis. *Papers, Reg. Sci. Assoc.* **41**, 29–41.
Therborn, G. 1976. What does the ruling class do when it rules? *The Insurgent Sociologist* **6**(3), 3–16.
Therborn, G. 1978. *What does the ruling class do when it rules?* London: New Left Books.
Therborn, G. 1980. *The ideology of power and the power of ideology*. London: Verso.
Thompson, E. P. 1975. *Whigs and hunters: the origins of the Black Act*. New York: Pantheon.
Thompson, J. D. and G. Goldin 1975. *The hospital: a social and architectural history*. New Haven: Yale University Press.
Tiebout, C. 1956. A pure theory of local government expenditures. *J. Polit. Econ.* **64**, 416–24.
Tribe, L. H. 1976. Intergovernmental immunities in litigation, taxation, and regulation: separation of powers issues in controversies about federalism. *Harvard Law Rev.* **89**, 682–713.
Tribe, L. H. 1978. *American constitutional law*. New York: Foundation Press.
Tribe, L. H. 1979. *Supplement*. New York: Foundation Press.
Tribe, L. H. 1980. The puzzling persistence of process-based constitutional theories. *Yale Law J.* **89**, 1063–80.

BIBLIOGRAPHY

Trubek, D. M. 1972. Max Weber on law and the rise of capitalism. *Wisconsin Law Rev.* **3**, 720–53.
Trute, B. and S. P. Segal 1977. Census tract predictors and the social integration of sheltered care residents. *Social Psych.* **11**, 153–61.
Tufte, R. 1978. *Political control of the economy.* Princeton: Princeton University Press.
Tushnet, M. 1980. Darkness on the edge of town: the contributions of John Hart Ely to constitutional theory. *Yale Law J.* **89**, 1037–62.

Unger, R. M. 1975. *Knowledge and politics.* New York: Free Press.
Unger, R. M. 1981. *Politics.* Cambridge, Mass.: Harvard University Law School.
Unger, R. M. 1983. The critical legal studies movement. *Harvard Law Rev.* **96**, 563–675.
Urry, J. 1981. *The anatomy of capitalist society.* London: Macmillan.
U.S. Department of Housing and Urban Development 1980. *Local financial management in the '80s: techniques for responding to the new fiscal realities.* Washington, DC: Office of Policy Development and Research.

Verba, S. and N. Nie 1972. *Participation in America: political democracy and social equality.* New York: Harper and Row.

Walker, R. and M. Storper 1978. Erosion of the Clean Air Act of 1970: a study in the failure of government regulation and planning. *Boston College Environ. Affairs Law Rev.* **7**, 189–257.
Walzer, M. 1983. *Spheres of justice: a defense of pluralism and equality.* New York: Basic Books.
Westergaard, J. 1977. Class, inequality, and corporatism. In *Class and class structure,* A. Hunt (ed.). London: Lawrence and Wishart.
Whiteman, J. 1983. Deconstructing the Tiebout hypothesis. *Environ. Plann. D.: Society and Space* **1**, 339–54.
Wilby, P. 1979. Habermas and the language of the modern state. *New Society,* March 22, 667–9.
Williams, R. 1976a. *Keywords: a vocabulary of culture and society.* London: Fontana.
Williams, R. 1976b. *Communications,* 3rd edn. Harmondsworth: Penguin.
Williams, R. 1977. *Marxism and literature.* Oxford: Oxford University Press.
Williams, R. 1981. *Culture.* Glasgow: Fontana.
Wilson, J. Q. 1975. The rise of the bureaucratic state. *Public Interest* **41**, 77–103.
Wilson, J. Q. 1978. *The investigators: managing FBI and narcotics agents.* New York: Basic Books.
Wilson, J. Q. (ed.) 1980. *The politics of regulation.* New York: Basic Books.
Wittgenstein, L. 1961. *Philosophical investigations.* London: Macmillan.
Wolch, J. and S. Gabriel 1981. Urban housing prices and land development behavior of the local state. *Environ. Plann. A* **13**, 1253–76.
Wolfe, A. 1977. *The limits of legitimacy: political contradictions of contemporary capitalism.* New York: The Free Press.
Wolfensberger, W. 1972. *The principle of normalization in human services.* Toronto: National Institute on Mental Retardation.
Wood, G. 1969. *The creation of the American republic, 1776–1787.* New York: Norton.
Woogh, D. M., H. M. R. Meier and M. R. Eastwood 1977. Psychiatric hospitalization in Ontario: revolving door in perspective. *Can. Med. Assoc. J.* **116**, 876.

BIBLIOGRAPHY

Wright, E. O. 1978. *Class, crisis and the state*. London: New Left Books.

Yates, D. 1982. *Bureaucratic democracy*. Cambridge, Mass.: Harvard University Press.

Yinger, J. 1979. Estimating the relationship between location and the price of housing. *J. Reg. Sci.* **19**, 271–90.

Young, G. 1976. The fundamental contradiction of capitalist production. *Phil, Public Affairs* **5**, 196–234.

Zola, I. K. 1977. Healthism and disabling medication. In *Disabling professions*, I. Illich *et al.* (eds). London: Marion Boyars.

Author index

Achard, P. 97–8
Alcaly, R. E. and D. Mermelstein 135, 145
Allderidge, P. 74
Allen, P. 75
Althusser, L. 15–17, 45, 61–2, 134
Althusser, L. and E. Balibar 62
Altvater, E. 31
Anderson, P. 47
Andrew, E. 98
Anscombe, E. 190
Arrow, K. 178
Arnstein, S. 100
Aviram, V. and S. P. Segal 79

Bailyn, B. 160
Barabba, V. P. 144
Bardach, E. 10
Barry, B. 156
Baumol, W. 19
Beard, C. A. 117, 128
Bennett, R. J. 16, 18–19, 52, 131, 133
Berger, R. 117, 160, 177, 181, 192
Bernstein, B. 85–6, 95–6
Bickel, A. M. 108
Binns, P. 108
Blackstone, W. 117
Bluestone, B. and B. Harrison 129
Boggs, C. 136
Bowles, S. and H. Gintis 133, 156
Brennan, W. J. 125
Brest, P. 7, 108
Broadbent, T. A. 133, 134
Brown, E. J. 117, 121
Brown, P. and C. Fraser 86, 90
Buchanan, J. M. 104
Buchanan, J. M. and G. Tullock 21, 104, 192
Bureau of the Census 145, 148

Calabresi, G. and A. D. Melamed 3
Castel, R. 61, 68
Castel, R., F. Castel and A. Lovell 61
Cave, N. S. 154
Chomsky, N. A. 91
Choper, J. H. 162, 172–3, 177, 184
Clark, G. L. 119, 132, 139, 150, 154, 191
Coase, R. 191

Cockburn, C. 42, 51, 133–5
Community Services Administration 145
Congressional Budget Office 145
Cooter, R. 191
Corrigan, P. 51
Cox, A. 105, 109, 122
Crosskey, W. W. 109
Crouch, C. 37–9
Crozier, M. 176
CSE State Group 39–40, 55
Cutler, A., B. Hindess, P. Hirst and A. Hussain 64

Dahl, R. A. 154–5
Dahrendorf, R. 22, 189
Dear, M. 79, 138
Dear, M., L. Bayne, G. Boyd, E. Callaghan and E. Goldstein 74
Dear, M. and G. L. Clark 148
Dear, M. and J. Long 100
Dear, M. and A. J. Scott 35
Dear, M. and S. M. Taylor 77
Deutsch, A. 71
Dillon, J. 142
Donzelot, J. 52
Downs, A. 18, 21, 156
Duncan, S. S. and M. Goodwin 133
Dworkin, R. 3, 106, 191
Dye, T. 21

Edelman, B. 112
Edelman, M. 85–92, 95–8, 101
Eisenmenger, R. W., A. H. Munnell and J. T. Poskanzer 144
Ely, J. 12, 106, 109, 163, 173, 177, 184
Engels, F. 62
Esland, G. 79–80
Esping-Anderson, G., R. Friedland and E. O. Wright 46

Federalist papers, The 163
Ferraresi, F. 56
Fish, S. 86–8, 93
Fiss, O. 7
Foucault, M. 64, 67–8
Frankel, B. 38, 46, 49, 52
Freedman, J. O. 108, 158

AUTHOR INDEX

Friedland, R., F. E. Piven and R. R. Alford 135
Friedman, L. M. 118
Friedson, E. 79
Frug, G. E. 139–40, 144, 170

Gabel, D. 51
Galanter, M. 107
Gaylin, W. 52–137
Giddens, A. 62–3, 65
Giglioli, P. 85–6, 91, 95
Giles, H. 96
Gintis, H. 110
Goebel, J. 118
Gold, D. A., G. Y. H. Lo and E. O. Wright 26–7
Gotkin, J. and P. Gotkin 75
Gough, I. 55
Gramsci, A. 17
Gregory, D. 7–8
Grob, G. N. 70–2
Gumperz, J. 95
Gunther, G. 124

Haar, C. and L. Liebman 170
Habermas, J. 7, 29, 32, 34, 38, 76, 96, 99, 109, 135
Hacker, P. 109
Hall, S. 99
Halliday, M. A. 91
Harsanyi, J. C. 155
Hart, H. L. A. 106, 109, 111, 139, 160–1
Hartz, L. 165
Harvard Law Review Association 126
Harvey, D. 3, 15, 62–3, 119
Harvey, D. and L. Chatterjee 20
Heller, T. C. 99–100
Hindess, B. and P. Hirst 64
Hirsch, J. 8, 31, 38, 47, 49, 56, 136
Holloway, J. and S. Picciotto 30–1, 34
Holmes, O. W. 108
Hookway, C. and P. Pettit 84
Horowitz, I. L. 40
Horwitz, M. J. 104–5 109, 116, 119, 121, 161
Hudson, K. 89–90, 92–3, 96, 99
Huntington, S. 12, 136, 158–9, 162, 185, 193
Hurst, J. W. 116, 124

Ignatieff, M. 67
Illich, I. 66–7
Inman, R. P. and D. L. Rubinfeld 148

Jessop, R. 24, 31–2, 34, 39–40, 45, 49, 51, 53, 56
Johnston, R. J. 10, 101, 137, 170
Jones, K. 73

Katznelson, I. 137
Kemp, R. 99
Kennedy, David 106
Kennedy, Duncan 104–5, 109, 114, 117
Kittrie, N. N. 68
Kress, G. and R. Hodge 85, 91, 95–6

Laclau, E. 26
Landes, W. M. and R. A. Posner 112
Lasch, C. 52, 136
Lemieux, M. 74
Lenin, V. I. 24
Levy, F. S., A. J. Meltzner and A. Wildavsky 20
Library of Congress 121, 124, 126
Littlejohn, G. 56

MacPherson, C. B. 155, 157
Magaro, P. A., R. Gripp and D. J. McDowell 74
Mahon, R. 54, 56
Maier, C. S. 173
Mandel, E. 16, 37–8, 41–2, 53–4
Marcuse, H. 91, 93
Martin, R. M. 39
Marx, K. 62
Marx, K. and F. Engels 24
McBain, M. L. 140
McKnight, J. 66
Michelman, F. I. 104, 162
Miliband, R. 11, 15, 26, 37, 45, 153
Miller, P. 61, 72, 74
Mollenkopf, J. 100
Morawetz, T. 106
Musgrave, R. A. and P. B. Musgrave 18

Nathan, R. P. 144
National Times, The 56
Nettels, C. 123
Nordlinger, E. A. 10
Nozick, R. 10, 23, 113, 132, 161, 163–6, 174, 188–9

O'Connor, J. 17, 29, 42, 135, 172
Offe, C. 29, 38, 46–7, 56
Offe, C. and V. Ronge 27, 29, 34
Olson, M. 10, 95
Olsson, G. 85
Orwell, G. 83–4, 88, 93, 99
Ostrom, V., C. Tiebout and R. Warren 131, 135
Oxford English dictionary, The 106

Panitch, L. 39
Paris, C. 132
Pashukanis, E. B. 108
Pateman, C. 154
Pateman, T. 96
Peet, R. 63, 132

AUTHOR INDEX

Piven, F. and R. Cloward 56
Pocock, J. G. A. 160–1
Poggi, G. 39, 54–6
Polinsky, A. M. 105
Portis, E. B. 45
Posner, R. A. 19, 44, 104, 109, 117
Poulantzas, N. 10, 17, 26–7, 37, 45, 54–5, 112, 153
Pred, A. R. 121
Putnam, H. 84

Rae, D. 20
Rawls, J. 10, 113, 154, 191–2
Reich, M. and R. Edwards 153
Rein, M. 100
Ribble, F. D. G. 120
Ricoeur, P. 84
Robinson, W. P. 85
Roemer, J. 3
Rosen, G. 68
Rosenzweig, N. 73
Rothman, D. J. 68, 73
Roweis, S. 136
Ryan, J. and F. Thomas 74, 76–8, 80–1

Said, E. W. 184
Samuels, W. J. 28
Sandalow, T. 140
Saunders, P. 38, 42, 48, 188
Saussure, F. de 84
Scanlon, T. 116
Scase, R. 38–9
Scherer, K. R. and H. Giles 86, 93, 95
Schmidt, P. 75
Scott, A. J. 35
Scull, A. T. 68, 73
Segal, S. P. and U. Aviram 77
Seley, J. and J. Wolpert 93
Sennett, R. 112
Shapira, P. 134
Sholley, J. B. 121

Siggins, M. 76–8
Simon, B. 68
Skocpol, T. 25
Smith, D. 170
Smith, N. and D. Wilson 84
Solberg, W. U. 129
Sontag, S. 92
Spencer, H. 127
Stepan, A. 54
Stern, R. L. 121–2

Teitz, M. B. 104, 107
Therborn, G. 16, 18, 34, 36, 46–8, 51–3, 55
Thompson, E. P. 110
Thompson, J. D. and G. Goldin 68
Tiebout, C. 153
Tribe, L. H. 118, 121–2, 125–7, 134, 142–3, 145

Unger, R. M. 106, 110, 112, 138
Urry, J. 30
U.S. Department of Housing and Urban Development 146

Verba, S. and N. Nie 10, 164, 185

Walzer, M. 183
Westergaard, J. 32
Wilby, P. 99
Williams, R. 53–4, 93
Wilson, J. Q. 10, 45, 176, 179
Wittgenstein, L. 85
Wolfe, A. 25, 32, 34, 41, 133
Wood, G. 160, 181
Woogh, D. M., H. M. R. Meier and M. R. Eastwood 74
Wright, E. O. 8, 36, 46, 54, 111

Yates, D. 17
Young, G. 119

Zola, I. K. 66

Subject index

accumulation 3–4, 5, 11, 18, 26, 28–31, 37–8, 42, 52, 119, 135–6, 152
apparatus *see* state apparatus and local state
autonomy 30–1, 55, 99, 162, 169, 173, 177–82, 185–90, 192–4
  legal aspects of 138–44, 149–52
  local 99, 131–6, 138–45, 148, 151–2, 171, 181
  political 9, 28, 31, 98–9, 111
  relative 11–12, 29–30, 38–40, 48, 56, 58–9, 111, 163, 175, 178–9, 181, 187–90, 192–3

bureaucracy 10, 16–17, 26, 38–9, 45, 54, 80, 91, 137–8, 152, 158, 176, 178, 193

capital logic school (*see also* theories of the state) 30–1
central state 100, 102, 133, 135
civil society 30, 40, 49, 161–2, 184
class 4, 12, 15, 24, 25
  conflict 25, 31, 110–11, 137
  exploitation 3, 11, 25–6, 29, 64
  power 155, 161, 178
  relationships 9, 11, 24, 26–7, 29, 31, 33, 37, 61–2, 64–6, 68–9, 95, 102, 104, 108, 110, 116–18, 133, 156–7, 169, 172, 174–5
class structuration 62–4, 76, 81
  social 64–6
  spatial 67–70
coercion 24, 27, 31, 38, 42, 102, 108, 112, 114, 134, 154, 163, 165, 170, 182, 190
commodity production 3, 4–6, 43
community mental health *see* mental health care
conservative theories of the state *see* theories of the state
consumption based politics (*see also* politics) 99–100, 171
control 60, 65, 67, 81, 98, 100–2, 112, 122, 128, 131, 133, 136–8, 141–3, 145–8, 160, 177–9, 181–3, 194
corporatism 31–3, 38–41, 55–6
crises 2–3, 12, 17, 29–30, 97, 99, 101, 119, 136–7, 151–2, 186, 189
  fiscal 1, 17, 29, 135, 138, 145, 176

crises—*contd.*
  of legitimacy 29, 35, 41, 98, 135–6, 138, 158, 172, 176
  of liberalism 168–74
  politics 11, 183, 185–7, 193
  management 38, 59, 95, 97–100, 133, 136–8

decentralization
  of commodity production 4–6
  democratic 105, 131, 157–9, 181
  and functions of government 135–7, 164, 171
deinstitutionalization (*see also* mental health care) 69–70
democracy 17, 29, 40, 84, 109–11, 131–2, 134–5, 139, 144, 151, 153–74, 177–9, 181–3, 189–94
  and consumption-based politics 99–100, 171
  defined 153–4
  decentralized 105, 131, 157–9, 181
  and electoral politics 101–2, 133, 172–3, 177, 183
  and legitimacy 153–4, 157–9
  theories of 18, 22, 131, 153–8

electoral politics *see* politics
élites 4, 12, 18, 25–7, 38, 40, 43, 67, 105, 154–5, 163, 175–6, 186–7
everyday life 1, 12, 60, 74–82, 98
executive sub-apparatus *see* state apparatus
expenditures *see* state expenditure
exploitation *see* class

federalism 1, 122, 124, 158, 163–4, 171–2
federal government 69, 74, 120–1, 122–5, 133, 158, 162–3, 171–2
fiscal crises *see* crises, fiscal
form of the state 2, 8, 11, 12, 18, 34–41
function(s) of the state 2, 7, 9, 11, 13, 18–19, 23, 25–7, 30, 33–5, 40–4, 136–7, 158, 164, 166–7, 170–2, 190–3

ghettoization (*see also* mental health care) 69–70, 76

SUBJECT INDEX

government *see* local, national, state government
government transfer payments 144–8

hegemony 11, 25, 95, 97, 136–7, 177
hermeneutics *see* methodology
historical materialism *see* methodology
human agency 2–3, 8

ideological state apparatus *see* state apparatus
ideology 17, 25–8, 34, 42, 45, 56, 64, 79, 105, 108, 112, 131, 133–8, 152–4, 156–7, 165, 168–9, 178–87
input–output models of state 29, 35, 152
institutional form of state 4, 6, 9, 11–12, 15–17, 27, 34, 87, 60–1, 107, 179, 181
instrumentalist theories *see* theories of the state
interpretation 7, 8, 34, 152, 157, 159, 183–7, 193
of language 86, 91, 95, 101
of law 108–11, 119
interpretive communities 95–6, 99–100, 102, 185

judiciary 15–16, 22, 40, 45, 90, 104, 110–11, 117–22, 125, 127–9, 142–3, 151–2, 172–3, 177, 180
and spatial integration 118–28
justice 20, 23, 28, 84, 105, 113, 115–16, 126, 154–5, 160–2, 166, 169, 175–94

language of the state 66, 83–103, 108, 112, 158
and crisis-management 98–100
and electoral politics 101–2, 137
grammar 94
and law 90, 105
linguistic theory 84–7
localization of political discourse 100–1
political language 83–4
social context 84–6, 88, 93–7
law and the state 104–30, 182–3
definition 106
and society 106–9
theories of 106–8
legal sub-apparatus *see* state apparatus
legislature 16, 72, 108, 140–2, 150–2, 184
legitimacy 2, 10, 28–9, 34–5, 39–40, 42–3, 59, 84, 88, 93, 101, 112, 133–5, 137–8, 157, 159, 162–7, 170–4, 176–7, 179–85, 187–94
crises *see* crises of legitimacy
of class structures 6
and democracy 157–9, 164
and fiscal dependence 144–8
moral claims to 168, 172
and self-determination 149–52

liberalism (*see also* crises of liberalism) 160–3, 173
liberal democracy 152–9, 173
liberal theories of democracy 163–6, 168, 170–4
liberal theories of the state *see* theories of the state
linguistic theory (*see also* language of the state) 84–7
local autonomy *see* autonomy and local state
local government 130, 139–41, 144, 151, 155, 158, 164, 166–8, 170–4
local state 42, 50–1, 57–8, 100, 102, 131–52, 162, 165–6, 171–2, 175, 180–1, 190
autonomy of 131–4, 138–43, 170–1
bureaucracy 137–8
definition 133
functions 42, 57–8, 136–8, 143, 158, 170
legal aspects 138–44
links with higher tiers of government 131, 133–40, 142–8, 151–2, 170
in Massachusetts 138, 140–2, 144–8, 170
in Michigan 139, 149–52
self-determination 149–52
as state apparatus 57–8, 131–3, 135–6, 138, 152, 177
theoretical considerations 131–8

marxist theories
and empiricism 8
of law 108–9, 128
and the local state 131–2
of the state 9–11, 17–19, 23–31, 131–2, 153, 159
classical 24–5
contemporary 25–35
(*see also* theories of the state)
Massachusetts 138, 140–2, 144–8, 170
materialist derivation theory 30–1, 33–5
mental health care 64–82
in Britain 72–4
and the client 74–6
and community attitudes 76–9
community-based 69–70, 74–7
history of 70–1
normalization 65, 69, 82
professionals 69–70, 73–4, 76–7
methodology 6–8, 108
empirical analytic approaches 7
empirical marxism 8
epistemology 7, 18
historical hermeneutics 7–8, 109, 128
historical materialism 2, 6, 18, 24
social theory 6, 161
society-centered theory 9–12, 16, 18, 26, 33, 132, 181–2, 185–6, 189, 194
state-centered theory 8–10, 12–13, 179, 181, 185–6, 194

SUBJECT INDEX

Michigan 139, 149–52
minimalist state (*see also* theories of state) 23, 113, 161, 189, 194
mode of production 15, 21, 33–4, 64, 111, 119, 137

national government 73, 133, 145–6, 158, 168, 171–2
nation-state 131, 133–5, 143–8, 162, 166–7, 169, 171–2, 177, 190
naturalism 108

policy 19–21, 67, 69–70, 78–9, 107, 112, 114, 116, 121–3, 134–5, 137, 139, 142, 144–6, 151, 154, 156, 159, 163–4, 170, 177, 180, 182, 184–5, 191
political language 83–5, 87–97
and crisis-management 98–100
definition 83
and power 97–8
structural characteristics 89–94
structural context 93–7
(*see also* language of the state)
political philosophy 92, 161–4, 166–8, 181
political sub-apparatus *see* state apparatus
politics 21–2, 61, 64, 71, 82, 92, 95–6, 98–101, 151, 155–61, 169, 173, 177, 183, 193
of change 183
crises 183, 185–7
democracy *see* democracy and electoral politics
electoral 97, 101–2, 133, 137–8, 144, 152, 173, 177
of interpretation 183
normal 183–5, 187
(*see also* electoral politics)
power
of contrectation 139
of imperation 139
of immunity 139–42, 144
of initiation 139, 142, 149, 184
legal 138–40, 144, 151
problematic of the state 2, 6, 14–35
production sub-apparatus *see* state apparatus
public choice theory 21–2
public city 70, 138
public expenditure *see* state expenditure
public finance 18–19, 42, 155, 167, 176, 189
public goods provision 1, 10, 18–19, 100, 131, 133, 167–8, 171–2, 189–90

radical transformation 176–8
relative autonomy *see* autonomy, relative
repression 34, 67, 112, 134, 152, 160, 178, 186
repressive state apparatus *see* state apparatus

reproduction 2–4, 11–13, 16–18, 30–1, 34, 41–4, 46, 58, 60–4, 67, 118–19, 126, 128, 132, 134, 136, 152, 175, 189
in mental health care 65–82
regional issues 5, 35, 107, 132, 137
rights
as contextual obligations 113–18
fundamental 125–6
individual 23, 28, 104–7, 109, 112–18, 121, 125–30, 139, 141, 143, 150–1, 153–5, 161–2, 165–6, 168, 173–4, 177, 183, 191
natural 106, 115, 151, 160, 166, 181

social justice *see* justice
social theory *see* methodology
social revolution and change 176–8, 180–7, 191–4
society-centered analysis *see* methodology
sociospatial processes 2–3, 8–9, 12–13
sociospatial structures 1, 9, 63, 78, 137
spatial
integration 4–5, 105, 109, 118, 123–5, 127–9, 152
jurisdiction 100, 118–19, 133
localization of discourse 97, 100, 102–3
organization 1–2, 103, 132, 156, 164–8
reproduction 63–6
structuration 67–70
structure 8, 63, 81–2, 104, 118, 129, 153, 171–2
state apparatus 1, 9, 12, 15–17, 26–7, 34–5, 35–61, 64, 74, 81, 83, 95, 98–9, 102, 107, 111–12, 115, 133–7, 176–81, 183–7, 191–4
administration 50–4
communications and media 50, 53–4
conflict between 56–9
consensus 43–4, 50–1
definition 49
and everyday life 75–82
executive 50, 54
health, education and welfare 50, 52
ideological 15–16, 45–6, 50, 52–3
information 50, 53–4
integration 43–4, 50, 52–4
legal 50–1
para-apparatus 49
political 50–1
production 43–4, 50–2
provision 50–2
psychiatric 67, 71–3, 75, 81–2
recent evolution of 55–9
regulatory agencies 50, 54
repressive 50–1
sub-apparatus 49
taxonomy of 45–54
treasury 50–2
state as arbiter *see* theories of the state

216 SUBJECT INDEX

state-centered analysis *see* methodology
state derivation theories 30–2
state expenditure 29, 42, 133, 144–8, 155
  social consumption 42, 52, 134, 137
  social expenses 42–3
  social investment 42–3, 52
state government 115, 140, 144, 158, 162
state as regulator and facilitator *see* theories
  of the state
state as social engineer *see* theories of the
  state
state as supplier *see* theories of the state
statization of psychiatric profession 60–1,
  70–4, 81–2
structuration of class relations *see* class
  structuration

theories of the state 15, 18–35
  as arbiter 15, 21–3, 189
  capital logic 15, 30–2
  of capitalist state 14–15, 23–33
  conservative and liberal 9–23, 33, 132,
    153

theories of the state—*contd.*
  corporatist 15, 32–3
  derivationist 15, 30–2
  instrumentalist 15, 25–9
  marxist 9–18, 23–33, 131, 153, 159
  materialist 15, 30–5
  minimalist 15, 23, 113, 161, 189, 194
  as regulator and facilitator 15, 19–20, 22–
    3, 104, 189
  requirements for 8–13
  as social engineer 15, 20–1, 23
  society-centered *see* methodology
  state-centered *see* methodology
  of state in capitalism 15, 18–23
  structuralist 15, 25–9
  as supplier 15, 18–19, 22–3, 131

uneven development 5, 129
urban 2, 5, 35, 63, 70, 107, 131, 135, 137

welfare 4, 16–18, 20, 43–4, 52, 57, 71–2,
  79–81, 92, 98, 138, 157–8, 180, 185,
  191
  state 74, 169, 172